Love & Dirt

DIANE ATKINSON lives in Shoreditch. She was born in the north-east and educated in Cornwall and London, where she completed a Ph.D. on the politics of women's sweated labour. She taught history at secondary schools in London before moving to the Museum of London, where she worked as a lecturer and curator, specializing in women's history. She is the author of two illustrated history books, *Suffragettes in Pictures* and *Funny Girls: Cartooning for Equality*. This is her first biography.

ALSO BY DIANE ATKINSON

Votes for Women

The Purple, White and Green: Suffragettes in London

Funny Girls: Cartooning for Equality

Mrs Broom's Suffragette Photographs

The Suffragettes in Pictures

DIANE ATKINSON

Love & Dirt

The Marriage of Arthur Munby & Hannah Cullwick

PAN BOOKS

First published 2003 by Macmillan

This edition published 2004 by Pan Books
an imprint of Pan Macmillan Ltd
Pan Macmillan, 20 New Wharf Road, London N1 9RR
Basingstoke and Oxford
Associated companies throughout the world
www.panmacmillan.com

ISBN 0 330 39228 X

1 3 5 7 9 8 6 4 2

A CIP catalogue record for this book is available from
the British Library.

Typeset by SetSystems Ltd, Saffron Walden, Essex
Printed and bound in Great Britain by
Mackays of Chatham plc, Chatham, Kent

For the loves of my life:

my parents, Peggy and Arnold Atkinson,

and my husband Patrick Hughes

Contents

List of Illustrations

Except where stated, pictures are used by kind permission of the Master and Fellows of Trinity College, Cambridge.

1. Arthur Munby in 1848. (Giles Munby)
2. Hannah Cullwick in 1853.
3. Playbill for *Sardanapalus*, 1853. (Theatre Museum / Victoria and Albert Museum)
4. Arthur J. Munby's self-portrait of 1860.
5. Hannah Cullwick in 1862.
6. Hannah Cullwick as a 'chimney sweep', 1862.
7. Hannah Cullwick in 1857.
8. A Lambeth 'dust-wench', 1860.
9. 'Pit broo wenches', 1863.
10. 'Flither lasses' at Flamborugh Head, c. 1860.
11. Mademoiselle Senyah, 1868.
12. Hannah Cullwick's hands, 1860.
13. Hannah Cullwick in mannish clothes, 1861.
14. Hannah Cullwick dressed up as a lady in 1864.
15. Hannah Cullwick as a Magdalen. 1867.
16. Drawing of Fig Tree Court, c. 1930. (Guildhall Library, Corporation of London)
17. Arthur Munby, 1891.
18. Hannah Munby in 1902.

Acknowledgements

My first duty is to acknowledge the large debt I owe to the Master and Fellows of Trinity College, Cambridge for their kind permission to publish the material contained in this book and photographs from the Munby Papers.

The Librarians of the London Library and the Guildhall Library for their expertise and unfailing courtesy.

Archivists at: Suffolk Record Office; York Reference Library; Wolverhampton; Warwickshire; Staffordshire Record Offices and in particular Mrs Healey at the Shropshire Record Office for her efforts in unearthing new material on the Cullwicks.

Thanks to Dr Claire Rider for pinpointing 6 Fig Tree Court and the Guildhall Library, Corporation of London, for permission to include the photograph.

The Trustees of the Victoria and Albert Museum for permission to reproduce the playbill of *Sardanapalus*.

Giles Munby for permission to use three pictures of his ancestor.

Sarah Lewis and Samantha Dicks at Adam Matthew Publications.

Deborah Cherry of Preston for her terrier-like search and find missions.

John Cullwick for all matters genealogical.

Dr Trevor and Dr Margaret Hill, local historians of Shifnal who were so generous with their knowledge and time.

Dr Michael Rowland's professional insights into the workings of the minds of Hannah and Arthur.

Holly and Hester Westley.

Alex Marengo.

My predecessors in the field whose work was an inspiration to write a biography of this odd couple: Professor Angela John; Dr Leonore Davidoff; Dr Liz Stanley; Derek Hudson; and Michael Hiley.

My agent David Godwin.

My editor Georgina Morley for her insights, patience and unbridled enthusiasm for the book.

Finally for my husband Patrick Hughes, my most heartfelt thanks. Always my biggest fan, his love and support are the size of Ayers Rock.

Preamble

'... before bed at ten o' clock I'd a capital chance to go up the chimney, so I lock'd up and waited till the grate was cool enough and then I took the carpets up and got the tub o' water ready to wash me in. Moved the fender and swept the ashes up. Stripp'd myself quite naked and put a pair of old boots on and tied an old duster over my hair and then I got up in the chimney with a brush. There was a lot o' soot and it was soft and warm. Before I swept I pull'd the duster over my eyes and mouth and I sat on the beam that goes across the middle and crossed my legs along it and I was quite safe and comfortable and out o' sight. I swept lots o' the soot down and it came all over me and I sat there for ten minutes or more and when I'd swept all around me as far as I could reach I come down, and lay on the hearth in the soot a minute or two thinking, and I wish'd rather that Massa could see me. I black'd my face all over and then got the looking glass and look'd at myself and I was certainly a fright and hideous all over, at least I should o' seem'd so to anybody but Massa. I set on and wash'd myself after, and I'd hard work to get the black off and was obliged to leave my shoulders for Massa to finish. I got the tub emptied and to bed before twelve.'

The chimney sweep was Hannah Cullwick, a maid of all work in Kilburn, London, in 1863. In Britain at this time a third of all females between fifteen and twenty-one were servants, whose employers ranged from the aristocracy at the apex of the social pyramid down to the likes of Hannah's boss, an upholsterer, who enhanced his social standing by joining the servant-employing class. Throughout her life Hannah worked at several levels and the diary she kept for her sweetheart is a rare insight into the daily drudgery and occasional kitchen frolics that were the lot of women who migrated to the major towns and cities of Victorian Britain.

London was the most powerful of magnets. Shropshire-born Hannah had arrived in the capital by way of a handful of country houses in her home county and Suffolk and Lincolnshire. She was one of hundreds of thousands of young women who came to London in search of work and adventure. 'Massa', her sweetheart, was Mr Arthur Joseph Munby from York, a gentleman and man of letters who had an unusual interest in the minutiae of working women's lives. We have him to thank for Hannah's lengthy descriptions of the rigours of her sixteen-hour working day. Without his encouragement, not to say insistence, our knowledge of a servant's life in the nineteenth century would be the poorer.

Hannah's sometimes daily diaries and regular letters to Arthur Munby throw arcs of light into the dark corners of Victorian servants' lives. The monotony of the work, the physical exhaustion, the pittance earned, the terror of losing a roof over one's head as well as a job created a great sense of insecurity. The suffocating lack of privacy, the fact that almost every hour of their day was under someone else's control, are all described. The Victorian chattering classes complained endlessly about 'the servant problem' but Hannah could have countered their arguments with plenty of examples from her own experience. Her writings show how vital it was for a servant to weigh up the master and mistress and the place as shrewdly and quickly as possible, otherwise misery loomed if a situation taken in haste proved quite unsuitable. Not all employers were tyrannical and overbearing, but many of them were: entering service at the age of eight, Hannah learned the hard way which kind of mistress was to be avoided. When she was fourteen she had a grim time as nursemaid to a vicar and his wife and their large brood of young children. But Hannah got on well with most of her employers: her willingness to do the work of two servants meant that in return they usually learned to turn a blind eye to her unexplained evening absences from the kitchen in pursuit of her love.

Hannah's diaries blow away the dust of our presumptions about life in service: for instance, her descriptions of having family and friends to stay the night without the permission of 'the missis'. Frequently a deaf ear was turned to sounds of partying from behind the green baize door on servants' birthdays and at Christmas, and sometimes wine was sent below stairs to lubricate the occasion. The master–servant dynamic was more complex than has been hitherto understood: life above and below stairs was not a one-way relationship.

But Hannah Cullwick was not a typical servant. She may have attended her local charity school between the ages of five and eight, but thanks to Arthur's tuition she became an accomplished letter-writer and a keen autodidact, dovetailing attendance at lectures on literature, biology and French conversation with the never-ending chores she did without the help of labour-saving gadgets and ready-made cleaning materials. She loved Charles Dickens's novels – *David Copperfield* was a particular favourite – re-reading them many times, often aloud to her fellow servants, and she dreamily identified with Thomas Hardy's Tess. Hannah was amused by *Pamela, Or, Virtue Rewarded*, Samuel Richardson's epistolary novel of 1740 about a servant who, on the death of her mistress, was relentlessly pursued by the son of the house but successfully resisted his increasingly desperate attempts to seduce her.

Hannah's on-going education gave her confidence and raised her spirits, which might have been lowered, or destroyed, by the tedium of her life and the danger of her scandalous romance with 'Massa' being discovered. Arthur Munby's insatiable interest in her working life and demand for more details and ever more pages meant that Hannah was under considerable pressure. At the end of a long, tiring day she would wait for the other servants to troop up to the attic or retire to their truckle-beds elsewhere in the kitchen, perch herself at the end of the scrubbed kitchen table, pick up her dip-pen and nervously and wearily start to write and tell him every single thing she had done that day. Over time she learned the best strategies to avoid the prying eyes and questions about what on earth she was putting down and to whom she was writing at such length at such an unearthly hour. When she had finished she would make her way up the servants' staircase to her attic room and fall into bed with the housemaid and, after only six hours' sleep, would rise again for another day remarkably similar to the one she had just scrubbed and scoured her way through. If she had no time to dash to the pillar-box, Hannah would give the envelope to the postman or pay a delivery boy to post it for her and hope he would not be able to read the name of the person to whom it was addressed, and not tell any of the other servants. At the end of the day the writing ritual would be repeated, and the next day, and the day after that.

Part of the pact that Hannah and Arthur drew up between themselves was that she would provide him with detailed descriptions of not only her back-breaking work, but the filthy state to which she had been reduced by her toil. She constantly told him how black she was, how sweaty, how animal-like in her strength. The dirtier and more unwholesome the work the better, for the ultimate reward for the almost fanatically zealous way in which she attacked the dirt would, he assured her, be her salvation in the eyes of God. She was therefore obliged to please three masters: her employer, her 'Massa' and God.

Hannah Cullwick expresses herself well on paper: whilst not always grammatically perfect, her writing is clear and vivid. Her output is detailed, vigorous and filled with character. Hannah's honesty, straightforwardness and native wit fill the seventeen volumes of her diary-writing and hundreds of letters too, brimming with metaphor and canny insights into her contemporaries whose reported speech was transcribed in the speaker's own dialect. Arthur was a connoisseur of regional accents and Hannah went to extraordinary lengths to add to his store of knowledge. He became an expert on the Shropshire dialect, frequently updating the glossaries he kept in the back of his notebooks, and the folk wisdom which gave an earthy and rustic quality to Hannah's writing charmed his own poetic sensibilities. In the early years she used the lowercase 'i' when writing in the first person; as her confidence grew, so did her use of capitals.

Hannah was generous with her talents: she wrote letters for her fellow servants and read the replies which would be quickly taken from the postman before the master or mistress could intercept them. Many employers regarded their servants as children with juvenile moral acumen and considered it their duty to treat them as such: wayward, at risk, and with no rights to privacy. Hannah's correspondence with 'Massa' was therefore not only onerous and stressful, but also fraught with the risk of exposure if his letters to her were opened and read by an employer. A quick glance at his handwriting, that of an educated man, would have revealed their scandalous relationship, and disgrace for them both would surely have followed.

Hannah's secret romance with 'Massa' broke every rule in the Victorian book. Their love for each other, leading to their marriage, offended every code of decency. We should not imagine that the Victorians were really so different to us: many men enjoyed pornography; prostitution was a considerable industry; there were many single mothers among the 'fallen women'. Arthur Munby was a friend of one of the biggest collectors of erotica of his day, and he himself had long-standing friendships with prostitutes. Like countless others he collected pictures of bare-breasted African women and scantily clad gymnasts showing a lot of leg and erect nipples peeping through their leotards. Munby's family and friends would have been shocked by his betrayal of their class by his 'misalliance' with a working woman. It would have offended them irredeemably and placed Arthur and Hannah beyond the pale of polite society. Whilst aristocrats and employers regularly seduced their servants, this resulted in marriage in only a tiny number of cases. Anyone marrying out of their class was altogether different from their peers. Hannah and Arthur's love subverted the Victorian hierarchy of class and turned it upside down in the most outrageous way.

CHAPTER ONE

Arthur Munby

ON THURSDAY, 1 MARCH 1827, the young lawyer Joseph Munby walked to St Helen's Church, Stonegate, York, to marry Caroline Eleanor Forth. The groom was twenty-three, the bride was twenty. In the chilly church the ladies were dressed in bonnets, shawls and fur muffs, the gentlemen in woollen overcoats and tall top hats. Trade between York and other ports was at a standstill owing to 'the great accumulations of ice in the river'.[1]

The newly-weds lived at The Terrace, one of three houses in Clifton, a village a mile out of York:

> At this village there is a ... pleasant place of entertainment called 'the Marquee Gardens' ... to which parties resort in large numbers during the summer season, both by land and water; where they can enjoy a little social intercourse, apart from the hustle of the city. A more retired and pleasant place of entertainment cannot be found within so short a distance from the City of York.[2]

In marrying Caroline, Joseph Munby married well: her father was the Reverend John Forth and her uncle, James Woodhouse, had been Lord Mayor of York three times. Joseph's father, a solicitor and once Under-Sheriff of York, had died in 1816, leaving his wife Jane with five children: Joseph was the eldest and at twelve years old had to grow up quickly.

Pretty Caroline Munby was devout, morally cautious, and

with her golden-auburn hair, an embodiment of 'the angel of the hearth'. Her accomplishments included flower-painting and playing the harp: 'she cared little for general subjects, nothing at all for politics: as for religion, she took all its details for granted . . . and believed as devoutly [in her husband] as he believed in God'.[3] Joseph was a devout Christian, played the organ in his church and was a philanthropist.

Two weeks after their wedding, Joseph's younger sister Jane helped the couple secure the services of a servant, Hannah Rooke, aged twenty-one.[4] On 19 August 1828, the Munbys' first child was born at home and baptized Arthur Joseph on 2 September at St Olave's Church.[5] Hannah Rooke became Arthur's nursemaid. Caroline and Joseph presumed that their son would become a lawyer like his father and his father before him, and his education was planned accordingly. The Munbys moved into York in 1831 when Arthur was three years old. The first picture of him, aged nearly three, is a silhouette made in 1831 showing a fashionably dressed little boy holding a whip.

Hannah Rooke was a loyal and trusted servant who worked for the family for twenty-eight years, helping Mrs Munby bring up her boisterous children who would eventually number seven – six sons and a daughter.[6] In 1838, the Munbys moved to 3 Blake Street, a smart house built by Caroline's uncle, the Lord Mayor. The family home was now next door to Joseph's office at 4 Blake Street.[7] The Munbys were living in the same street as the Assembly Rooms, in York's best district: they were at the centre of the city's social life. The other six children were: John Forth Munby, born in 1831; George Frederick Woodhouse in 1833; Frederick James in 1837; Joseph Edwin in 1839; Caroline Elizabeth in 1844, and Edward Charles in 1845.[8]

By the time his sister was born, Arthur had been at school for two years: he had a tutor at home, shared with his younger brothers, but did not start formal schooling until he was fourteen. In 1841 John Simpson, aged twenty, lived in at Blake Street and prepared him for St Peter's Grammar School in the Minster Yard.[9] The school amalgamated with the Proprietary School at Clifton which had opened in 1838, 'a handsome and Gothic edifice in the Collegiate Style'.[10] Arthur moved to the new school in Clifton in 1844 and left in 1846, aged eighteen. The Reverend A. W. Brown was hired by Joseph Munby to coach Arthur for his entrance examination to Trinity College, Cambridge: a first step on the ladder to becoming a lawyer and joining the family business.[11]

Arthur's adolescent years were typical of growing up within an upper-middle-class family: there was a variety of female servants, daily prayers for the family and servants and regular church attendance. His mother was an affectionate woman who had a 'gentleness of spirit' and a

> *singular power of loving.* Her whole being dwelt always in
> the region of the affections: her husband first, and all her
> children next, so equally, that each of us might also feel as
> if he were her only child. And though she was firm
> and judicious as a mother, her love was so tremulous and
> tender, and her health so delicate always, that each of us
> felt it might kill her, if he went into the army or navy, for
> instance, or went away very far or for very long.

Perhaps Mrs Munby's health was 'delicate', as the result of having a child about every two and a half years. Hannah Rooke's service meant that Arthur's mother was spared the most onerous aspects of childcare. Munby's father was in love with his wife:

> ... she was his first love, and he was hers: and all his
> life ... she showed his love, not only in all greater
> matters, but in a thousand little fantasies of affections and

courtesies, which we only knew of by degrees or by accidents. Even her name – Caroline – he continued to emphasize in all things: he used the letters of it as symbols, in arranging his library and his music: he planted the village [Clifton] street with a line of trees – Chestnut, *E*lm, *M*aple, alternately, which in full leaf represents her initials over and over again.[12]

Joseph may have been an exacting father. He had assumed responsibility early and expected his sons to behave in a similar way. From his earliest years Joseph Munby was a driven man. As well as establishing his legal practice, he became Clerk to the Magistrates in 1836, and clerk to the County Gaol Sessions for the county of York and Clerk to the Visiting Justices in 1845. Joseph Munby was involved in all the major philanthropic and cultural activities of York: he was a founder of the Yorkshire School for the Blind, Secretary to the York County Hospital, on the committee of York's Bluecoat School and of the School of Art, a friend and supporter of York Ragged Schools and the Yorkshire Philosophical Society, and Secretary to the York County Hospital.[13]

His son Arthur Munby studied classics, mathematics and theology at Trinity College from 1848 to 1851, and graduated with an ordinary degree. He lived in room L5 in New Court and formed several life-long friendships.[14] Founded by Henry VIII in 1546, Trinity has always been one of the foremost Cambridge colleges. Arthur's student accommodation was built in the Gothic style of the early nineteenth century; Trinity's chapel was mid-sixteenth century, but the interior had been drastically altered in the 1720s and 1730s; Sir Christopher Wren's library dated from the late seventeenth century, and for a man with a great interest in poetry,[15] Arthur found the Backs a perfect setting for contemplative walks along the banks of the River Cam.

During Arthur's first year at Trinity, his father embarked on a project to move his family from Blake Street to a new house in Clifton. The foundation stone was laid in 1849 and in 1850 the Munbys, the six children still at home and their six servants moved in. Clifton Holme was 'an impressive two-storey grey brick house' which demonstrated Joseph's standing.[16]

Meanwhile, Arthur's social horizon at Trinity was expanding: his friends Robert Spencer Borland, Cuyler Anderson, Alfred Kennion and Francis Joseph Moore all became clergymen. Others included Vernon Lushington, who went into the law; William Ralston was a Russian scholar and Richard Buckley Litchfield was a civil servant who joined the Ecclesiastical Commission in Whitehall in 1859.[17] While at Trinity Munby started writing poetry, some of which he published in his collection *Benoni* in 1852, and he became influenced by Christian Socialism. One of the few extant pictures of him is from his Trinity years: this drawing shows him aged twenty, fashionably whiskered and coiffed. In 1851, armed with a degree and a stack of poetry books, after another tearful leave-taking with his mother and with his father's words ringing in his ears, he left Clifton Holme for London, and a career as a barrister. (Plate 1)

CHAPTER TWO

Hannah Cullwick

ON 23 JUNE 1833, Charles Fox Cullwick and his wife Martha, née Owen, walked from their home and saddlery business in Shifnal High Street, Shropshire, to St Andrew's Parish Church with their new-born daughter in their arms.[1] Their three-year-old son James and more Cullwicks and Owens followed behind. Vicar John Brooke baptized Hannah, a name meaning 'God has favoured me'. She had brown curly hair, blue eyes and rosy cheeks, and her godmother was Anna Maria Dorothea Eyton.

Hannah's parents, Charles and Martha, had married at St Andrew's Church on Christmas Eve 1829, signing the marriage register proudly, in Charles's case with an arty flourish; Martha's signature was altogether smaller, sweeter and shyer. The bride wore her best frock, 'a primrose with pink sprigs'.[2] Her sister Eleanor Owen signed as a witness, but David Rowton, the second witness, could not and made a cross as his mark. The wedding party walked briskly to the couple's new home in Shifnal High Street.

Charles Fox Cullwick, baptized on 13 November 1803, was the eleventh and youngest child of William and Susannah, née Fox. The Cullwicks had been saddlers for generations: William Cullwick senior is listed in *The Universal British Directory of Trade, Commerce and Manufacture* and trained his sons in his trade. They were a lower-middle-class family and had been burgesses or freemen with the right to vote, which had first been granted to Charles's great-great-grandfather, a tailor in Bridgnorth, Shropshire, in 1647.[3] In 1828 Charles Fox Cullwick could vote in parliamentary elections, at a time when this was denied to most Englishmen and all Englishwomen. His saddlery shop was in the busiest street in this bustling town. Eighteen coaches a day passed through because Shifnal was the half-way point on the London to Holyhead route and its wealth was derived from the business that geography had bestowed on it. The road to Holyhead was known as 'the Irish road'.[4] Business would continue until the coming of rail travel sidelined Shifnal. The Royal Mail, the Emerald, the Old Prince, the Prince of Orange, the Prince of Wales, the Union, the Hibernia and the Wonder! stopped at The Jerningham Arms and The Star, purpose-built coaching inns dating back to the eighteenth century.

Charles's neighbours in the High Street represented all the trades Shifnal needed in the late 1820s: there was Samuel Blud, the skinner; the tailor William Swann; Jane Peake was a dressmaker and milliner, in competition with Ann Swann and Harriet Wilkes for straw hats. There were butchers, bakers and candlestick-makers, and druggists who provided patent remedies for those who could not afford the services of a local doctor. When Hannah was born her mother had been attended by one of the two Shifnal surgeons, probably Samuel Fletcher who was in the High Street.

In 1838 Charles Dickens visited Shropshire and used his memories of Shifnal in *The Old Curiosity Shop* as a place visited by the weary Nell and her grandfather before they reached her final resting place at Tong Church:

They came to a large town, where the wagon stopped and where they spent a night. They passed a large church [St Andrew's]; and in the streets were a number of old houses, built of a kind of earth or plaster, crossed and re-crossed in a great many directions with black beams, which gave

them a remarkable and very ancient look. The doors, too,
were arched and low, some with oaken portals and quaint
benches, where the former inhabitants had sat on summer
evenings. The windows were latticed in little diamond
panes, that seemed to wink and blink upon the passengers
as if they were dim of sight . . .[5]

Saddlers were important. In 1828 Charles Fox Cullwick
was one of four in Shifnal: The others were Ann Parker,
who was running her husband's business after his death,
Thomas Lloyd and Moses Smith.[6] Saddlers served a seven-year
apprenticeship and wore a working uniform: a bowler hat,
wool jacket and a leather apron reaching to the ground. The
status-conscious also wore a waistcoat and collar and tie.

Hannah's mother, Martha, was an Owen through and
through: both her parents, John and Anne, were born Owen.
Her father was from Shifnal, her mother from Albrighton,
a hamlet nearby.

In 1800, the year of Martha's birth, Shifnal was treated to
a performance of 'the celebrated ventriloquist Mr Lee Sugg'.
For a two-shilling ticket he promised to:

> convey his voice from one pocket to another with much
> ease to himself and to the astonishment of others; con-
> verse with his lips closed and count any number, and no
> person will discover any alteration to his features
> although a candle will be held to the performer's mouth;
> throw his voice to a face held at great distance from him
> which will answer any questions put to him and sing
> God Save the King, and he will converse with the assist-
> ance of his internal orator as if four persons were in his
> company, two voices as if from outside the door and two
> on the inside, so truly astonishing as to be allowed by
> the admirers of this gift of nature to be the wonder of the
> world.[7]

Like her mother, Martha became a servant; her father was a maltster and sometime soldier in the 18th Light Dragoon Guards. He died in March 1821, aged sixty seven, and was buried at Tong: her mother returned to domestic service in her mid-fifties. In March 1839 she died aged seventy-four, an inmate at Preston Hospital, at Preston-upon-the-Wild-Moors, a village of 200 people. Founded in 1716, this almshouse was built under the terms of the will of Lady Catherine Herbert, to provide a home for twelve respectable women and girls. Priority was given to respectable widowed servants. Martha's mother had free accommodation, a pension of £26, two tons of coal a year and a small garden for her own use.

Martha Owen worked for just one employer, the Reverend John Eyton, of Eyton Hall, Eyton-upon-the-Wild-Moors, and his wife Anna Maria. Starting in 1814 as a housemaid to a family of nine children, Martha moved up the servants' hierarchy to become lady's maid (earning £12 a year) to Anna Maria and her three daughters, and was much favoured by Anna Maria Dorothea Eyton who was born in 1815. The Eyton children were orphaned in 1825 when their mother died, their delicate father having predeceased her in 1823.

In 1833 Anna Maria Dorothea was happy to be Hannah's godmother. Her first gift to Hannah was in her name:

> she stood to me and named me as much like herself as my mother would let her. Her own name was *Anna Maria Dorothea* and she wanted mine to be the same. But my mother said it was too much out of the way for mine, and all it sh'd be was *Hannah* and that'd be a scripture name and a plain name and still something like my godmother's. So that's how my name came to be Hannah – as plain a name for a *servant* as could be.[8]

Later Hannah remembered her godmother, by then Mrs Neave, visiting the charity school she attended in Shifnal.

The patrons of the Blue Coat School for Girls, the Moultries of Aston Hall, were close friends of Hannah's godmother and readily accepted her as a pupil. It was an honour to have such an esteemed sponsor who provided her first uniform, a blue serge sleeveless frock, a white tippet, white frilled cap, straw bonnet, a yellow waistband and leather badge with her number printed on, two aprons, one blue-checked for weekdays, white for Sunday.[9]

The school was housed in a modest building, still standing, which had been endowed in 1716 by Beatrice Jobber for

> clothing, instructing six poor children, daughters of widows, or such other poor people of the parish of Shiffnall . . . not to be under the age of seven years, nor to stay at school after the age of fourteen . . . the mistress to teach the children to read the English tongue perfectly, and say the catechism, and to sew plain work, and mark and knit; and she was to be allowed three pounds yearly, and to have the benefit of the children's work (over and above what should be necessary for making and mending their own clothes) . . . the six poor girls were taught to read and work.[10]

To thank the Moultries for their largesse the 'Bluecoat girls' could expect to be called on Saturdays, in their livery, to weed their gardens. Sometimes they were rewarded with a penny; often Hannah was given a slice of bread and cold meat. On Sundays they were expected to attend St Andrew's Church in their uniform, and sit in a special gallery.

Although she felt shy wearing her charity wench's uniform, Hannah was grateful for the instruction her teacher Miss Mary Woodhouse provided. She attended the school from 1838 to 1841, when she left for home carrying the sampler she had made: she was literate, a good reader with a sound knowledge of the Bible, a competent knitter, very good at sewing, later able to make a man's coat, but shaky at arithmetic all her life because they had never been taught 'summing'. It was often the practice in charity schooling not to teach writing and arithmetic. This omission aimed at allaying the concerns of those who feared the dangers of a literate and numerate labour force at a time when England experienced periodic outbreaks of social and political unrest.[11]

When Hannah returned home on the day of her godmother's visit to her school, she discovered that Mrs Neave had

> sent a butler to our house with a Bible for me and a new print dress for mother, and she and me was to go up that evening to the Hall to see her. I remember it because she seemed so grand to me and I polished my shoes as well as ever I could and I trotted up by my mother as fast as possible on purpose to see my godmother who was a *lady*! She kissed me I know and gave me cake and wine was brought on a tray, but I canna remember the face very clear. I made a nice curtsey and was sorry when I came away and wondered when I should see her again.[12]

In fact Mrs Neave never saw Hannah again, but she continued to take an interest in her god-daughter. Her elder brother, the Reverend Robert William Eyton, would later give Hannah a job in 1847 as nurserymaid at his vicarage at Ryton, just three miles from Shifnal.

Hannah remembered her father as a tall and overpowering man with a bad temper and a fondness for drink, who was violent with his wife and children. Martha was pious, kind and long-suffering. At her mother's knee Hannah acquired her sense of humility and her pride in working for 'bettermost folks': 'I used to think as gentlefolks was made of quite different stuff to us common folks; and mother said as poor folks like us had no right to pronounce wer [our] aitches. Her never did, nor father.'[13]

Martha taught her children their place on the social ladder: 'As for service, why I was born and bred a servant! My mother was a servant afore me; and so was all my aunts and uncles: all on [of] them gentlemen's servants. An' I reckon it's no shame to stick to what you was born.'[14] Hannah pictured her mother as a stoic woman:

> mother used to wear a large white cap with strings and a short cotton frock, and a white kerchief round her neck, tucked in at her bosom, and a large blue-checked apron, and strong shoes. She looked so nice in it, for she was very gentle, and her hands were long and thin, but very hard inside; for poor mother used to work hard after she married – harder nor she did in service . . .'[15]

The family relied in part on the small sums Hannah and her elder brother James could earn by scaring birds, picking peas or potatoes or stones, and used the horse manure they collected from the roads to fertilize their vegetable patch on a piece of 'poor's land' their father cultivated. They kept hens and chickens and pigs to fatten and kill. Typically, 'half a pound of bacon and 'taters every day' was the diet for the whole family, and 'just a bit o' meat on Sundays'. On occasion Martha would send Hannah to the nearest 'big house' where she was to beg for a bowl of dripping 'cause we was so poor you know. Eh, I used to think how grand it ud be if I could coom to be a servant in a kitchen like that.'[16] When Martha was going to have a child she was reduced to having to ask for 'The Bag' of baby clothes from Aston Hall. Because of her long service with the Eytons, Martha was loaned baby clothes and candles, offered only to the respectable poor in the parish: 'there's everythink in it for a newborn baby; and yo've got to send 'em all back, clean washed at the month's end, aye and candles too, they send'.[17] At other times Hannah was sent to beg for bones and suet at the kitchen door of St Andrew's vicarage.[18]

Hannah had to intervene when her father was about to hit her brother James and her mother: 'I often did wi' poor mother, when Father was a-goin' to beat her; I coom in between, and says "yo' shanna do it!" and then he beat me instead o' her.'[19] A local woman told Hannah as a child how her mother had 'saved thirty pounds, but Father had it all – spent it. Eh! her never was happy after the first fortnight; her run away from him, and came back, but never had no more joy in him.' Hannah remembers her mother as 'too religious – always praying and sad, and seemed never to care for Father to kiss her nor us neither'.[20]

Hannah's memory of the day she left home for her first job was that her father beat her so that she would not want to return. A while later he sent her his love via a woman who called at Hannah's place of work. Perhaps her father's temper was excited by drinking. Martha often said how 'thankful she would be if she could be sure of eight shillings a week, and she never could be sure of even five shillings a week. And that with five children to keep.'[21] They had to take in lodgers, sometimes four or five navvies building roads and the new railway line through Shropshire. Was the saddlery business in trouble? In 1836 Charles moved his premises to the Market Place and in 1840 his elder brother William is also listed as a saddler, perhaps called in to help his younger, struggling brother.

On 6 June 1841 a census enumerator called at the Cullwick home in Shifnal High Street, and provides a snapshot of Hannah and her family just after her eighth birthday. Her siblings were eleven-year-old James, Richard, aged five, and two-year-old Ellen. There were five lodgers: Thomas Reid, a saddler, aged fifty; Thomas Main, a thirty-year-old cabinet maker; Joseph Ravensfell, a paper-maker aged twenty; John Hughes, a carpenter, aged thirty, and Charles Pulley, a Scottish paper-maker, also thirty.[22]

By 1841 Martha had four children. In 1843 and 1844 she gave birth to two more, of whom one survived. On 15 May 1843, baby Mary was born and baptized three days later, and two days afterwards died of 'weakness'. Vicar Brooke performed the burial. Her father took a month to register her birth: Mary was recorded as having died before her birth was entered in the official record.[23] The fifth child was born on 12 July 1844 and baptized Mary Ann (known as Polly) on 2 September at the Wesleyan Methodist chapel.

The seventeenth-century house where Hannah was born in the High Street, Shifnal, on the site of what is now 20 Bradford Street, is no longer standing (many of Shifnal's streets were renamed in 1898 by the local landowner, the Earl of Bradford).[24] It was one of those black and white brick and timbered houses noted by Charles Dickens on his visit in 1838, when Hannah was starting at the charity school. The two-storey house was substantial, with eight bedrooms, four of which were in the garret where the lodgers slept. It was a dark house with small windows. The upper floors were reached by 'corkscrew stairs'. There was a parlour where the lodgers had their meals, often waited on by Hannah and her mother: the family ate in the kitchen close to the open range on which Martha cooked. The lodgers paid three pence a night, but Martha does not seem to have made much money: 'the navvies . . . built the line . . . but mother was so gentle, they used to cheat her'.[25] When Hannah was six or seven, a lodger and his wife almost burnt the house down: Hannah had to run for help and the tenant who discovered the fire had his whiskers burnt off.[26]

Charles's saddlery shop was at the rear of the house. Water was drawn from a pump in the yard and there was a garden which was home to their two pigs. Hannah gathered leaves in the lanes to feed the pigs; helped her mother go 'leasing' or gleaning when the harvest was gathered, and gathered sticks to eke out their supplies of coal.

Hannah grew up to be a tomboy. She was a good runner, winning school prizes of sixpence which she gave her mother. She put her running abilities to good use by calling at the bigger houses in the area and offering to run their errands for them: for this she earned food, usually bread and a slice of beef, and sometimes a penny as well.[27] Martha would make bread and Hannah 'carried it on her head up the street to the baker's', to Lydia Scarrott's premises in the High Street.[28]

If the hens they kept had an obstruction in their crops, Hannah's father taught her how to cut the crop open, remove the blockage and sew it up. She saw their own pigs killed at the annual pig-killing feast, an important date in the calendar of rural life. As a child she had helped ewes to lamb and sows to have their litters. Poverty haunted Hannah's memories for the rest of her life: 'When I was a little wench, I seed so much poverty i' my own home, I made up my mind as I never would be poor not if savin' could stop it. Nor I never thought to get married; not till I'd saved a goodish bit i' service.'[29]

On Hannah's eighth birthday in May 1841, she left the charity school and started her first job. It was a 'petty place' where she was taught domestic service. This was a gentle introduction to the world of work: her mistress was Mrs Phillips, the wife of Andrew Phillips, a solicitor in Market Place, a thoughtful woman who was responsible for acts of kindness to Hannah and her brothers and sisters. Although socially superior to Martha Cullwick, Mrs Phillips was described by Hannah as a friend of her mother's.[30] She had no children of her own, and she trained Hannah, fed, clothed and housed her, and paid her a small wage. Hannah was there for two years during which she teached me how to do everything properly, to wait at table, to wash up, to clean silver and indeed everything so as she said there wasn't a job I couldn't do as well as the cook or housemaid . . . she used to take me with her for a ride or a-fishing. I carried the stool and minded the little dog.[31]

Hannah's uniform was a lilac cotton print frock which she made up herself, under her mistress's instructions, from material bought in Birmingham, and a white cap which had a double frill round the face and tied 'with hood strings under the chin'.[32]

In 1843 Hannah was no longer needed, and Mr Phillips gave her her first sovereign, with which she bought 'a brown straw bonnet, a pair of boots, a white shawl with sprigs, two pairs of stockings, a cap and two flowers to go in it'. She returned home delighted to see her mother and James, Richard and Ellen, but dreading living under the same roof as her father.[33]

Hannah found a job as a 'pot girl' at The Red Lion, a coaching inn, working for the Edwardses, a couple her mother knew. She earned a shilling a week and tips. The Wonder! mail coach changed horses at The Red Lion. Hannah's job included doing all the dirty work and waiting at table. When the coach came in, 'I had to serve the passengers . . . many's the tuppence I had off the gentlemen, for fetchin' 'em glasses of ale; and the ladies give me two pence for showing them the closet [lavatory].'[34]

Hannah recalled the scenes when pit wenches (girls who shovelled coal at the surface of the mines in nearby Ketley) arrived at The Red Lion at the beginning of the summer to catch the Wonder! to travel to work in the market gardens in Middlesex, having been laid off from their usual work. They had walked five miles with their boxes on their heads: 'their sweethearts came with them and blubbered and kissed the coach wheels as it went off and shouted, "Molly, keep thy legs close, till thee comes back." '

The Red Lion would be in an uproar. The coalminer sweethearts would get drunk 'and fight and hug the wenches'.[35] Hannah did well when she went round with a pewter plate after dinner 'curtseying and saying, "Please sir, remember the waitress . . ." and some of 'em give me a half penny, some a penny, and sometimes they chucked me under the chin cause I was a lively wench and tall o' my age.'[36]

In 1844, after eight months, Hannah had to leave The Red Lion. Her father was unhappy at her working there. Mrs Phillips agreed to have her back, even though she feared that it was not respectable to hire someone who had worked in a public house.[37] Hannah stayed here until Mrs Phillips died in June 1847. Knowing that she was dying, her mistress gave Hannah some of her things, and made her husband promise 'to be a friend to all of us children – Martha's children she called us', which he honoured by opening a savings account for each of the Cullwick children. Before she died Mrs Phillips pointed out Martha Marshall, a young Sunday School teacher, to Hannah, and confided that her husband planned to marry Martha as soon as he could after she had died. Hannah and the other servants followed their mistress's coffin to the churchyard wearing the mourning clothes she had provided for them in her will.[38]

In September, Hannah, now fourteen, moved three miles to Ryton Rectory to work as nursemaid to her godmother's brother, the Reverend Robert William Eyton, who now had a family of three young sons: William, aged four; Robert, two; and Philip, a baby of six months. Hannah's wages were £5 a year. The Reverend Eyton, who was one of the principal landowners in the area, was compiling his *Antiquities of Shropshire* at the time, and had the care of the 200 souls in his tiny parish, which had forty-one houses. Hannah remembered her time working for the Eytons at Ryton as the most miserable of her life: the only highlight was a visit from her mother who had walked across the fields. Soon after this Hannah was visited by a neighbour of the Cullwicks, Philip Blud, a cobbler, who told her that her father had died of 'fever'. She was shocked when Blud returned a few days later with the news of the death of her beloved mother:

> but nobody told me of her being ill else nothing'd o' kept me away. I should o' run across them fields and all the three miles in half an hour I *know*. But when Philip Blud came on the Saturday evening and said she was dead I thought it was no use though I axed to go, and all my strength seemed gone and when the missis called me out of the schoolroom from minding the children . . . into the dining room and told me I fell on the floor and she left me to cry to myself. I prayed heartily that it mayn't be true or that she'd come to life again. After a time I got up and come out – I saw Philip standing in the passage and I said, 'Is it true, Philip?' He said 'Yes.' I said, 'Where are the children?' He said, 'Up at your Uncle Owen's.'[39]

Hannah knew that her brother and sisters were safe with Owen Owen, her mother's brother, who was a beer retailer in Shifnal High Street. But the future looked bleak: her youngest sister, Mary Ann, was only three years old. Both Charles and Martha Cullwick had died of typhus fever within two weeks of each other. Charles had died on 20 November and was buried four days later: Martha passed away on 4 December and her friend Ann Howell, who was with her when she died, attended the funeral the following day.[40] The husband and wife were buried in the churchyard of St Andrew's but there was never any money to erect headstones to their memory.[41] The Reverend Eyton's wife, fearful of the 'fever', would not allow Hannah to attend her mother's funeral, or visit her brothers and sisters. Years later she recalled the night she heard of her mother's death:

> ... all night I was praying that she may come to life again ... it seemed as if my care for life or work was all gone. I'd bin thinkin' how I should work and make *her* happy for she sh'd have all my money. I'd quite lost my love for livin' ... Miss Dudley, the governess, was very kind to me and talked to me nicely and told me that I should get over it. But I said I don't think *I ever* shall.[42]

The Cullwick children were spared but the family was broken up. James, aged seventeen, had started his wheelwright's apprenticeship with Richard Pointon and was living with his master, his wife and young baby and two lodgers in Shifnal High Street. Richard Cullwick was eleven and it is probable that he was sent to live with his Uncle William Cullwick and Aunt Martha, to start his saddler's apprenticeship at Horseley Fields in Wolverhampton. Ellen was just eight and taken out of school and sent to her first job in domestic service. Mary Ann, aged three, went to her Aunt Elizabeth Cullwick, a spinster in her mid-fifties who lived at Haughton just outside Shifnal.

After the funerals Hannah's Owen and Cullwick relatives divided up the family possessions: Hannah was given her mother's rush-bottomed chair and her few clothes. She was alone and penniless and spent an unhappy winter at Ryton. She wore her mother's clothes for years, not caring how old-fashioned they looked, enjoying feeling close to her mother. Trying to make sense of what had happened, she often recalled an ominous event:

> An' I remember one day in the parlour, when we was all havin' tea, a mouse came on the table and ate some of the

bread; father catch'd it, and tied a bit o' red round its
neck, and let it go again. But it was a *sign*. It's a sure sign
of a death, when a mouse lets you catch it; and them two
[her parents] died soon after.[43]

It was a harsh winter and the work was hard but Hannah
was used to that: it was Mrs Eyton's odd, cruel behaviour
which disturbed her. 'But what I couldn't bear was the Missis
rushing at me as she did with her wild-looking eyes, and I
told my aunt it was very uncomfortable and she told me to
leave.'[44]

In June 1848 Hannah climbed aboard a horse and cart
with her box and went to work for an aunt and uncle who
had a smallholding near Newport, Shropshire. It was a
stop-gap measure and Hannah soon found another job,
working as a nursemaid to the five children of William
Liddle, a lawyer, and his wife, who lived in a substantial
eighteenth-century house in High Street, Newport. She was
paid £5 a year. Hannah stayed with this family for fifteen
months and in the summer of 1849 saw the sea for the first
time when the Liddles took her and the children to South-
port for their annual holiday. By the end of 1849 she had
moved to Langton-by-Wragby, Lincolnshire, to work as a
nursemaid for the Scotts, a curate and his wife and five
children, for £8 a year. She was encouraged to move there by
a cousin who was a housemaid at the Scotts'. 'Places' were
often got by the recommendations of a network of family
and friends.[45]

Hannah was happy at the Scotts': she liked the work, the
children and their parents, and she enjoyed eavesdropping at
the boys' lessons with their governess. While she swept and
dusted the nursery and cleaned the grates, she learned of
Cicero and Demosthenes and memorized the Greek alphabet
by peeping into their school books. She was thirsty for knowl-

edge and read a lot during the time she worked there.[46] The Scotts liked her but felt she was too young for the job and regretfully asked her to leave, though not before giving her the good 'character' essential in securing another place. There was a more disturbing reason too: egged on by the other children, Hannah had foolishly pushed their brother Roddy into a pond. The Scotts were upset about this but did not punish her as severely as they might have. This was Hannah's last post as a nursemaid. She was mortified by what she had done, but armed with a good reference from the kindly Mrs Scott, in early 1850 she went to work for the first time in a country house, Aqualate Hall, two miles east of Newport, near the Shropshire and Staffordshire border, the home of Sir Thomas and Lady Louisa Boughey.

Now aged seventeen, Hannah was tall – five feet eight inches – and strong and healthy. Her robust rustic looks would have helped her in getting the job of under-housemaid: employers favoured servants from the country who were believed to have greater stamina and better morals than girls from the town who were said to be flighty and harder to discipline. Hannah was one of two under-housemaids employed to clean the house with two charwomen, and was paid £8 a year. Sir Thomas paid the twenty-five servants personally: they went into his room one at a time at the end of every month.

Arriving on the back of a carrier's cart, Hannah was impressed by Aqualate Hall, which looked spectacular. It was a romantic Gothic mansion, with crenellated battlements, towers, spires and mullioned windows. Built in 1633, it had been extensively 'new modelled, rebuilt and considerably enlarged after 1798' by Sir Thomas's grandfather.[47]

Mrs Beeton's *Book of Household Management*, which set very high standards, describes how housemaids and their underlings, like Hannah, should perform:

'Cleanliness is next to Godliness', saith the proverb, and 'order' is in the next degree; the housemaid, then, may be said to be the handmaiden to two of the most prominent virtues. Her duties are very numerous, and many of the comforts of the family depend on their performance; but they are simple and easy to a person naturally clean and orderly, and desirous of giving satisfaction.[48]

The 1851 census gives a picture of the household. Sir Thomas Boughey was forty-two years of age, his wife was forty-four. There were eight children: the daughters, Anne, Louisa, Lucy and Selina, were sixteen, twelve, five and four respectively, and the sons were Robert, eight, Walter, six, Francis, two, and Henry the baby. The hard-pressed children's governess was a thirty-seven-year-old German woman. The two ladies' maids were Grace Crawley, aged thirty, from London, and Ann Badger, twenty-one, from Shrewsbury. The four nurses were all from Shropshire: Eliza Channock and Ann Blakeway were both aged twenty-four, Hannah Titley was nineteen and Margaret Bott, twenty-three. Hannah's fellow housemaids were twenty-eight-year-old Mary Morris of Pembrokeshire and Mary Slack, twenty-three, of Shropshire. Two of the three kitchenmaids were local – Harriet Pugh, aged twenty, and Ann Wheeler, twenty-eight; nineteen-year-old Mary Ann Bradbury was from Staffordshire. Mary Evans, the dairymaid, aged twenty-six, was Welsh.

William Rowley, the butler, aged forty, was from Somerset. The cook was a married man, born in London, John Jones. There were three footmen, John Fox, aged thirty-eight and from Shrewsbury, and Samuel Ray, twenty-eight and John Harvey, twenty-five, both from Staffordshire. John Hickman of Wellington, the brewer, was thirty-one years old. James Mercer, the coachman, was from Staffordshire and below him were four grooms: William Jarrett, James Wall and George

Jones, all local and in their twenties, and William Harrison, the eldest, from Chelsea.[49]

Housemaids got up at five or six o'clock in the morning in the summer and seven in the winter: they had to work noiselessly to clean the house, empty grates and light fires before the family rose. Then they took hot water upstairs for washing and bathing, lit the bedroom fires and emptied the chamber pots. Water-closets were a new-fangled luxury, and many employers continued to use chamber pots while servants used earth closets in the back yard. Taking hot water and coals into gentlemen's bedrooms could surprise both parties. Hannah remembered:

> I had to see gentlemen stark naked . . . I had to take up the visitors' hot water, and light the fire i' their bedrooms for 'em to get up by. I always knocked at the door first of course; then he says 'Come in!' and so I come in, and theer he'd be standing naked in his bath. [Hannah continued with her work] . . . It was my place to light the fires; so I just used to kneel down on the hearth wi' my back to him till I'd done; and then I backed out of the room.

This happened several times at Aqualate: 'I didn't know who they was but o' course I never looked at 'em, and it did me no harm.'[50]

Hannah was dismissed from Aqualate after eight months. Lady Boughey saw her and another housemaid fooling around as they cleaned the sixteen copper kettles and dismissed them both. Hannah was distraught at the thought of losing the roof over her head, and at leaving her female friends and some of the young male servants behind. She begged her ladyship to reinstate her, even offering to work for no wages:

> Well I did fret so to have to leave that grand house, with a nice park to look at and all; and I made bold and axed

to see her ... and I made such a humble curtsey and I says to her 'Oh my lady, I am so sorry to leave! If you would please let me stop without any wages, I'd do my best and be thankful!' but she tossed her head, for she was a proud lady, 'Oh nonsense, you don't suit me – you must go.'[51]

Graciously enough, Lady Boughey gave Hannah a good character, recommending her to Lady Louisa Cotes, a friend at Woodcote Hall, sixteen miles from Shrewsbury. The job was for a scullion, a demotion to the bottom rung of the ladder of domestic service.

Woodcote Hall was the seat of John Cotes, magistrate and Deputy Lieutenant for Shropshire and Staffordshire, and his wife Louisa, grand-daughter of the late Lord Liverpool, Prime Minister from 1812 to 1827, who had been one of Queen Victoria's bridesmaids. The house was 'a handsome mansion ... pleasantly situated, and surrounded with park-like grounds ... the garden and ornamental grounds comprise an area of upwards of forty acres'.[52] The Coteses had four daughters and two sons. Hannah joined a household of twenty indoor and outdoor servants but her lowly duties kept her in the scullery and away from the family and the servants like Amelia Barbary, the governess, and the housekeeper, Hannah Mold. Harriet Pheasant was lady's maid to Lady Louisa. There were three nurses to look after the children, Mary Tyan, Maria Peak and Elizabeth Baxter. The three housemaids, Ann Goosney, Hannah Hayes and Emma Jones, were all young women in their twenties, as was the dairymaid Emma Hulse. A kitchenmaid, Ann Hayes, was immediately above Hannah in the pyramid of service. Richard Luscombe, the butler, was at the apex, below him was the young French cook, Monsieur Charles Quinevit, from whom Hannah received her orders. Joshua Swallow, aged thirty-two, Robert Truman, thirty-four, and twenty-year-old Henry Whitehead were the footmen. The coachman was Edward Upstone, and a sixteen-year-old lad, Thomas Jones, was the groom [53]

A scullion earned the lowest wage: Hannah earned £8 a year. Mrs Beeton described the work:

> . . . to assist the cook; to keep the scullery clean, and all the metallic as well as earthenware utensils . . . If she be fortunate enough to have over her a good kitchenmaid and clever cook, she may very soon learn to perform various little duties connected with cooking operations, which may be of considerable service in fitting her for a more responsible place.[54]

Hannah had barely settled into her new place when in April she and Monsieur Quinevit were sent to London to get the Coteses' house ready for 'the Season'. The work was hard but life was sweet and it was Hannah's first visit to London.

CHAPTER THREE

26 May 1854: A Defining Moment

IN THE SUMMER OF 1851 Arthur Munby, now twenty-three years old, graduated from Trinity and came to London to join a profession in which he was not interested. He arrived in London with mixed feelings caused by the rigours of being called to the Bar and excitement at being away from home and the pressures placed on him by his father. He lodged with James Chamberlain, a solicitor, at 36 University Street, between Tottenham Court Road and Gower Street and enrolled as a student at Lincoln's Inn on 11 June.[1] His pupillage was in the chambers of a future Lord Chancellor, Hugh Mc Calmont Cairns, who was noted for being a 'lucid lawyer, and philanthropist'.[2] Munby soon made friends with R. D. Blackmore, another Bar student, who later wrote *Lorna Doone*.

In 1851 London was full of people flocking to see the thoroughly modern Great Exhibition and the exhibition hall which soon became known as 'The Crystal Palace'. This fabulous glass and iron structure displayed examples of manufacture, science and culture from Britain, the Empire and the rest of the world. Six million visitors, three times the population of London, visited the exhibition during the five and a half months it was open. Many were conveyed on excursions arranged by Thomas Cook and enjoyed the light refreshments supplied by Mr Schweppes.

Hannah Cullwick did not go to the exhibition: she was only entitled to a half-day off a week, usually a Sunday afternoon after all the dirty work had been done, and the exhibition was closed on the Sabbath. The Coteses stayed at 24 Grosvenor Street for two months, the entire household returning to Woodcote Hall at the end of June. Whenever she could, Hannah slipped away from the kitchen and explored the grand streets of Mayfair, doing the errands quickly in order to see as much of London as she possibly could. It was the biggest, noisiest place imaginable. Grosvenor Street was one of the best streets of the Grosvenor Estate, built in the 1720s. In 1735 it was an address of people of distinction, with aristocrats making up a third of its residents. By 1851 it was not quite so grand: the Coteses' neighbours, included, to the right, Madame Barenne, a milliner, Thomas Sheppard, tailor, two Members of Parliament, an upholsterer, dentist and solicitor; and to the left, William James Palmer, a tailor and robe-maker, and two doctors, Caesar Hawkins and George D. Pollock.[3]

At Woodcote Hannah had led an almost subterranean existence. She lived 'in a rough outhouse next the kitchen with no window to look out and could only get out through the coalhole unseen'.[4] One of her jobs was to dig the coals in the cellar and had to go to great lengths to get a breath of fresh air:

> and of an evening when I was tired of being in the scullery and still daren't ask leave of cook, I used to climb up the heaps of coal into the chimney or shoot of the coalhole and squeeze myself up through the trap at the top in the yard, and I rin in the fields, and then go down again.[5]

There was plenty of male interest in Hannah. The servants either teased her or made sexual advances or both: the French cook seems to have regarded her as his special pet, kissing her when he felt like it. One of the gardeners, though attracted to her, was disappointed that she was only a scullion and advised her that he could not possibly consider romance unless she was promoted to upper housemaid at least. The butler behaved quite differently when they were on their own: 'he would offer her sips of wine; and once snatched a kiss, as a reward for a glass of sherry'.[6] Her master showed his friends round the kitchens when Hannah was there – she once heard one of them remark, 'I say, Cotes, what a damn fine girl!'[7]

Once her dress caught alight as she tended the kitchen fires alone. She had the presence of mind to take off her burning skirt and lie down on the stone floor and 'rolled herself to and fro until the fire was out'.[8] On Sunday afternoons she would run across the fields to her old place, some three miles away, to see her friends there, and Jim the postillion would escort her home. She was nineteen and ready for romance, but not with Jim:

> I liked him for company, but I didn't ever want him for a sweetheart, just cause he was a little short chap and again he wasn't steady enough or worth having so I only talked to him like a mother. He only twittered and laughed at me whenever he came with me and in the carriage to Woodcote I tried to see him and my fellow servants teased me about him . . . but I couldn't help thinking as it was very good for me to leave Aqualate just on *his* account, cause I might o' got fond of him against myself.[9]

Whilst Hannah did not want Jim the postillion and was not attracted to any of her fellow servants, she was emotionally needy, and in her rare time off she 'felt lonely and I begun to wish I had somebody to love and to love me'.[10] She attached great significance to reading her tea leaves every morning and interpreting omens. While she was at Woodcote she 'saw a man's face as clearly as could be in the fire. I showed him to Emma [the kitchenmaid]. She said, "Ah, one of us will see somebody like that someday." It was such a nice, manly face with a moustache. I little thought I should see such a face.'[11]

Hannah spent some of her time working at Pitchford Hall, seven miles south of Shrewsbury, about twenty miles from Woodcote. Lady Louisa Cotes inherited this property, a sixteenth-century timber-framed country house built in the 1570s, on the death of her father. Pitchford was a village of fewer than 200 people, its name derived from its ancient bitumen spring, and Hannah's place of work was 'exceedingly picturesque in appearance, and the grounds are beautifully diversified and richly wooded'.[12] At certain times of the year, the Coteses would decamp with their servants to Pitchford which was more convenient for the balls and the social whirl of Shrewsbury. As a local dignitary, John Cotes was expected to host balls with his wife and be seen in the county.

The first photograph of Hannah was taken while she was working at Pitchford in 1853. As was customary, she had her likeness taken in her Sunday best. She looked stiff and serious as her head would have been held in a clamp to prevent it moving during the long exposure. She wore her best frock and frilled white cap, which she had probably made herself, and a bonnet and cape. She might have walked, or hitched a ride, to Shrewsbury to have her picture taken. (Plate 2)

Hannah was back in London at Grosvenor Street for the 1853 Season. As usual, the cook, Monsieur Quinevit, was there. As they worked together one afternoon in June he told Hannah about a play that was being performed nearby at the Princess's Theatre in Oxford Street and gave her the evening off to see it.[13] This was the first time she had ever been to the theatre: the experience was so thrilling it defined her life ever after. (Plate 3)

She would have turned left into New Bond Street and walked up to Oxford Street, then turning right she would have crossed Regent Circus, reaching her destination at number 73. The building had started life as a bazaar and exhibition hall in 1830 and was converted into the Princess's Theatre in 1836 in honour of the then Princess Victoria. In 1850 Charles Kean, son of Edmund Kean, took over the management of the theatre and and staged a series of Shakespearean revivals and melodramas. Kean's decision to stage Byron's tragedy *Sardanapalus*, written in 1821, was shrewd and timely. During the late 1840s much archaeological evidence of ancient Babylon and Ninevah had been unearthed by Austen Layard, and by 1851 these discoveries were made available in popular books to a public thirsty for knowledge of this distant world. Kean had historical reference for the sets and costumes of *Sardanapalus* at his disposal and was determined to exploit a growing interest in all things classical. Improvements in gas lighting meant that all the resources were in place for Kean and his designer, Mr Grieve, to stage a spectacular production which would entertain and educate an audience of more than 1,700 people a night. The play is a vivid tale of mad love. Sardanapalus was the king of Ninevah and Assyria, and a tragic, romantic hero in the Shakespearean mould; his subjects had grown restless and even bored during his largely peaceful reign and were itching for war. He was a sybarite and hedonist who gives voice to Byron's democratically inclined views. Sardanapalus is poetic and weak, has no appetite for war, and is madly in love with one of his many slaves, Myrrha, who loves him in return. He makes no secret of this love to his wife, telling Myrrha: 'thy own sweet will shall be the only barrier which ever arises betwixt thee and me ... my chiefest joy is to contribute to thine every wish. I do not dare to breathe my own desire, lest it should clash with thine ...' and 'I had rather lose an empire than thy presence.'[14]

Sardanapalus's family despair of his excessive love of Bacchus and loathing of war: he is a life-lover, certainly not

a war-monger, as would normally be expected of a king. He
tells Myrrha he would like to:

> . . . lay down the dull tiara,
> And share a cottage on the Caucasus
> With thee, and wear no crowns but those of flowers.

The extent of their love is made clear in Myrrha's response:

> Master, I am your slave! Man, I have loved you! –
> Loved you, I know not by what fatal weakness,
> Although a Greek, and born a foe to monarchs –
> A slave, and hating fetters – an Ionian,
> And, therefore, when I love a stranger, more
> Degraded by that passion than by chains!
> Still I have loved you . . .[15]

Because love knows no boundaries, Myrrha is in love with
a king even though she is a republican and a democrat and
asks herself why she loves him:

> Why do I love this man? My country's daughters
> Love none but heroes. But I have no country!
> The slave hath lost all save her bonds. I love him;
> And that's the heaviest link of the long chain –
> To love whom we esteem not. Be it so . . .[16]

The text describes Myrrha's strength and the king's weakness: he calls her 'Joy's true herald' and 'gentle and austere'.
Once he has banished the troublesome rebels, her role is to be
tough with him, and when he eventually goes into battle, she
is happy to go too. When the palace is invaded she stays and
fights with him. Sardanapalus tells her, 'My chiefest glory shall
be to make me worthier of thy love.' The madness of their
love has overtaken her such that 'I loved until I half forgot I
was a slave.'[17] Sardanapalus wants to marry her and make her
his queen and is moved by the way she has empowered herself

through her love: 'I did abase myself as much in being your paramour, as though you were a peasant' . . . and 'I feel it [the abasement] deeply – more deeply than all things but love.'[18] An exhausting battle follows and they both decide to commit suicide: she insists on dying on the funeral pyre with Sardanapalus: he climbs onto it first and she lights the flames and then springs forward, throwing herself into the inferno.

Newspaper accounts of the 1853 production are full of praise and give an idea of how mesmerizing an impression this play would have made on an inexperienced twenty-year-old woman like Hannah. No expense had been spared on attention to historical detail:

> Mr Grieve and artists of the highest ability have been engaged in the production of the splendid scenery, the groupings, the processions and the movements of the dancing girls have occupied the unceasing attention of that prince of ballet-masters, Mr Oscar Byrne, whilst the machinery-man, the property-man, and the perruquier have found ample room for the exercise of their industry and ingenuity.[19]

Hannah sat in the gallery in a sixpenny seat (a day's wages) and was transported. It was hot and dark and bright in the theatre and the play was most exciting thing she had ever seen:

> After marching and counter-marching, the stage is lined, and *Sardanapalus* enters, accompanied by Myrrha, in a splendid chariot drawn by two horses, magnificently caparisoned. An umbrella of gold hues hangs suspended above the car and the slaves fan with peacock tails the recumbent and luxurious monarch. He is elegantly attired . . . rings in his ears. Bracelets on his wrists and across his biceps. A scarlet robe fringed with gold, and beneath a shirt of satin. Myrrha is attired in a plain white robe of

graceful form . . . a buzz of admiration from the ladies of the audience marks their sense of the magnificent dress and trappings.

The author of this review is unimpressed with Charles Kean as Sardanapalus in the first half of the play – 'he is not effective in any speech he has to deliver in acts one, two and three' – but was pleased to report his performance did improve, it seems under the influence of his wife who was playing Myrrha:

> A beautiful and exciting dance by the whole of the corps de ballet is here very deservedly encored . . . Mrs Kean . . . plays with her accustomed sweetness and appreciation of the beautiful. Her soothing to rest with the lyre the wounded monarch, is unsurpassed and unsurpassable.[20]

Kean's acting improves with Act 4 where he 'rises far above his former self. He is now and from this period to the final consummation something like a Kean.' While wearing copies of Assyrian dress of the period, Mrs Kean and the other ladies of the company did not take off their corsets and vast petticoats for the production.

Hannah walked back to Grosvenor Street on air. She identified immediately with Myrrha, and resolved that she too would be a slave to a master, that this was the only kind of love that she would seek:

> and when I see that Myra [sic] as was the king's slave, you know, I *was* took with her! I never thought of him having a wife, so as her love was wicked; but I thought, if I was to love anyone, *that's* what I should like: for him to be above me, and me to be his slave, like Myra.[21]

Hannah and Myrrha were both unfree but independent. Although Hannah was not owned by her masters, she was a young woman alone in the world, with no family home to return to if she lost her job. Myrrha had been wrenched from her own people and culture, and Hannah identified with this. It had been a total theatrical experience, tragic and romantic. From this moment on Hannah desired only a master–slave relationship like that of Myrrha and Sardanapalus. Nothing else would do as a model for love.

At the end of the Season the house in Grosvenor Street was shut up and the family and servants returned to Shropshire. During the years Hannah worked for the Cotes she did her best to keep in contact with her siblings: by the early 1850s James was a wheelwright; her younger brother Dick had left his apprenticeship with their Cullwick relations in Wolverhampton and walked to London; her sister Ellen came to work at Woodcote at Hannah's recommendation; and Polly, the baby of the family, was living with their Aunt Elizabeth at Haughton. Hannah walked across the fields to visit them both.

> carrying with her a big hare, two rabbits and a plum puddin' . . . 'All the servants [at Woodcote] had roast beef and plum puddin' on Sundays – us under servants and all; and Emma the kitchenmaid and me used to save our puddins to give away. And I'd axed the keeper to give me summat for Aunt and he give me the hare – throwed it under the sink for me; and the underkeeper gie me the rabbits. Aunt *was* pleased wi' 'em. And her used to keep a loaded gun in her cottage, you know and shot rabbits.'[22]

In 1854 Hannah was back in London again for the Season, and with Monsieur Quinevit's permission she had a visit from brother Dick on her twenty-first birthday on 26 May. She walked part of the way home with him to his lodgings and kissed him goodbye, and as she crossed Oxford Street to take the back streets back to Grosvenor Street 'a gentleman spoke to me and I answered him – that was Massa's face that I'd seen in the fire but I didn't know it again, till a good while after'.[23] She was wearing a lilac cotton frock, white apron, blue shawl with red and white spots, and a black bonnet with a white cap inside.[24]

The gentleman was Arthur Munby, roughly the same height as Hannah, with brown hair and a moustache, and out and about enjoying his hobby – collecting information about working women. The streets of London bustled with all sorts of women: servants on errands, milliners and dressmakers delivering finished garments, fruit and flower-sellers, prostitutes, shop-girls, milkwomen, charwomen and laundresses, rag-pickers. Munby collected them, or rather the stories of their lives, and their likenesses too. He started his collection of photographs of working women in the mid-1850s. Disillusioned with his barrister's pupillage and struggling to qualify for the Bar, he would walk for miles to study his subject, and then approach the woman and question her about the detail of her working life. This was the spirit in which he approached Hannah in Oxford Street. He spotted her from a distance and moved to catch up with her. Years later he would recall in detail how she looked and behaved on that day: 'her clothing, her large bare round ruddy arms and her laborious hands were those of the humblest servant, but her lovely young face was queenlike in feature and expression' and

> she carried a red bundle, hardly redder than the arm that held it. A robust hardworking peasant lass, with the marks of labour everywhere: yet endowed with a grace and beauty, and obvious intelligence that would have become a lady of the highest. Such a combination I had dreamt of and sought for; but I have never seen it save in her.[25]

Munby spent the next fifty years of his life collecting information about thousands of women. Sometimes he had their pictures taken, or bought pictures of women to fill a gap in his knowledge or collection, as if they were a rare or endangered species.

Hannah was as impressed with Munby as he was with her. They arranged to meet again. He bought her a blue shawl which she would treasure for the rest of her life as a 'sacred relic'. This odd couple were smitten with each other. The physical attraction between them was overpowering, but Hannah's modesty was such that she found it hard to understand why Arthur was attracted to her and was taken aback by his words. After they met, and while she was still at Grosvenor Street, she would:

> run upstairs from my scullery up to our attic (and it was a long way too) when I'd a chance and look at myself in the glass theer, an' wonder however you could come to love me, the simpleton.[26]

Their first kiss confirmed her feelings for him. She loved his mouth and sweet breath: 'Aye that's why I kissed you first when yo' axed me. It was to see what your mouth was like . . . I knowed you was good by the feel of your mouth. An' I couldna love no man if I didna like his mouth.' Arthur was fascinated by regional accents and would have been attracted to hers which was West Staffordshire, not so nasal as that of Wolverhampton and the Black Country.[27] Suddenly the summer of 1854 was giddy for both of them. They met as often as she could escape from her duties but the time came for the Cotes to return to Shropshire.

Although they wrote to each other while Hannah was still in London, and after she returned to Shropshire, no letters survive from the first stage of their love affair. We have to rely on their reminiscences years later of those early heady days, and on the poems Arthur wrote about Hannah. His unhappiness in his profession was balanced by his interest in working women, and then, from the summer of 1854, transformed by his secret love for Hannah. He had hoped his poetry could earn him a living if he dared go against his father and abandon the law, but the reception of the poems in *Benoni* had not encouraged him. He also took an active interest in the Working Men's College newly founded in 1854 in Red Lion Square.[28]

Hannah and Arthur's romance had to remain a secret, otherwise they would have been undone. It was unthinkable for a man of Arthur's class to be able to have a respectable relationship with someone so far down the social ladder as a servant. Sexual favours, yes; marital bliss, no. Hannah's status as the lowest type of servant made matters worse. His parents, family and friends would have been shocked by his choice. Her people would also have looked askance at the situation and worried about Hannah's long-term future. If the Coteses had found out they would have dismissed her on the spot, it was such a social solecism. There were 'misalliances' which were often written about in the press in great detail, but they were scandalous, and it would have taken a braver man than Arthur Munby to tell the world of his love for a woman as 'low-born as Hannah'. The Cullwicks were not quite the peasant stock that her ruddy and rustic appearance might have suggested. But Hannah did not wear her family tree on her sleeve, and the years of humility taught at her mother's knee, and as a Bluecoat girl, made her at ease with her low station. She had no ambition to move up the social ladder, even if it would end her life of hard work and provide her with the status of being a 'lady'.

Hannah was overjoyed at having found romance, and perhaps a master to whom she could be a slave, but she had to keep these feelings to herself. It was dangerous to confide in one's fellow servants. Politics and gossip below stairs could be fevered. When Arthur's letters arrived at Woodcote or

Pitchford they would have been noticed: when she collected letters at the nearest post office, the clerk would wonder who could be writing to Hannah in an educated hand. There was little privacy in a long, busy day to write love letters. But she managed.

In the autumn, while she was at Pitchford Hall, Hannah managed to get an afternoon off to meet Munby in Shrewsbury, the nearest town, and relatively easy for him to reach by train. She paid precious pennies for a ride on a cart on the six-mile journey to an appointment on the banks of the River Severn.[29] They discussed the immediate future, arranging that she would leave the Coteses, visit her relatives in Shifnal for two weeks in January, and then travel to London and look for a place so that they could see more of each other.

She spent most of her stay at her Aunt Elizabeth's cottage in Haughton with her sister Polly who was now ten years old. While in Shifnal she wrote to Munby, and at his suggestion started a diary of her days, paying particular attention to her various tasks. Her days here were spent sewing, baking bread, feeding her uncle's cattle, child-minding, preparing meals, going to church, reading, getting to know Polly, and catching up on news of the Owens and the Cullwicks.[30]

On Monday, 22 January 1855 Hannah waved goodbye to her aunt and Polly, carried her box to Shifnal and caught the train to London and an uncertain future. Furtive and nervous, Munby met her at Isambard Kingdom Brunel's new Paddington station. He could not openly greet a social inferior such as Hannah. They had to make signals and eye movements to acknowledge each other until they found themselves behind closed doors. She had to walk behind him and speak to him without attracting attention. If she had walked with him, passers-by might have made insulting remarks to her, not him. Working-class as well as middle-class folk were capable of expressing hostility to a relationship such as theirs which threatened all social mores.

For the next three weeks Hannah stayed at the Servants' Home in Clare Market, just off New Inn Square, in a tiny, cold room, sleeping on a straw bed, for which she paid five shillings and sixpence a week while she looked for a new situation.[31] Munby probably secured her place there with his personal recommendation.[32] Armed with a good character from Lady Louisa Cotes, Hannah looked for work near to where Munby was lodging, but could find nothing to suit and was worried about spending her tiny savings.

At this time she adopted her lifelong name for her sweetheart, 'Massa', a phonetic transcription of the Shropshire pronunciation of master, which was used for the head of a family or business. Recalling this time, Hannah gives a hint of the fetishistic behaviour that would come to dominate their lives and give them both pleasure and pain: 'There Massa came to see me again, and there was where I first black'd my face with *oil and lead*.'[33] Munby loved Hannah 'blacking up' as a chimney sweep, smearing her face and body with black lead (used to clean ranges and stoves). He was not just fascinated by the work that women did, he loved to see them dirty from their labours. This suggests the unfolding of a bizarre scene: the preparation of the materials, Hannah smuggling him into her room, and then her 'blacking up' to please themselves.

In the depths of winter Hannah left London at five o'clock one morning to travel to Henham Hall, a hundred miles away in Suffolk, to work as a kitchen-maid for Lord Stradbroke. She would never forget 'how miserable I felt when Massa wished me goodbye'. It was a bitterly cold three-hour journey from Shoreditch station. On arrival she boarded a horse-drawn coach for a further three-hour journey to the lodge gates, where the laundrymaid met me with a man and a cart for my box. The housekeeper [Mrs Smith] stared at me but didn't speak at me for ever so long and then said to the charwoman, 'She looks young' and then to me, 'You can go in the laundry for some tea and then come in and get his lordship's dinner up.' I'd made her a curtsey and when she made no answer I thought I was sure she was unkind and my heart began to fail me, but the servants was nice in the laundry and I made haste and put on my cotton frock and cap and apron to be in the kitchen by six. Mrs Smith was most unkind to me in the ordering and I was ready to say I'd go back [to London] in the morning. I told Bill the groom but he said, 'Never mind her, she's drunk and doesn't know what she's about – you stop and you'll get on alright', and as it was winter and so far back [to London] I thought I'd stop.[34]

Hannah gradually settled into her new place: it was a promotion from being a scullion, and she was proud to work for a lord. Stradbroke was the 2nd Earl and Lord Lieutenant of Suffolk who had succeeded his father in 1827, and an elderly bachelor (he married in 1857, aged sixty-three). His mother, the Dowager Countess, was the mistress of the household. Henham Hall, five miles from Southwold, had been the country seat of the Stradbrokes for 300 years. The local hamlet numbered 101 people. The Hall was 'a mansion of considerable elegance and is surrounded by a very extensive park' and had been rebuilt after a fire in 1773.[35]

Hannah was happy for most of the eighteen months she was at Henham although she was up at five in the morning and not in bed until eleven. From her attic bedroom she could sometimes see the sea and she appreciated her surroundings. It was a household of sixteen servants and she made friends with another Hannah, a laundry-maid, Bill Harvey the groom, and Mary and Rachel, also housemaids. The housekeeper, Ann Smith, was a spinster in her forties, and like all 'upper' servants of a certain age, was addressed as 'Mrs' though she was not married. Her drinking and poor health caused her to be irascible with all the servants, not just Hannah.[36] The Countess, who died in 1856, aged eighty-seven, made a lasting impression on Hannah as she went back to London to die:

> she wished us a kind goodbye and said how she thought it'd be the last visit to Henham so she gave us servants a new cotton frock and half a sovereign and the upper housemaid and the laundrymaid a whole one and a stuff frock each. The lady gave me good advice. I wasn't to mind the housekeeper's temper . . . 'and be careful whom you choose for a husband'. And after the Countess had shown me the pictures in her room which she had painted and used to get up ever so early for the light, she took my right hand in her delicate one and said goodbye.[37]

In April 1855, Hannah was delighted to learn that she and her friend Mary Clark the housemaid, one footman and William Patmore the butler, were to be sent to London where the Stradbrokes would spend the Season in their house at 32 South Street, just off Park Lane:

> I thought I was lucky I sh'd see my Massa again. We had orders and started early one fine morning. The butler rode in the same carriage with us and talked quite freely and joked with us but I was thinking mostly of who I should see when I got to London.[38]

Hannah described number 32, which, like the Coteses' house, was part of the Grosvenor Estate, as 'a nice little house'. By the mid-1850s the directories show how mixed very smart neighbourhoods could be. The Stradbrokes' neighbours included the Dowager Countess Sandwich, Lieutenant General Hare-Clarges, Lady Grenville, Lady Cardigan, Lady

Featherstonehaugh and the Honourable George Matthew Fortescue. There was a public house, The Carved Lion, at number 30, and further down the street were several lodging houses: Jesse Buggins ran one at number 11.[39]

Hannah's duties in London included waiting on the butler and the London housekeeper, cleaning their sitting room, all the areas below stairs and the front steps. It was this last duty which held a thrill for Hannah and Massa. The summer of 1855 was the beginning of his voyeuristic trips to see her at work: at a prearranged time he would stand at a discreet distance so as not to attract attention and, choosing a different vantage-point each visit, watch Hannah scrubbing the steps leading up to the front door. It gave Arthur a particular thrill to watch her doing this lowly work in the public gaze and she enjoyed doing it for him. The secrecy of their affair gave them a frisson of excitement and sustained their romance on those occasions when they could not speak to each other:

> When she came out of that door, in white cap and cotton frock, homely and bare-armed, carrying her pail and scrubbing brush, and knelt down in the street and cleaned those steps and flags ... how I chafed in secret that I could not take her away and give her the rank that seemed her due. And yet nothing could be more fresh and charming than the Homeric simplicity of acts like these done by such a maiden . . . the untaught ease and loveliness of movement with which she beautified even such degrading work as the scrubbing of street steps.[40]

These were the highlights of Hannah's stay in London: the times Arthur could snatch from his working day to watch her work were supplemented by other visits, two or three times a week, when they would daringly walk together in Hyde Park, which was at the end of South Street. She also visited him at a room he rented in the Temple into which he moved in November 1857.

> And when I could I axed leave for the evening and went to the Temple where Massa had shown me the way and axed me to go *if I liked*. Of course I was shy at first, but I wasn't *afraid*. I forget whether I'd begun to wash his feet then or not, but it wasn't long afore I did. I was glad o' that as well as any other jobs Massa found me to do, both for being useful and for showing my humility and that I never wanted to be set up.[41]

On her return to Henham Hannah nervously requested Mrs Smith the housekeeper to ask Lord Stradbroke if her sister Ellen could have a job as a scullery maid. He interviewed Hannah about her family, enquiring if any of her brothers were soldiers, and hearing from Mrs Smith what a good worker Hannah was, he agreed. She wrote to Ellen at Woodcote telling her the good news and sent some of her savings for her sister to buy new clothes.[42]

Hannah settled into the rhythms of a kitchen life determined by the seasons of the year: the autumn meant pickling walnuts and bottling fruits grown on the estate. Mrs Smith was often confined to her room, which led to a happier atmosphere in the kitchen, although one of Hannah's duties was to cook her meals and she was a difficult woman. Ellen joined the household in the autumn, and there were Massa's letters to look forward to. When they were loving she was happy, but he did expect her replies to be prompt and include detailed descriptions of the work she did. This was a difficult request, given how busy her days were and the little privacy she had in which to sit down and write. Hannah was bereft on days when she got no letter from Arthur and overjoyed when she did: but his replies could be critical and this upset her. He expected her to write in much more detail about how she spent her days. He could also criticize her behaviour with the other servants. The whole business of letter-writing was a problem: it was hard to please her Massa without incurring the displeasure of Mrs Smith, and the curiosity of her new friends. Describing Monday, 20 August, 1855, she wrote:

> Did my washing this morning. Taking the seeds out of currants all the afternoon . . . the maids asked me to go and have a game of cards with them in the laundry. I almost shrink from writing that last sentence for I'm afraid you won't like to know that. But I shall not do it again.

Four days later she was 'in trouble about my letter and writing an answer in time for today's post'. The following day is a heartfelt entry in her diary: 'I've not been happy today. I've thought so much of the letter I wrote yesterday and am anxiously expecting the answer, yet I dread its coming.' The post took two days to reach Henham from London and this added to Hannah's misery. A week after she had written to Munby she was anxious: 'I have felt very wretched today and wondered whether I should have an unkind letter in the morning, or whether it will be an angry one.' She received a letter from him the next day, and she was so overjoyed at its contents she could not put her feelings into words for her diary.[43]

Munby was finally called to the Bar on 17 November, after a four-year slog.[44] His father must have been pleased. The tensions between Munby's private and professional lives spilled over into his letters to Hannah, causing him to vent some of his frustrations on her. While he was relieved to be pleasing his father, decisions about his future now loomed, and a career in the law seemed inevitable. He did a certain amount of conveyancing, but a dazzling future in the legal profession was not to be. He did his best, however, and kept up with his hobbies: wrote poems, corresponded with his family and friends from Cambridge, collected more working women and enjoyed his dangerous romance with Hannah. For keen letter-writers like Munby life was made easier in 1855 with the introduction of pillar-boxes: the first ever was not far from his lodgings, on the corner of Fleet Street and Farringdon Street. There were now ten collections a day, starting at nine in the morning and ending at ten at night. This innovation of street collection and door-to-door delivery was the idea of the writer and post office employee, Anthony Trollope. Before this one had to take letters to a receiving office and collect them from there, or rely on freelance collectors who would deliver them for a gratuity.

Munby spent Christmas with his family at York, while Hannah remained at Henham Hall. The Munbys probably wondered when Arthur would marry: there was no obvious love in his life. He was twenty-seven, a barrister, and making his way in the world at last. He would have had to invent a fake identity for the young woman – it was clearly a female hand – who had written to him last Christmas and this. With frequent practice, Hannah's charity-school handwriting improved. It was clear and confident and would have passed as that of a 'lady'.

In the spring of 1856 Munby paid his only visit to Hannah at Henham. He probably stayed at The Angel Commercial Hotel in Halesworth and walked over on a Sunday to Wangford where he knew she would be attending St Peter's Church. It was an odd visit as it was hardly possible for them to speak to each other without being noticed in such a small place where strangers were commented on immediately. Undaunted by these difficulties, Munby positioned himself so that he could see Hannah and watch her and the other Stradbroke servants troop into the church and sit at the back.[45] But on the way back to his hotel he got hopelessly lost and irate: 'Massa came to see me at Suffolk and lost his way back to his hotel . . . and he told me if I stopped there he wouldn't come again.'[46] Munby's harsh ultimatum worked and Hannah informed Mrs Smith that she wanted to give notice and leave at the end of the forthcoming visit to London. She regretted leaving Ellen and her new friends but felt she had to obey Massa. This was the second time that Hannah had encouraged her sister to go and work with her and then left: this inevitably led to a resentment on Ellen's part which was never resolved.

Hannah had to wash the the vast dinner service and put it away for the summer, clean and pack any items needed for the London house, and leave the kitchen at Henham spick and span. She swept the kitchen chimney and 'filled a box with soot for my hands to bring with me to London'.[47] She brought the soot to indulge Munby's love of dirt. Back in London, she and Arthur saw each other when circumstances permitted. A few days before her twenty-third birthday Hannah was confirmed at St George's Church in Hanover Square: as it was Munby's idea, there is every likelihood that he was present in the congregation, watching her.[48]

On Wednesday, 26 August Hannah started her new job as a maid of all work for a Jewish family in Westbourne Park. She does not tell us their name or address, only that her mistress was 'Mrs G'.[49] She responded to a newspaper advertisement, taking up this new situation immediately to earn £16 a year. On her arrival at half past nine in the evening,

> the housemaid showed me upstairs to our bedroom and when I had got all my things up she left me with a light [a candle] and I stayed there sometime arranging my things and when I come down into the kitchen I had supper. I then helped the housemaid to mend stockings till we went to bed.[50]

Hannah was happy here and enjoyed her new role as maid of all work. She liked her mistress, who often came to help with the cooking in the kitchen, and although the work was arduous, she was in London and near Massa. A typical day would start at half past six in the morning and include lighting the kitchen fire; cleaning the boots; sweeping the hall and scouring the front steps; cleaning the privies; preparing and cooking all meals and washing the dishes; scouring the scullery; making up fires; knife-cleaning; and some cleaning of the rooms above stairs that were not the work of the housemaid. The working day rarely ended before half past ten at night.[51]

It was not too difficult for Hannah and Arthur to meet, but having to take her time off on Saturdays, and not Sundays, to suit the Jewish Sabbath was not convenient, and she left after working there only six weeks. Hannah's 'missis' was not happy at her leaving so soon.[52] During her short time at Westbourne Grove Hannah made an important friendship. Unhappy at being in Henham Hall without her sister, Hannah's sister Ellen had followed Hannah to London and found lodgings with a family in Clerkenwell called the Smiths. Hannah spent time there with Ellen and made friends with Mrs Emma Smith and her daughter Sarah. Mrs Smith, a widow from Suffolk, and her daughter, became a surrogate family for the Cullwicks: Ellen, Hannah, Dick and Polly all stayed there whenever they were in London and 'out of a place'.[53] Mrs Smith seems to have been a mother-substitute, reliable and wise, a few years older than Hannah's own mother would have been if she had lived. Sarah Smith would remain a friend to the Cullwicks long after her mother died. The Smiths' house at 6 Wingrove Place (parts of which survive as Skinner Street), which was in a rough, working-class neighbourhood, came to be Hannah's London home. In times of crisis she lodged there and worked to pay for her keep.

In October Hannah went to work for Thomas Jackson, an upholsterer, and his wife, at 25 Beaufoy Terrace near the Edgware Road, again as a maid of all work for £16 a year.[54]

Mrs Beeton was unusually sympathetic towards the maid of
all work:

> perhaps the only one of her class deserving of commiser-
> ation: her life is a solitary one, and in some places, her
> work is never done. She is also subject to rougher treat-
> ment than either the house or kitchen-maid, especially
> in her early career: she starts in life, probably a girl of
> thirteen, with some small tradesman's wife as her mistress,
> just a step above her in the social scale; and although the
> class contains among them many excellent, kind-hearted
> women, it also contains some very rough specimens of the
> feminine gender, and to some of these it occasionally falls
> to give our maid-of-all-work the first lessons in her
> multifarious occupations. By the time she has become a
> tolerable servant, she is probably engaged in some respect-
> able tradesman's house, where she has to rise with the
> lark, for she has to do in her own person all the work
> which in larger establishments is performed by cook,
> kitchen-maid, and housemaid, and occasionally the part
> of a footman's duty, which consists in carrying messages.[55]

Beaufoy Terrace was a short walk from open fields yet to
be devoured by housing. The Jacksons were a young married
couple and hoping to go up in the world. They employed
Hannah and a housemaid called Ellen, and sent the washing
out to a local laundress. It was a Pooterish street. Life here
was very different to Hannah's previous places: everything was
scaled down – the size of the house, garden and the household
of servants. But she was pleased to be closer to Massa. Within
a few weeks of starting to work for the Jacksons, at Munby's
instruction, Hannah had her likeness taken at a local photographer's studio, probably at Joseph Henry Cave's studio at
17 Portman Place, a short walk away.
    Munby liked to see her, with her sleeves pulled up as if she

had been interrupted at work. Hannah's apron was dirty from her morning's work and she wore a white cotton cap, the servant's badge. She looked unflinchingly at the photographer, at life. As yet there was no leather 'navvy strap', as she and Munby called it, on her right wrist: the symbol of his ownership which she was happy to wear.

Hannah's diaries are descriptions of a working life driven by routine and the tyranny of the clock. Her long days are relieved by Massa's letters, and their clandestine meetings. She struck up a relationship with the postman in order to intercept letters being delivered in case the Jacksons learned of those letters she received, and their frequency. They would certainly have remarked on the educated hand which had written them.

A typical day of the five years Hannah worked at Beaufoy Terrace is as follows:

Saturday, January 10, 1857: Blacked the grates. Lighted the fire. Had breakfast. Sent up the parlour breakfast. Cleaned the hearth. Washed the dirty things up in the scullery. Cleaned the front hall and steps. Cleaned the boots and knives, the stairs, watercloset, and passage. Went on some errands. Plucked a pheasant and roasted it and got ready for dinner at six o' clock. After dinner I washed up and cleaned the kitchen and scullery on my knees. Went to bed at twelve o'clock.[56]

In 1857 Hannah and Arthur made the first of many visits to 57 Oxford Street, where, directed by him, she was photographed in various guises by a German 'photographic artist', Philip Fink. Hannah was familiar with Oxford Street from her stays in London working for the Cotes and then the Stradbrokes. If they had left Fink's studio and turned left they would have arrived at the Princess's Theatre where she had seen the play which was the inspiration for the images that she, Munby and Fink would concoct. In the picture of her sitting on the floor Munby has instructed Fink to crop him out of the photograph. They are his knees which Hannah leans against and his hand on her shoulder: he was in no danger of being recognized. This is a woman at the feet of a man who 'owns' her. (Plate 7) Munby wondered if Hannah would pass as a lady, but no Victorian ladies wore slave chains to which only their sweethearts had the key. At Arthur's wish Hannah wore the chain to which only he had the key for twenty years.[57] (Plate 6)

Sunday afternoons were the time for Hannah to see Arthur. She would slip away after the chores were done and had to return at ten o'clock. Employers insisted that their servants had no 'followers', men friends visiting the house. Mrs Jackson tolerated her taking time off at other times too, and would sometimes give her permission to go out at short notice when Arthur had sent her a note to say he would meet her in the fields nearby. The Jacksons were easy-going employers, thoughtful and generous, often giving Hannah and Ellen small treats such as tickets for special outings and tips for extra work when they had been entertaining friends. On 14 February, Hannah managed to spend some time with her Valentine at the end of a busy day:

> Blacked the range and lit the fire. Dusted the breakfast room and cleaned the kettle and got breakfast ready. Cleaned the hearth and birdcage [for eight birds]. Washed dirty things in the scullery. Cleaned the knives and boots. Sent the breakfast up at eleven o'clock. Went to . . . the shops with orders. Got dinner ready. Cleaned the front hall and steps on my knees. Scoured the stairs and passage. Cleaned the kitchen floor and scullery on my knees. Cleaned my candlestick. Washed up in the scullery. Went out for a short time with Massa and came

in and got supper ready. Cleared away afterwards and went to bed.[58]

Hannah was able to have her brother Dick and Emma Smith to tea in the kitchen regularly, and to entertain her youngest sister Polly when she came to London.[59] Aged thirteen, Polly was in London for the first time, en route to her position as a shop-girl in Ipswich.

On 18 February the Jacksons gave Hannah most of the day off and Arthur took her to the Crystal Palace, now relocated in Sydenham. This outing was part of Munby's programme of supplementing Hannah's meagre charity-school education: she enjoyed reading and he regularly sent her 'improving literature', such as the writings of Hannah More, the spokes-woman for 'the domestic ideology of the two spheres', and Mrs Gaskell's *Mary Barton*, and took her to exhibitions, museums and art galleries. After she had lit the fires, cleaned the hearth, sent the breakfast up, washed the dishes and cleaned the boots and knives, she dressed in her Sunday best and caught an omnibus to London Bridge station where she met Arthur at midday:

> It was a fine day – we walked about a good deal and we looked at a great many things and he told me about all we saw but chiefly about the architecture and the pictures and the antediluvian animals. Massa was much pleased with my hands because they were red and coarse and I don't think he was ashamed of me but he would have been if he had seen anyone he knew. We came home before nine o'clock and I stayed with him till ten and I got home before eleven and stayed up till twelve for Mr Jackson.[60]

On 11 June the Jacksons' first child, a son, was born. Hannah noted that her mistress 'was taken ill' soon after seven o'clock in the evening. Mr Jackson went for Mrs Warwick, a local midwife, and at ten o'clock Hannah was sent to collect 'Dr S' in a hansom cab. Hannah worked through a long night and started the next day without any sleep:

> We sat up and I was busy getting the tea and supper ready for the gentlemen and cutting sandwiches. I went to the chemists at three o'clock. I walked nearly to Hyde Park before I could get a cab to take me to Marlborough Street and the man was fast asleep inside the cab and and I had a great deal of trouble to wake him. When I got home again I was busy getting breakfast for all the different people and that begun my Friday's work.[61]

During 1857 there are several references in Hannah's diary to her chimney-sweeping. The Victorians consumed vast amounts of coal for heating and cooking and professional sweeps were regular visitors to all Victorian homes. But Hannah, unnecessarily, cleaned the kitchen chimney herself to show Munby how hard she worked, and to make herself as black as possible. She appreciated Arthur's love of the contrasts between their lives, and by sweeping the chimney she was exaggerating the difference. She was underlining her status as slave, and his as master. She kept the chimney-sweeping a secret from the Jacksons: once she forgot to wash her face and when she answered her mistress's call, 'I went upstairs with a black face but I didn't know it and Mrs Jackson said, "Oh what a black face you've got," and I said I had been cleaning the saucepans.'[62]

Hannah rejoiced in emptying the slops from the chamber pots, loved scrubbing out the water-closet and the floors and steps on her hands and knees, and revelled in using her bare hands to clean the horse manure from the foot-scraper at the front door. Many thousands of horses on London's streets meant that dung was everywhere:

Swept and cleaned the front door and the flags and the scraper with my hands, and curb [sic] stone. Cleaned the kitchen passages and scullery and water-closet and swept and dusted my bedroom and emptied the slops. When I had done my work I took the [tin] bath into my room and had a wash all over.[63]

She was stared at and the butt of remarks about her dirty appearance and eccentric behaviour. But she was unabashed: 'shook the curtains and doormats and swept the front hall and flags and the steps. Cleaned outside the front door with my Belgium cap on and people stared at me very much but I didn't mind that.'[64]

There are moments of a kind of ecstasy in getting as dirty as she could, and telling her Massa about it. One Saturday in October,

the sweep came at three o'clock and swept the kitchen chimney. I was got very wet and dirty cleaning the paint[work] and kneeling on the floors and the soot was all over the floor and I had to kneel in it to clean it up so I was as black as a sweep all but my face and that was very dirty . . . cleaned the passage and water-closet on my knees.[65]

On 10 November Munby signed the tenancy of 6 Fig Tree Court in the Temple. His father approved of his choice of chambers and agreed to pay the rent of £50 per annum for the rooms on the first floor of a seventeenth-century building.[66] These were domestic and professional premises: Munby shared his address with five other men, four of whom were barristers like himself: Edmund Grimani Hornby; Donald Malcolm Logie; John Berry Torr; Henry Thomas Wroth and Frederick Thomas Jennings.[67] Hannah and Arthur had their first chance of real privacy, but her visits to him would have to be carefully timed if the couple were not to be undone.

A week after Munby moved in he took Hannah to a concert. Mrs Jackson allowed her time off at short notice:

> cleared the dinner things away and made the kitchen fires up. Cleaned myself and asked leave to go out. Went out just before four o'clock and Massa met me soon after. We walked to Hampstead and from there we rode into London and then he took me to a concert. We heard some beautiful music and a great deal that I didn't understand, but I liked it very much. I was obliged to come away early and I got home at thirty minutes past ten. I didn't wear any gloves and there was a lady sat by me who noticed my coarse hands very much and she looked at it most contemptuously, but I held it out all the more for her to look at and it pleased my Master very much.[68]

The following Sunday evening they went to church together. He met her at the back gate, not the behaviour of a middle-class man of letters, more the 'follower' of the servant girl that she was. They avoided going to the nearest church in case Hannah was recognized and the Jacksons got to hear of her sweetheart:

> After the service we went for a walk together and whilst he was sitting on the little bridge and me kneeling by him we talked about several things . . . of my being a charity school girl . . . and it pleased him very much. And I told him about the other two servant girls who live next to me being such neat tidy girls, always clean when at work and cleaning the steps with white aprons on – so different to me and that pleased him too and I was very much pleased with Massa too and I could always talk freely to him if I

could always feel free as I did then and when I think he loves me very much.[69]

The year 1857 ended with Hannah feeling content with her place and in love with her Massa; he travelled north to York for a family Christmas. Arthur and Hannah were not able to see each other in 1858 until 27 January, and then she could only slip away for a short time. She became adept at dovetailing her workload and the demands on her time made by her brother and sister with Arthur's sometimes sudden appearances at the back door. Servants in such a small house as the Jacksons' lived and worked closely together: they usually shared an attic room and often the same bed, so it was possible for a fellow servant to find out more than one might wish. There was also the slave chain round Hannah's neck, usually concealed beneath her dress, but undressing for bed made it difficult to hide. Her description of her first date with Munby in the New Year gives an idea of how she juggled her life:

Blacked the grates and lighted the fires . . . cleaned three pairs of boots, fed the birds, cleared away and washed up the breakfast things. Made up the fires. Mrs Jackson went out with the baby . . . washed up in the scullery, cleaned the knives. Had my dinner [lunch]. Swept the front hall and shook the mats. Swept the stairs, passage and cellars. Cleaned the front steps and the flags on my knees and the front door and scraper. I cleaned myself and my sister [Ellen] and cousin came to see me. I got the tea. The nurse came home at six o' clock and then we spent the evening together. Massa came at eight o'clock and I went out with him for a short time. Came in and got supper and then I walked a part of the way home with my sister for she was going to her new place [as a nurse] on the morrow. Wished her goodbye and came home again. Sat up at twelve for Mr and Mrs Jackson and then I went to bed.[70]

Hannah's sister did not settle at her new place and came to nurse Mrs Jackson who was in bed with a bad throat. The Jacksons knew Ellen quite well: she had spent the night a few times, sharing the attic room with Hannah. Between them the sisters nursed Mrs Jackson and the baby back to health, and armed with a good character from Hannah's grateful 'missis', Ellen left for another situation as a nursemaid in Notting Hill Gate.[71]

In the evening of Monday, 29 March a special dinner party took place in the kitchen at Beaufoy Terrace. The Jacksons were out for the evening and the coast was clear:

> cleaned the kitchen hearth, washed my hands and face and sat down to sew till Massa came at six o'clock. I got his dinner ready and waited on him and cleaned his boots. We had a nice evening together and he played the piano for me. Mrs Jackson came back at half past ten and we waited up till twelve for Mr Jackson.[72]

Hannah must have been confident of Mrs Jackson's habits to risk such a potentially dangerous scenario. It went smoothly: the fear and thrill of discovery was an ingredient in her secret life with Munby. His chambers could not guarantee privacy but sometimes Hannah would visit him at Fig Tree Court and perform as a servant.

At the end of May Arthur was pleased to become an unpaid teacher at the Working Men's College, at 45 Great Ormond Street. He taught a two-hour Latin class on Thursday evenings; Vernon Lushington, his old friend from Trinity, taught English Composition, and new friends, the socialist and art historian John Ruskin and the artist Dante Gabriel Rossetti, were members of the council.[73]

In the summer of 1858 Arthur was photographed with his younger brother Joe who was studying at Trinity. His 'Dundreary' side-whiskers were extravagant, and if he seemed pompous, perhaps it was the tall top hat, the academic gown, and the long exposure time needed in studio portraiture which helped determine his mood.

Stoical as Hannah was, the monotony of her life could sometimes depress her. On the last day of June she summed up the last four weeks: 'I have cleaned ninety-two pairs of boots . . . been very dirty often. Been to church but once in the month [with Arthur] and then not to the service. I don't think I've been out anywhere except on errands. Read very little indeed.'[74]

Renovation work at the Jacksons' house gave Hannah and Ellen a welcome distraction. Hannah was attracted to one of the workmen, Bill, and told Munby of her feelings in her diary. As well as preparing the house for Bill and his workmates, she and Ellen were cleaning up after them and fetching their beer from the local public house:

> the men were at work fixing a bath in the dressing room so I had to fetch their beer . . . One of them is called 'Bill' and he is I think clever. Mrs J went out after dinner [lunch] and when I had cleaned away the things he played a polka and then some beautiful sacred music. His fingers were very dirty and stiff from his work but he did it well for all that. The men had tea with us in the kitchen.[75]

Hannah was never shy to admit to her encounters with other men. Although she had decided that Munby was the only man for her, mentioning others was a reminder to him that men found her attractive. She described conversations in detail and the occasions when she had to wrestle men off. Hannah's writing about Bill worked because three days later Arthur visited Kilburn: 'Met Massa at church. We went in and came out and then went in the fields. Had a little talk and stayed there until nine and then I came in.'[76]

The Jacksons gave Hannah and Ellen a treat of five shillings each and one day in July 1858, they met Emma Smith at London Bridge and went to the Crystal Palace. This was probably Arthur's idea. He was present but could not speak to her:

> Massa was there but I could not be with him. Lost my sister once and did not meet him for a very long time. So altogether it was a very unpleasant day ... went into a public house and had some ale and then Richard [her brother] and his friend saw us on the omnibus and we had a pleasant ride home.[77]

There is no record of when Hannah introduced Arthur to Ellen. There could have been concern on Ellen's part about her sister having this suitor. She may have feared for Hannah, or she might have been jealous of her happiness. For whatever reason, Hannah was unable to spend the day with Arthur *and* her sister and her friend Emma.

On Wednesday, 14 July, Arthur suggested that Hannah and Ellen go to see *The Merchant of Venice* and that Hannah leave the play early so they could be together. Hannah was tense about asking her mistress's permission to go out and reacted badly to her less than enthusiastic agreement:

> Mrs Jackson grumbled at my asking leave to go out although I left nothing to do nor anything to cook, and I spoke a little hasty to her I'm afraid and apologized as well as I could and then I went out. I rode in the omnibus ... went to my sister [in Notting Hill Gate] and had tea with her and then we all went to the play together ... which I was delighted with. Massa came there and so I

went out before it was over that I might speak to him and to get home sooner.[78]

In the middle of December Mrs Jackson had another baby. The household was growing larger and Hannah's work increased. Although a nursemaid had been employed to care for her employers' first child, Hannah's diary describes looking after him a lot. The Jacksons also started keeping chickens at the bottom of their garden, which became Hannah's responsibility. She volunteered to tend the garden and grow vegetables for the table as well.

Mrs Jackson not being well. Lit the fire and got the breakfast ready soon after nine. Washed up in the scullery and cleared away the breakfast things. Made the beds and cleaned the knives. Got ready a large dinner. Sent it up at four o'clock. Cleared away and washed up the dishes. Helped to get the tea. Cleaned the kitchen tables and hearth and read after tea ... I sat up till two o'clock. Took up supper. Mrs Jackson confined of a baby daughter and I went for the doctor.[79]

There is a long gap in Hannah's diary-writing from the end of 1858 to 1863. Fortunately Munby started a diary in January 1859, but thirty-five years later, in 1894, he re-read his diaries and tore out thirty-one pages from 1859 and seventy-eight pages from January to August of 1860:

All the excised passages in this and other volumes, had references, so far as I can remember, to my darling Hannah, now my wife. They described the hours we spent together; and the training and teaching that I gave her; and the work often of the lowest and most servile kind, which she – a maid-of-all-work – of her own accord did for me, to show her love in her own way.[80]

Presumably Arthur's embarrassment at their passion and private moments was the cause of this. The diary was started at Clifton Holme. He did not return to London until 29 January and brought with him a strong urge to get married:

> walked by the river to the station . . . reached London at six-thirty. Commonplace journey – nothing going on in the fields along the line: ploughing nearly over, turnips all gathered, the whole country quiet for two hundred miles . . . where are the people? showery day with high cold winds. [Hansom] cab to Temple: found the rooms looking very warm and bright, with lamp and fire, and a warm welcome from Mrs Mitchell the housekeeper: felt however for the first five minutes a new sensation, nympholepsy, the longing for a wife. Probably the result of cheerful family life and endearments.[81]

The diary for 1859 says nothing about his working life, and this is true of all his diaries: his professional life was not allowed to impinge on his private thoughts and hobbies. Wherever he went he took a notebook, pen and pencil, and made notes and sketches about working women he met. Maybe Arthur Munby used his hobby to distract himself from his sometimes gloomy thoughts. He visited his family, made friends with Louisa Baker, a milliner, went to bachelor parties, smart tea parties, soirées at Ruskin's home in Denmark Hill, and to the Isle of Wight for a weekend in April.[82]

Louisa Baker was his first recorded specimen. He 'caught' her in the winter: one evening he spent hours alone with her in her humble lodgings off the Euston Road. She repaid the money he had lent her which had helped her move out of her previous 'wretched back rooms'. Thanks to his loan and better wages, Louisa's circumstances improved and she was still 'respectable': milliners and dressmakers had a reputation for resorting to prostitution when work was hard to find, and

Arthur's help to a pretty, 'deserving' female was typical and would be repeated. He wondered at the incongruity of being able to sit alone with twenty-two-year-old Louisa at no cost to his reputation, or, it seemed to hers. Such a situation would not have been tolerated in his social circles unless they were closely chaperoned, and he concluded that the difference in their class made their friendship acceptable: 'with men of her own class it would be indelicate to associate as friends; for modesty is an affair of *class* as well as sex, and with them such intercourse would certainly be misconstrued'. Arthur felt comfortable with Louisa and justified his motives:

> if however they be honourable in such a case friendship and trust may grow between him and her of a kind she could not in her position get elsewhere – sisterlike and yet with just enough of sexual consciousness to make it romantic without being unsafe.[83]

Arthur had helped her over a lean patch and they discussed her future: Louisa was at pains to show her disapproval of her colleagues' chatter about 'their gentlemen friends who give them presents to take them to casinos'. He tut-tutted but was also excited by the vivid life which working girls and women could access through their sexuality.

In the middle of July he took an excursion by train and boat to Boulogne for the weekend. He noted the closure of Vauxhall Pleasure Gardens a week later. At the end of the month he saw an old friend, a 'fallen woman', made good. Sarah Tanner had been a servant, became a prostitute, then turned businesswoman. Arthur had met her in 1854, 'a lively, honest, rosy-faced girl, virtuous' when she was a maid of all work to a shop-keeper in Oxford Street. A year or so later he saw her in Regent Street, and remarked on her 'gorgeous apparel', asking how she had come by it. Sarah had grown tired of domestic service, and wanting to 'see life and be independent', decided to become a prostitute. She: 'saw no harm in it: enjoyed it very much and thought it might raise her and perhaps be profitable'. Sarah took up her new profession with much 'energy', saved money and took lessons in letter-writing. Within five years she had earned enough to give up prostitution and buy a coffee house near Waterloo Bridge. Arthur was proud of the ambition of a young woman who had made a success when so many others had failed.[84] In August his travels took him back again to Wigan (his first visit had been in 1853) where he conducted the first of his interviews with the 'pit-brow lasses' of Lancashire. Arthur's obsession with working women's clothes and his careful recording of what they wore, and how, is illustrated by his account of his visit to Kirklees Hall pits on 19 August:

> A hooded bonnet of padded cotton, pink, black or blue striped shirt open at the breasts; a waistcoat of cloth, generally double-breasted but ragged throughout, fustian or corduroy or sometimes black cloth trousers, patched with all possible materials except the original one, and stout clogs. Round the waist is tucked a petticoat of striped cotton, blue and black, rolled up as a joiner rolls his apron; it is never let down, and perfectly useless, only retained as a symbol of sex.[85]

Arthur travelled home that summer to celebrate his father's fiftieth birthday and returned to London anxious about the family's finances. On 19 December he had some news to please his father: he accepted an appointment with the Ecclesiastical Commission and was to be a civil servant. His barrister's training over-qualified him for this humdrum position, which paid a modest £120 per annum, but there were enough good things about the job to cheer him up at the end of the year.[86] A friend from Trinity, R. B. Litchfield,

was already working there, and may have recommended him
to the Commissioners. Life with Hannah was good though
unnerving. He was still her Massa and she was his loving and
willing slave.

CHAPTER FOUR

'I am a dreamer and observer'[1]

IN A SEVENTEENTH-CENTURY panelled room in the Temple, London, the oak floor is uneven and low winter light creeps through the leaded windows. A fire burns in the grate and gilded frames twinkle. At first sight they are icons. But they are not religious subjects. These photographs are dotted around the room, propped up against books, on shelves, on the mantel, on the desk, anywhere where there is space for them to be admired. A small leather locket, padded with red velvet, is held shut with a gilt hook. In it is a picture of a pre-Raphaelite woman who was carried around in the owner's breast-pocket.

Thirty of Arthur Munby's collection of women were examples of his interest in social reform. Five of them were of Hannah. She is depicted seated with a carpet brush in her hand; scrubbing steps, looking over her shoulder at the itinerant photographer;[2] 'in her dirt' at the Jacksons in Kilburn; and it was her picture in the locket, a picture so admired by Dante Gabriel Rossetti that he asked to meet her.[3]

Hannah was not the only servant whom Munby displayed. In seven of ten anonymous pictures young women are portrayed wearing their Sunday best. There is a pretty girl in Richmond, Surrey; two London maids of all work; a housemaid in Gravesend; a bonny girl up from the country; a servant in Dartford and a maid in Bethnal Green. Three others have been photographed in their working clothes: a kitchen-maid at an hotel in the West End and two maids of all work, one at a Bermondsey coffee house, the other at a public house in Dartford.

Three others are of coal-mining women, about whom Munby was an expert: a Shropshire pit girl in her best clothes; Jane Brown from Wigan, twenty-five, bare-armed; and Ellen Grounds, a pit-brow lass, a 'broo wench', with whom Munby enjoyed a close friendship – so close that a photograph of them together escaped Munby's weeding out of images of himself. Ellen wears her best clothes, earrings and brooch.

Annie Barn and her sister-in-law worked in the herring sheds in Filey, East Yorkshire, and Munby got their picture when he visited Annie's mother one afternoon. He admired the photograph of the girls in their work aprons which hung above the fireplace and Mrs Barn gave it to him. Not all Munby's photos were of pretty young women, however: an old girl from Whitby, a life of hard work in the fishing industry etched on her face, hangs there too.

One framed photograph of a black woman was of special interest to a man who loved his sweetheart to be as black as possible. He had a small collection of images of black women, mostly naked Africans, and a 'nigger street dancer' photographed on Derby Day at the Epsom races. Also peering out from a golden frame were a rosy-cheeked farm servant from Shropshire, a paper-mill worker in Dartford, and, rare for him, a woman with a man, 'a country girl and her sweetheart'.[4]

Munby enjoyed Charles Dickens's work but they never met: he sometimes saw Dickens striding about London but was too shy to approach him. Munby's letters and diaries give the tiniest scraps of information about his professional life – his ink was mostly spent on his life's hobby: big, strong and dirty women. As soon as his working day was over he was out of the door to socialize and teach and walk for miles, making mental notes that were written up later, documenting women. They were everywhere – walking, bumping into him, trying to sell him their wares, propositioning him, doing their work, spotted from afar going about their business. Munby loved looking at women, following women, making friends with them, giving them small tips and collecting their pictures to update his notebooks on the progress of their lives. It did not matter where on the ladder of the working class they were, they obsessed him. To our ears Arthur Munby's words can make him sound pompous: but he was a kind man, broadminded and wanting to learn as much about the mores of working women as he could.

He could also sound Pooterish. He took himself too seriously and expected others to do the same: his letterhead – *virtus suum tutamen* – means 'integrity was his safeguard'. And yet on the first day of 1860 he wrote a ditty which made light of his dreams to become a poet:

> He was a Simple Barristere,
> Unknown to wealth or fame;
> In Fig Tree Court his chambers were,
> And Munby was his name.[5]

Although Munby's job at the Ecclesiastical Commission was undemanding and unfulfilling, at least it did not involve practising the law, which he loathed, and it gave him time to work under the blotter undisturbed. The working hours were civilized, from ten till five: the ambience was agreeable and the workload was light. (Plate 4)

The Ecclesiastical Commissioners had been established in 1836 to supervise the financial affairs of the Church of England; to draw diocesan boundaries; and to address complaints about its vast administration. Their new clerk embarked on his career with resignation. He despaired of the bureaucracy

and the meanness of the Estates Office: a first, rare outburst
conveyed a frustration he struggled to overcome:

> in which schemes for the rearrangement of Church prop-
> erty are prepared, and all manner of applications to the
> Commissioners as landlords and patrons are dealt with.
> The schemes appear to be fair enough, though the Eccle-
> siastical Commission always bags a share on all capitular
> sales: as to the rest, their contributions to parochial wants
> are, as far as I can judge, niggardly – seldom exceeding
> five pounds; and various rules apparently exist, e.g. as to
> never subscribing to clothing clubs. . . . A most complex
> system of registration and management has grown up also
> in the Office, inversely proportioned to its age: 'forms' for
> everything, accurate queries and setting forth of facts: very
> judicious doubtless, but highly exasperating to the appli-
> cant, who can't get his chancel rebuilt for want of a
> straightforward answer.

After five weeks Munby was sent to the Augmentations
Department. There was more interest here, but he found
aspects of his new duties depressing:

> Here are received and answered all applications from
> clergymen for increases of poor livings and buildings of
> parsonages. The work apparently is less formal and system-
> atic, being strained down (or up) to the level of the
> unpractical parsonic mind: sad enough in its revelations
> of clerical straits.[6]

On the third day of his new job, Munby saw an old friend,
Mary Sullivan, 'Queen of the dustwomen', in the street. She
thought she was twenty years old, but could not be sure, and
was 'small-featured and pretty, yet huge and stalwart as a
navvy'. Mary had her creel of perquisites on her head above
her 'crushed dingy bonnet'. She wore a yellow flannel mason's
jacket, a short ragged skirt and a dirty apron,

picturesquely looped up, and between this and her strong mud boots, her legs were protected, the one by a piece of carpet tied on with string by way of a gaiter, the other by wisps of straw twisted loosely round the calf and ankle. And so full-chested, square-shouldered, with her hands in the pockets of her jacket she strode on erect, manly, loud, thundering on the pavement . . . into whose broad black palm, rough with cinders, hardened with toil, I dropped the welcome trivial coin.[7]

Dust was a valuable commodity in Victorian London: contractors paid parishes for the right to collect household rubbish. In 1861 it amounted to 3½ million tons, mostly coal cinders, from the fires which kept Londoners warm and cooked their meals. The dust was piled into great mounds, to be sifted by an army of young girls and women. The Victorians were devoted recyclers. Coal dust and soot were used as fertilizer, cinders in brick-making, and tins and iron pots and pans were melted down for re-use; oyster shells were used in the foundations of buildings; old boots and shoes were bought up by the manufacturers of Prussian blue dye.[8]

Munby's interest in the dustwomen and their mounds predates by four years Charles Dickens's depiction of dust as a symbol of the waste of urban existence in his best-seller *Our Mutual Friend*:

> It was a cloudy night and the black shadow of the Mounds made the dark yard darker . . . Cautiously along the path that was bordered by the fragments of crockery set in ashes . . . they could hear him at his peculiar trot, crushing the loose cinders as he went.

> On reaching the right mound Boffin

> tucked up his cuffs and spat on his hands, and then went at it like an old digger that he was. . . . Then he stopped,

looked down in the cavity, bent over it, and took out what appeared to be an ordinary case bottle; one of those squat, high-shouldered, short-necked glass bottles which the Dutchman is said to keep his courage in. As soon as he had done this, he turned off his lantern, and they could hear that he was filling up the hole in the dark. The ashes being easily moved by a skilful hand, the spies took this as a hint to make off in good time.[9]

On 6 January 1860 Munby learned that a seamstress he had befriended, Jessie Harrison, had fallen into prostitution. He visited her at her lodgings and she greeted him with her 'hair dishevelled and her brown stuff frock unhooked; looking gentle and girlish but somehow not so innocent as before'. Jessie told him that she had been able to move from her attic to the first floor by supplementing her earnings with the help of a 'friend – a gentleman who had spoke to her and came very often to see her'. Anxious to get rid of her unexpected visitor, she told Munby her 'friend' was due at any moment – although her appearance suggested that he was already upstairs. Munby walked home saddened that Jessie, who had been the May Queen of her village, had made this career move which would, he felt, deny her what every woman might expect, 'all hopes of home and marriage'. He was not morally outraged that Jessie had made this decision, however, and accepted it was hard for her to survive on wages of eight shillings a week.[10]

Later that week Arthur Munby visited Hannah in Kilburn. It was risky: servants were not allowed to have men friends or 'followers' visit their place of work and for him, a gentleman, to be found courting her would have been doubly scandalous. It was dangerous and exciting: if the Jacksons had walked in, the consequences would have been dire for both of them:

One day I went to see her at her own suggestion . . . for
the family were all absent and she wished to show me her
work . . . the kitchen she had to scour, the big kitchen
grate that she blacked, and the chimney she had swept . . .
the hole in which she had cleaned the boots and knives
and the scenes of many another sordid but necessary task.
And she took me upstairs and showed me her attic, a little
bare room with a blue-checked quilt on the bed and one
chair and a common washing-stand in the corner with a
jug and a basin . . . there was no looking-glass in the
room. . . . Then as I came downstairs she opened by way
of contrast, the door of her mistress's luxurious bedroom.
On the bed lay a ball dress of black gauze and lace with
crimson garniture; and this made me wish to see for once
how Hannah would look in a lady's condition. I told her
to put on the ball dress . . . she took off her own servant's
dress and put on that of her mistress. It was too short and
too narrow for her and it would not meet around her
healthy rustic waist; still she was able to wear it; and
seeing a rose in the room I brushed at her hair in a lady's
fashion and placed the rose within it. Thus she stood
before me to be looked at; smiling and slightly blushing;
feeling awkward and strange in that unknown garb, but
not looking awkward at all but most graceful. I gazed at
her in a kind of rapture; so lovely a figure she was, so
ladylike, so sweet, that I longed to take her away from her
slaving and make of her a lady indeed. . . . She tore off
that strange . . . finery . . . and hurried me down to her
kitchen where she could feel properly clad and at home.
And it was this incident more than any other thing, that
made me wholly and for ever hers.[11]

Munby enjoyed seeing the London milkwomen in their
working uniform, a reminder of an arcadian past surviving in
the heart of an industrialized city. His favourite was 'Queen

Kitty', Kate O'Cagney, whom he had known since 1852. She was 5 feet 10 inches tall, and graceful, and she wore a straw bonnet, shawl, cotton frock and stout boots. He failed to persuade her to have her photograph taken at a studio near to William Sim's dairy in Jermyn Street where she and 'Rosyface', 'Coolie' and 'Brown Duchess' worked. Munby knew that his hobby was unusual and that his interest in such 'unwomanly' women was eccentric. Early on in 1860 he confided to his diary:

> In Fleet Street as I went out this afternoon there appeared two phenomena totally uninteresting to the well-regulated mind, but very satisfactory to mine; the one, a tall strong woman of thirty in a battered bonnet, a thick coarse shawl and a short print gown that showed her big bespattered ankle boots; striding – not tripping – across the muddy street, she walked on at a man's speed among the huddled crinolines and Sunday clothes, looking neither right nor left, but holding her head up for all the heavy rain, and swinging her great arms from the shoulder like a man; the other, a young milkwoman, her cans swinging beside her, her yoke with her master's name painted legibly thereon, upon her shoulders, trudging on indifferent to fashion and to weather with no cover from the rain, save a kerchief over her bonnet. Any rainy day in London one may see women like these and he who does pass by indifferent one should pity and deplore. I do neither, but beholding, rejoice to see the strength of their womanly endurance.[12]

Hannah's deteriorating appearance worried Arthur. She visited him one day and was too 'dirty and unkempt' even for his taste: when she produced a photograph of herself in her Sunday best from her days with the Cotes family in Shropshire, he was shocked at how far she had dragged herself down to please him. Five years of menial work and cooking over smoky fires had given her a weatherbeaten look, but she was not distressed, rather proud and was

> *pleased* that she is now 'so much rougher and coarser' because it pleases me, she thinks. Truly, every smear and stain of coarseness on her poor neglected face comes of *love*. And now it is high time that all this discipline should cease but I have no means of ending it! To be a smart parlour maid even a lady's maid are distinctions far above her reach: she would smile incredulous if I proposed them.[13]

Arthur Munby believed that Hannah Cullwick was really from a higher social caste than the one in which she found herself, and loved hearing about her encounters with men who complimented her on her high-born features. If only she had been a lady, their lives would have been easier: but Arthur would not have loved her. As they travelled to the Haymarket Theatre one evening to see a pantomime, an old man sitting next to Hannah on the omnibus said to her that he supposed she was 'very low'. She proudly replied that she was a maid of all work. He went on: 'Ah, but you have better blood in you than you know of . . . I can see by your profile that you have got good blood in you. Has nobody belonging to you ever been better off than you are?' Hannah replied, 'No, Sir, I never knew of anything but what I am.' Arthur, proud of the compliment to her, was also suspicious of the man's motives:

> And so he doubtless went home to tell of the waif of wrecked nobility he had picked up – so low too. Well, I don't care to find ancestors for her, nor to love a kitchen maid because she is *not* a kitchen maid, yet it makes me glad to think of this little story, glad and sorry – that being what she is she should have a sweetheart like me who is yet so helpless to raise her above the kitchen.[14]

One picture in Arthur's chambers stood out from the rest: a young girl's direct look demands attention, her pinched face is tired. (Plate 8) One gloomy Saturday in March 1860, Arthur Munby had set off from Fig Tree Court on one of his weekend walkabouts. At four o'clock he caught a boat at the Temple Pier to Westminster. On board he met an elderly farmer on his first visit to London who 'applied to me to know the meaning of the various wonders around'.[15] On their right were Somerset House, the Adelphi Pier, Great Scotland Yard Wharf. Munby may have pointed in the direction of his office. Next, the India Office and the site for the new Foreign Office. Beyond Waterloo Bridge the air was filled with the shouts of stevedores unloading at the Belvedere Coal Wharf. Passing under the Hungerford Suspension Bridge, there was the sweet smell of hops brewing as they passed Providence Wharf, then timber yards between the river and Waterloo Station. At Westminster Munby alighted and walked across Westminster Bridge to the south bank. As he left the bridge he

> found a group of dustwomen resting on their way home. They were leaning against the parapet on which they had placed their large creels of refuse that they carry on their heads. It occurred to me that this was a good chance of obtaining a photograph of a woman of this class in working dress.

Arthur was nervous when he asked a dustwoman to accompany him to the Lambeth studio of Mr F. Lindsey, and enlisted the help of Lindsey's doorman, or tout, an ex-soldier. Arthur had guessed the woman's suspicion when the doorman returned with her: 'seeing me she quickly ran away again'. She was brought back and the session began:

> grinning and wondering, she tramped up the stairs like a ploughman. I followed: and in a little room that served as

a showroom and parlour, I found the photographers, two respectable young men and two girls, their sisters apparently, who were seated at needlework. The dustwench, all in dirt as she was, had plumped herself down in a chair by the door, and sat silently staring: and the disgust and astonishment with which the two milliners looked at their coarse masculine sister, was very amusing. Rapidly noting the contrast, but speaking as if the whole affair were a matter of course, I said to the young men who had preserved an air of businesslike indifference to my fair friend, 'Can you make me a portrait of this woman?' They agreed and 'this woman' was marched up to the glasshouse [the studio at the top of the building].

Munby's description of this new specimen and the way he acquired her offer an insight into why she was special enough to be exhibited in his study:

She was a stout rough Irish lass of two and twenty, with big muddy boots and a ragged cotton frock looped up over a grey kirtle [skirt]; her neck and chest protected by a thick brown kerchief. Her arms which were strong and full were bare; but she carried a man's heavy corduroy jacket over her shoulder – a filthy thing black with coal dust. Indeed as she was fresh from ten hours of work among the dust and cinder heaps, her clothes and arms and face and hair – which her battered bonnet left uncovered – were all smeared and powdered with a dull dingy blackness. She put on her jacket at my desire, and sat down, holding her tin dinner can in one hand, and thrusting out her strong feet before me: and when I had posed her thus – which I did with my gloves on, seeing how dirty she was – the lens was uncovered.

The light that day was poor and the young woman had to sit still for several seconds. She was an obedient model, apparently not moving 'even her eyelids'. When it was safe for her to move she 'drew a long breath and said, "Eh!, well, that *is* punishment! that's wuss that a day's work, that is."' The exertion of doing nothing had made her eyes water and she 'took out a tattered handkerchief (an unusual luxury!) and rubbed them; wiping off as she did some of the many strata of dust upon her face'. After getting a few details from her, Arthur paid her a shilling for her trouble. He was fascinated by the conditions in which she and other dust-wenches worked. He found them 'picturesque', even when they wore 'pieces of black crepe tied tightly over their faces, making them look hideous, and giving them small protection'.

This girl was employed by the dust contractor John Easton at his yards in Lambeth for 9 pence to a shilling a day, working from seven in the morning to five at night, four o'clock on Saturdays: '"Sir, we stand at the dust heaps out o'doors, rain and all weather; often gets wet through; but I put my jacket on when it rains."' Easton's Yards were on Shot Tower Wharf, shared by the lead manufacturers Burr Brothers.

Two weeks later, Arthur watched a woman intently at the Paddington dustyards,

> picking out the broken plates, rags and other treasures and throwing them into her private creel behind her, shook and riddled her sieve, raising thereby a new cloud of dust and threw the residuum on one side, while the finer dust fell round her. And so doing such work, they stand there each embedded in her dustheap without the least protection from the cold and rain.[16]

Judging by his many working-class women friends, it is clear that Arthur did not lack the confidence to approach strangers and make long-lasting relationships. But he could also be shy: even though he was brought up by maids, and had Hannah as a sweetheart, he could be bashful of young and pretty female servants. He was sexually excited by these fit young women who performed intimate tasks, such as emptying slop-pails and bringing hot water to men's bed-rooms. On the evening of 23 April 1860, at a musical party in Kent,

> a significant incident occurred to me about bedtime. It became necessary for me to retire for a space; but the other men servants had gone to bed and amongst the intricate passages of the old house I could nowhere find the spot I wanted. So, encountering in the hall the waiting maid, a rustic damsel, I had no resource but to ask her the way. An unpleasant process, with much hesitation and awkwardness I strove by delicate circumlocution to hint to her of my needs: but the girl's rude [simple] mind could not comprehend them – she looked at me with respectful wonder, and at last I was obliged to say bluntly 'Can you tell me where is the watercloset?' She would blush I half thought and stammer and I should regret having said it. Not at all. It was only the reflex of one's own training that made me think so. She looked full in my face and answered briskly, 'Oh yes, Sir. I'll show you the way,' and she led me to the door – with perfect possession.[17]

In the middle of June, during his first summer at the Ecclesiastical Commission, Arthur's parents, 'the father and the mother' as he called them, and his brothers George and Joe, came to London to see how he was settling in: they also visited Caroline at her boarding school in Brighton. Arthur was relieved to say that he had passed his Civil Service examinations, a necessary stepping-stone in any bid to escape from his job in Whitehall Place. He took his mother to see for the first time the chambers in the Temple for which her husband paid the rent. She stayed for hours, 'talking of gossip and how Fred had requested permission of the father to marry Miss Latimer, the governess'.[18] This was a 'misalliance'. Governesses inhabited a limbo: sometimes they were the daughters of the middle class who had fallen on hard times, or they could be from further down the class ladder. Arthur may have toyed with the idea that his parents would not object to his relationship with Hannah. But this was fantasy: though governesses were indeed servants, they were educated, whilst his love was a maid of all work.

Arthur's mother would have mentioned his nursemaid Hannah Carter, née Rooke. She had left the Munbys in the late 1840s to marry a carpenter: but by 1851 she was a widow and working for the family again. In 1860 she was lady's maid to his mother, and second in the hierarchy of five servants at Clifton Holme; finally she became the housekeeper, a reward for her years of service.[19] This Hannah, the first in Arthur's life, exerted a life-long influence on his feelings. As a young woman she had bathed and nursed him: he spent more time with this woman than with his own mother. It is clear from his diary that she was very special to him. Perhaps she was a big, strong woman and he may have had his first sexual feelings with her. Arthur's dutiful visits to his family every summer and Christmas were also the opportunity for meeting his old nurse Hannah again.

Go back to the panelled room and open the clasp of an album of Arthur's *cartes de visite*. He had several hundred photographs altogether, but this is a compilation of forty-four big, strong 'pit broo wenches' from the Wigan and St Helen's coalfields. Each picture is interleaved with pink tissue, the mounts shaped like church windows. Here are 'Mary, greaser' from Hindley, Lizzie Hedley, a 'riddler', of Ince Hall Pits and Ann Morgan, a 'filler', posing in their working clothes and holding shovels and sieves, the tools of their trade. Other photographs were taken at the pit brow, not in front of the painted backdrops of his usual photographers, Robert Little, Miss Louisa Millard and Charles Craig of Wigan. (Plate 9) Whilst Arthur knew about coal-mining women in all the British coalfields, including the 'tip girls' of South Wales, he had a special affection for the Lancashire 'pitbrow lasses' whom he regarded as 'heroines'. During the 1860s he followed the debate on whether to ban females from working at the surface of coal mines with indignant and well-informed interest. Many of the pitbrow lasses were his friends and he championed their cause, writing letters to the Select Committee on Mines set up to investigate their working lives, whose evidence he heard on at least eight occasions at the House of Commons in 1856 and 1866.[20] He lobbied the chairman and several Members, passionately defending the women's right to work where and when and for how long they wanted. In 1842 women and children had been banned from working underground in Britain's coalmines, and in the 1860s, a generation later, another coalition of campaigners, including some feminists, criticized women undertaking such physically demanding, allegedly morally degrading 'unladylike' work, and demanded their removal from the workforce.[21] To his contemporaries, Munby's championing of their cause may have seemed eccentric: if they had read his diaries, his behaviour would have become clearer. After much debate the pitbrow lasses' work was spared from legal interference until the 1880s when the clamour to exclude them from the coalfields was rekindled again. But the Mines and Collieries Act of 1887 only laid down that females had to be at least twelve years old to work at the pit top.

Arthur Munby had friendships lasting thirty years with some of the pitbrow lasses: two favourites were Ellen Meggison, who appeared in his poems as 'Boompin' Nelly', and

Ellen Grounds, in whose gilt-framed picture in his room she wore her uniform of

> a bonnet . . . striped shirt, open at the breast: a waistcoat . . . [and] black cloth trousers . . . [and] stout clogs clasped on bare feet.[22]

Arthur would walk for miles to see his friends, to watch them and ask them about their work, to coax them to meet him at Miss Millard's and other studios to have their likenesses taken. In thirty years of interviewing he found that the pit brow lasses were unanimous that women should be allowed to go back underground: they were not afraid of the hard work, and the wages were far better than at the surface. This was in the context of a campaign to get them removed from the coalfields. He liked to hear about their private lives too, if they had sweethearts and plans to marry, and he had learned on his earliest visits that coal miners were suspicious of him: more than once he had to be rescued by the pitbrow lasses from being attacked by men who were displeased with him. If the miners had read his diaries they would have been uneasy at his interest in 'their' women's physicality, their strong and dirty bodies, and his excitement at seeing the exposure of their sinewy black arms when their sleeves were rolled up to the shoulder:

> a fine tall girl of twenty . . . broad shouldered and strong limbed: her bonnet stuck in top of her head . . . her waistcoat open and her shirt unbuttoned at the breast for heat . . . she moved at full trot with her barrow full of coke, or strode about with her pickaxe on her shoulder: the sweat running down her face and beading her bare chest.[23]

Arthur amassed over 250 pictures of pitbrow lasses, scouring the shop windows of photographers' studios. Local 'photographic artistes' were also interested in the subject and this helped fuel Arthur's enthusiasm and build his collection. Many of the pictures showed the women in their Sunday best, and Wigan's Mr Little and Miss Millard may have wondered why Mr Munby was so insistent that his subjects be only photographed in their dirty work-wear. In late August 1860, Arthur rounded up a couple of his friends to be photographed. Grateful for the shilling, a day's wage for a half an hour's 'work', one woman stipulated that she would only have her picture taken on condition that it would not be displayed in the photographer's window: ' "if mah feller should see it, he'd abat kill ma" '.[24] Often, when in Wigan, Arthur found he was the object of curiosity: 'people turned round to look at me and made wondering remarks . . . in the streets of Wigan a man with a beard and leggings is a much more singular object than a blackfaced woman in men's clothes'.

On 1 September Arthur was back in London, rested from his family holiday in York and invigorated by his rambles around the Lancashire coalfields. He arranged to meet Hannah outside 57 Oxford Street, the premises of Philip Fink: he walked from his office, she came by omnibus from Beaufoy Terrace. Some of the photographs taken that day 'of her in working dress and attitudes' give a glimpse of their secret world. Arthur was pleased with Hannah's readiness 'to be posed, handled and discussed to her face; the coarseness of her hands examined and the best mode of showing them displayed'.[25]

Sleeves rolled up, biceps and leather strap on display, Hannah pretends to scrub the floor and looks at her lover as if seeking confirmation that what she is doing is correct. In another scenario, Arthur was cropped out of the shot entirely except for his boot in Hannah's lap which she is polishing. The wallpaper backdrop hinted at a middle-class parlour, but a parlour from which he disappeared, years later, after cutting the photograph in half. Hannah's hands were her pride and joy – were a testimonial to hard work whenever a new place was sought. As well as their character from a previous employer, all servants' hands were examined for their worth. (Plate 12)

When the session was over Hannah and Arthur returned to Fig Tree Court: the Jacksons were on holiday and for the first time Hannah stayed overnight. It was 'a dangerous experiment which I had much considered, and almost feared'. As soon as Arthur had returned from his travels he had gone to Kilburn and stood in the street watching Hannah clean the windows, 'looking almost picturesque and pretty', and had then crept into the house to see her do some of her dirtiest work where 'her arms were wet to the shoulder and her ragged skirt was wet through' and 'she begged me to stay with her'.[26] He had wanted to stay but was afraid that their celibate state would be compromised: he now relented and allowed Hannah to stay with him in the Temple. It was a testing time for both of them:

> I learnt somewhat of physical temptation and of resistance. But she never knew what I was learning. I had not calculated myself. And when she had gone to rest under my roof, in a bed that was not mine, I went in and kissed her rosy face as it lay on the white pillow and smiled . . . and I left her to her virgin sleep.

Years later he recalled some extraordinary scenes in the Jacksons' home. On one of their tours of the house, she proudly showed him the privy she cleaned and declared: '"If you was to tell me to strip myself and jump into this *privy I would do it!*"' Arthur was startled, thinking it a 'strange speech, to be addressed by a beautiful maiden to her lover! But the beautiful maiden was only a servant of all work; and she had devoted herself to her lover and fondly called herself his slave.'[27] On these visits Hannah wanted to show Munby what she would do to please him:

> I went up like a reg'lar sweep, wi' my back again' one wall, and my knees again' t'other. Of course I had my head in a bag; and I was welly [almost] naked, only drawers on, and a sack on my back to keep it from the bricks; but as for the other wall, my knees was rough and hard wi' scrubbin', so they didna mind it. I went up till the chimley got too narrow, and theer I fun' a ledge full o'soot, and I sat on it and rested; and then I sweep the soot down all round me wi' my arms and my brush, and then I coom down the chimley in a reg'lar cloud o'soot; the grates and the hearth was full o'soot when I got down to 'em . . . and then I washed mysel' all over i' my scourin' pail, one leg at a time; and then I put on my nightgown, and went up to my attic to bed.[28]

The day after their visit to Fink's, Arthur took Hannah to Eastbourne for the day. On their walk to Beachy Head he worried that they had so little to say to each other:

> would that we could have *talked* too! But there is no alternative – meditation, loneliness, *intelligent* companionship. I be alone and yet not alone, in the worst sense of the word – who shall say how depressing it is! . . . She is full of mute untaught admiration: she opens her store of sandwiches in the cliff, and thinks she makes me happy. And you *ought* to be happy, alas the result is other than happy, is very disheartening as you walked down to the train with her in the ruddy evening, watching how meek and gentle she is, and yet how hopelessly cut off, in all but heart, from you. Heart: is that all, is that enough? It seemed so as we came home on the train.[29]

Arthur's love for Hannah was driven by an overwhelming attraction to women who were dirty and dishevelled, and his visit to Rouget's, his favourite restaurant near Leicester Square, in the middle of December, a few days before he left London to spend Christmas with his family, is a reminder of the strength of his atttraction. After supper he found himself clambering down a dark staircase and exploring the 'low rude foul-smelling cellars'. Through a gap in a wood partition he was excited to see a young scullion, like Hannah when they first met, working in dirty surroundings:

> an arm and hand were visible – wet, dirty, muscular, apparently a man's – holding a ragged cloth. Their owner peeped round the corner hearing me . . . a young girl, comely and robust . . . she was washing the plates from which I and other strangers had eaten . . . I considered her a moment . . . though she is thought too low to notice. . . . The den where she wrought was low, damp, ill-smelling, windowless, lighted by a flaring gas jet: and full in view, she had on one side a larder hung with raw meat, on the other a common urinal; besides the many ugly dirty implements around her.[30]

One very cold afternoon in January 1861, Munby left work and crossed Hungerford Bridge to see what was happening on the river. The tide was at half ebb and blocked with 'wide floes of snow-covered ice'. The river traffic had stopped: a steam tug which had been trapped in the ice was being freed to cheers as he took his place on the bridge and looked down at Whitefriars Dock. He was amazed to see female mudlarkers scavenging in the river: 'wading barefoot and thigh deep, under the barges through the frozen ice-covered mud'. A newcomer stood by Munby as she decided where she might find some stray coal, 'a young woman . . . with a creel on her back', and then she walked round to the side of the dock and:

> climbed down the dust shoot into the barge loading with rubbish; took off her shoes there and slung them round

her neck; and then let herself drop over the side of the barge and barelegged into the mud. Thence with long strides she waded through the mire and water, among the dead cats and broken crockery, towards the river until, stooping almost double, she disappeared in the mud and darkness under the side of a coal barge.[31]

Early in 1861 it became clear that Hannah would have to find a new place: her employers, the Jacksons, were in financial difficulties: 'the family got bigger and Mr Jackson got poorer through extravagance and had to leave his business'.[32] They would have to leave London and offered to take Hannah with them to Haslington, in Cheshire, but she did not want to leave her sweetheart. In desperation, she suggested cutting off her hair, wearing men's clothes and masquerading as Massa's valet. This was not realistic, but a photograph taken at Fink's on 13 February shows that Arthur was intrigued enough by the idea: 'Met Hannah there by appointment and had three photographs taken of her ... in bonnet and shawl, full length with me and ditto in men's clothes.'[33] (Plate 13)

Arthur's friendship with Dante Gabriel Rossetti, whom he had met in the mid-1850s, in the early days of the Working Men's College, introduced him to the world of the pre-Raphaelite Brotherhood. On 24 February 1861, Arthur and a couple of friends were invited by Rossetti to tea at his studio by Blackfriars Bridge where he showed them drawings of his wife, muse and a milliner, Elizabeth Siddal, and 'read his sister Christina's charming poems, and some of his own'.[34] William Holman Hunt, one of the founders of the Brotherhood, was a man Arthur had liked from their first meeting, finding him 'a most unaffected, good natured and gentlemanly fellow'.[35] They met frequently at Alexander Macmillan's literary evenings or 'tobacco parliaments' at the publisher's offices in Covent Garden, and at one of these soirées Arthur heard from Hunt how one of his biggest works, *The Finding of the Saviour in the Temple*, had nearly been destroyed in a fire and was saved by Lady Seaton offering her Indian shawl as a fire blanket.[36]

Arthur inhabited a different world with Hannah. They had pet names for each other and in all their years together she only called him Arthur once, using 'Moosiri', a variant on the respectful Massa, when other people were around. He would call her 'Una', meaning 'one'; 'Reine' when she seemed very queenly and 'my Juno' after the Roman goddess, the wife of Jupiter.[37]

At Easter Hannah moved to her new place as kitchen-maid for the family of Mr Dodshon Foster, a beer merchant, at 22 Carlton Villas, on the other side of the Edgware Road. Arthur would often watch her scrubbing the nine stone steps which led up to the front door. Her change of job involved little upheaval: she knew the area well, and the lovers' visits remained the same. She earned £15 a year, and two shillings a week beer allowance, the usual 'perquisite' for many servants. Hannah described it as a hard place. There was plenty of dirty work, sometimes too much, but she stayed there three years. A situation had to be intolerable for Hannah to leave of her own volition. During her first summer at the Fosters, she went with the family for their two-month summer holiday in Brighton, then a fashionable sea-bathing place with almost 14,000 residents: the Fosters rented a house at 10 Royal Crescent which had full views of the sea.[38]

Hannah was in Brighton for her twenty-eighth birthday and Arthur visited: it was a Sunday and she had the afternoon off. Earlier in the day she slipped out of the kitchen and ran down to the beach where she spent half an hour with him, arranging that he would return later and discreetly collect her for her 'Sunday out'. They spent the afternoon 'in a shady spot' near the race-course: at six o'clock she went to church and back to work and he caught the train to London.[39]

During the summer Arthur's social life continued apace, but left him feeling empty and jaded:

> My interest in balls is dying out: they enable one to draw out and study the characters of women and to blow off one's superfluous bitterness under the guise of polished deference: that is all. But always to be among the sparkling froth atop of society has one sad delight, in that it keeps vivid before me that gentle misplaced creature who lies grovelling among the dregs: that toiling maid of all work who might have been a drawing-room belle, and is a kitchen drudge. Her love, her humble devotedness are more than ever valued in the presence of their opposites.[40]

By July the Fosters had returned to London and Hannah resumed her routine of visiting Arthur at his chambers. One Saturday they met in the usual cloak-and-dagger way:

> she came out in her evening dress [uniform] – a white apron and a sleeved frock – under her bonnet and cloak, passing me without speaking and hurrying on ahead that she might not be seen to belong to me, she waited in the quiet lane till I came up: and even there when anyone appeared she dropped behind, poor child, and wished she had brought her basket, to look more like my servant bearing my purchases. Her meek acceptance of her inferiority is charming: but it only makes more sad to me the irritating anomaly of such a situation. After leaving the lane, we crossed the Great Western and the Hampstead Railways and found a pleasant path through some rich meadows, green and silent, with well wooded hedgerows. Here on a stile I sat while she told me of her kitchen life

– her floor scrubbing and her boot cleaning and how 'rough and ignorant her fellow servants think her'.[41]

They kissed and canoodled and Hannah pestered Arthur for a date when she might sweep his chimney. A week later he called on her briefly to ask whether she had been 'a good slave' that day. One of Hannah's days was much like another, the highlights were the chance to show him the work she did while the Fosters and all the servants were out: 'she begged me to come in and round to the back of the house that I might through a window see the kitchen and scullery where she spends her life and the pots and pans which for my sake she loves to clean'.[42]

Hannah could be impulsive. She often slipped away from her kitchen work to visit Arthur, even for a brief moment. Sometimes she was not able to speak to him – it was enough just to see him, and let him see her. She was prepared to dash around London on foot, just to see Arthur. When she had a compulsion she had to go, risking dismissal if her absence was noted. These unexpected visits always pleased and sometimes unnerved Arthur in case their secret was revealed.

In August Arthur Munby was on holiday in Devon staying at the Clarence Inn, Ilfracombe. One sunny day, waiting to catch a coach, he noticed a woman at the edge of the crowd trying to slip away unseen. She was a 'tall young woman, well but simply drest . . . her figure was erect but elegant, but her head was bent down and she wore a veil of preternatural thickness, which hid her face thoroughly'. He wondered if she had scrofula or cancer. Before she could escape he pursued her to find out 'as gently as one might' the nature of her condition. Checking that no one could see her, she meekly lifted her veil for him, a stranger, and

> disclosed one of the most hideous faces I ever saw. Scarce to be called a face – for it was covered with sores and

redness and was ghastly as a skull. The eyes were drawn downward and shrunken in their sockets; the nose was long since gone; the rotting lips were drawn back and showed all the teeth and gums.[43]

Harriet Langdon had lupus vulgaris, tuberculosis of the skin, with ulcerating facial lesions, especially round the nose and ears. She had a 'noble figure', wore a dainty bonnet and her face was framed with soft brown hair. Arthur determined to see her again and find out more. Two days later he tracked her down to a tenement on the outskirts of the town where she described her 'affliction' and how she had lived as a leper for twenty years since she was eight years old: 'no childish amusements for her, no girlish gaiety and pride of person or dress, no womanly companionship and love . . . she has always been shut out from all society'.

Arthur acknowledged his own 'repulsive fascination' in studying a face which had been destroyed by disease, 'like a coin that had lost its image'. Her face was

> even worse than it seemed at first sight: the eyes being full of sores, besides being distorted. And the hideous hollow in the centre of her face where the nose had been, was foul with fetid mucus which was absolutely offensive. She *could* not know how horribly ugly she was as she sat there . . . she absolutely *smiled* at times.[44]

Harriet told him she had been to London once for treatment but had to return to Devon when her father died: her few friends were too poor to help, and she now earned a meagre living as a needlewoman. Arthur offered to use his network of friends and charitable connections to take up her case, gave her a shilling which she was reluctant to accept, and left.

In December 1861, the country heard of the death of Prince

Albert from typhoid and was 'struck dumb with sorrow'. On Sunday 15th, Arthur went to a mourning service at the Temple church with a female friend and her little daughter, and was taken aback to see Hannah's face in the throng outside:

> I saw among the crowd of ladies . . . one very different to them, and dearer than them all. She was standing behind a footman and policeman in her black straw bonnet and coarse grey shawl and gown – nothing else, not even gloves. I had to pass her without looking – talking all the while with the unconscious ladies on my arm. I had to see her gazing at me, without so much as wishing to be noticed, all which gave me such a pang – such a sense of bitter sweetness of my enforced relations with her, that I could scarcely keep up the appearance of polite attention.[45]

Distracted, he had to walk the mother and daughter along the Strand and show them onto an omnibus, and was discomfited when he noticed that Hannah was following them. Seeing him walking with these women, she was not jealous, just curious, and content to follow Arthur back to his chambers unacknowledged. She would not take the arm he eventually offered, preferring to follow a few steps behind.

Arthur was excited by his cravings to see her, and frightened of them too: he would make many trips to Kilburn during the eight years she worked there. Many times he set off in the hope of a glimpse, a glance or even some stolen time together. On 20 December he wrote bitterly: 'So I to Kilburn to see my Hannah – a miserable way of meeting at best, afraid for her sake and my own to be seen together by some gossiping eavesdropper but she cannot come to me.'[46]

Hannah's Christmas was a day like any other but with extra work. Arthur was in York and she looked forward to his return early in the New Year, so that they could engage in a favourite annual ritual of theirs, counting the number of boots she had cleaned:

> More than a thousand pairs does this dear drudge clean every year. Big men's boots, small-footed ladies' boots, she carries them down to her hole in a foul heap and brings them up bright and clean – the dirt and dust of them transferred to her own poor face and hair.[47]

While Hannah's life was mundane, Arthur's was vivid and full of incident. On 7 January 1862, he was walking near the British Museum in Bloomsbury and was picked up by a tall young woman who he soon discovered was an artist's model:

> She stopped, waited, looked at me in a grave and diffident way, and seemed though without the least immodesty to expect that I should speak to her. I did so therefore, when she affected to mistake me for someone else . . . but with a manner dignified and distant. This mistake being disposed of, the situation became awkward.[48]

Munby was too excited to walk away and offered to 'accompany her as far as his route and hers agreed', whereupon her behaviour changed completely and she linked arms with him 'unasked' and abandoned her ladylike demeanour, and 'grew all at once lively and amorous; a turn for which I was scarcely prepared'. Nervously he interviewed her. She was new in town from Manchester: she posed for 'busts and full lengths, different postures, anything'. He could have guessed the answer to his decorous question if she was 'taken draped generally, or, ahem, nude, *naked*'. She replied 'right out, "*Oh, I have often been taken naked.*"' Arthur learned that she modelled at the Royal Academy where she earned 10 shillings for a morning's sitting, more than a week's wages for many working women. She assured him the artists did not take liberties with her, it was a trade for them as it was for her and that she liked *'it very much'* to pose naked. She gave him a special insight into her life up north:

> a ball given by some private roué there, to which she and eight other girls, all models went. 'We were all naked', she explained, 'everyone, *men and all* – the ball was given for that very thing.' 'Do you mean that you had *no clothes on whatever*?' 'Not an item,' she cried, 'and it was such a bit o' fun.'

Arthur added that this admission was the 'climax' of her story: but he had been embarrassed that passers-by had heard her talking: 'uttering her shame . . . to my frequent discomfiture'. He was relieved to say goodbye and reflected on her unusual situation. He was both shocked and aroused:

> for though such women may be vicious, they have no need for prostitution for money; and their voices take the form either of callousness and shamelessness such as I have described, or of a passionate lustfulness quite different from the mercenary advances of a woman of ill-fame.

London's streets teemed with people scurrying to earn a living, others, many of them 'friendless girls' who had been lured to the capital but had failed to make their way and were destitute. Arthur was shocked by two runaways he met one cold and rainy January day in Covent Garden. His eye had been drawn to them by their wretched appearance of 'utter squalor'. They were:

> well-grown lasses of eighteen, but they stooped and shambled like women oppressed with care: their clothes were filthy rags – the cast-off refuse of a ragshop, the more hideous because they had once been 'genteel'. Their shoes and bonnets were worn out, their hair uncombed and tangled, their skins unwashed. They moved along together listless, without an object, looking at no one.

These girls eked out a hand-to-mouth existence, living at the Friendless Refuge in Playhouse Yard, near Blackfriars Bridge. They were turned out every morning after a breakfast of 'a bit of bread and some coffee' and walked about till they were allowed to return at night. One of the girls was from Reading and had run away to London 'for a lark' and dared not go back. She had 'been on the streets', a prostitute, until her clothes had become too ragged and now was 'not fit' to work. Arthur gave them some advice and sixpence each.[49]

Munby's social life and hobby of recording working women were framed by his love affair with Hannah. His thoughts turned constantly to her: from January 1862 he was increasingly troubled by the effects of the programme he had devised for her, to get salvation through hard work. She carried on cheerfully scrubbing away and debasing herself further at the Fosters', exulting in doing the filthiest of work with a religious zeal. The boot-counting scene triggered a period of gloomy and guilty introspection on Arthur's part, and a decision that it was too late to 'put her away from her slaving'.[50]

Even the sentimental celebration of St Valentine's Day could inflict pain on Hannah, and thereby Arthur. On 14 February 1862, Hannah's fragile serenity was dented by the cruel comments of her fellow servants at Carlton Villas: triggered by a sarcastic Valentine card sent by Neal the gardener, and snide remarks by her fellow servants Rachel and Mary about her red hands and her ragged, dirty appearance, Hannah broke down on her visit to Fig Tree Court. On her return home the Fosters reprimanded her for being late: her love-life and work were crowding in on her. Afraid of losing her job and home, she felt bullied and afraid. Her colleagues' jibes were in part caused by her extreme frugality: she spent little on her clothes – she was happy to wear Arthur's cast-off boots. Her sister Ellen 'wouldn't hardly walk down the road wi' me the other night, she said she was so ashamed o' me in my bonnet and shawl and she *knew* I hadn't a better one to put on'.[51] Arthur calmed down 'her semi-hysterical weeping' and after a cup of cocoa the master–slave dynamic was restored and calm returned. She 'fetched the ewer and towel and knelt down and washed my feet', kissed him and left, running to get home in time.

A visit to Hannah a week after her Valentine's Day upset caused Arthur to wonder at the strength of his love for her. He pressed the Fosters' kitchen bell once, the signal that he was loitering close by, and Hannah dashed out and ran past him in the street. She was a tall, lithe figure, 'clad in the humblest ... dress and looking ominously dingy even in the gas light'. It was a freezing cold night and she wore no shawl or bonnet and was

> reeking from her coarsest labour: her white cap was almost black; her cotton frock was damp and drazzled, her striped scouring apron hung round her wet through and foul: her hands too; and the leather strap on her wrist was wet and soiled; her bare arms were all begrimed and blackened with the unctuous soot from the kettles and the saucepans and such like, her face was even clouded with similar blackness and her hair was dusty and unkempt. She stood before me and rejoiced that I should see her in her dirt. A strange creature one would say, to excite admiration and love in a man of my education and refinement. Materfamilias would look in her with utter disgust.[52]

How, he asked himself, could a man who had been 'fancy-fed, first with the velvet-cheeked golden-haired ideals of youth and then with the intellectual beauties that manhood worships' fall in love with such a 'dirty servant of all work'? He could justify it, 'knowing what she has done for me, and what is the motive of her drudgery – knowing how every rag on her back and every smear on her face is a symbol of love and self-sacrifice'.

At Easter Hannah, who was exhausted, had a change of air when she and the other servants were sent to Brighton to prepare 10 Royal Crescent for the Fosters' holiday. Arthur was worried about her and visited her immediately, lodging in a cottage nearby. She failed to make their first assignation, so he wandered among the holiday visitors and 'the London whores of high degree', and waited, hoping to see her. They did not meet until the following day, Easter Monday, after she had to work extra time for her afternoon off. Hannah was pragmatic about their situation: '"no one shall know, I shall seem as if I don't belong to you"', accepting that because of the difference in their class they could not walk arm-in-arm. But Arthur insisted that they walk together, and Hannah was proved right: 'It was a hard and miserable condition and at first I walked by her side, towards the Downs, but the people turned round and stared at her and me.' Hannah was adept at the subterfuge and seemed to enjoy it:

> And so, though she was with me all the time, it was as though she was not with me, she walked behind me as before and sat apart and spoke by stealth and looked another way. All this apparently seemed natural to her: she did not feel humiliated by it. But I was chafed beyond measure at this concealment and restraint and all the more because they were necessary. . . . We took refuge behind a wall in a ploughed field for our hurried final talk and then we walked down into the town, as before, though at the corner of the street we did shake hands and part.[53]

After months of negotiation Arthur Munby secured Harriet Langdon's admission to the Royal Free Hospital in Gray's Inn Road. Founded in 1828 'for the free admission of the sick poor', it had been known as the London General

Institution for the Gratuitous Care of Malignant Diseases; Queen Victoria had asked that it be called 'The Free Hospital' when she first became patron. On 30 April 1862, Arthur, Harriet's sister and her sister's husband, a coachman, were waiting to meet Harriet at Paddington Station. Arthur took her by omnibus to the hospital, 'carrying between us her luggage, which was simply a bundle, roughly tied up in a cloth and fastened with a cord'. He stayed for her first consultation with the surgeon, Mr Selwood, whom, he noticed, flinched when he examined Harriet's face. Later he told Arthur that he had never seen such a bad case of lupus: '"The nose is gone. It is horrible – quite impossible for her to go anywhere or be seen by anyone."' Mr Selwood offered small hope of a cure but agreed to treat her.[54] Over the next ten weeks Arthur visited Harriet most Saturdays and slowly her condition improved: 'she removed the bandages and showed me that the sores were fast healing. The sight of her lost nose, which used to be horribly diseased, is now a ghastly hollow indeed, but clean and wholesome.'[55] Arthur busied himself trying to find Harriet paid employment, and bought her a mask from Lewis and Henry Nathan's costume company to cover her damaged face.

One day in June Arthur took Hannah to have her picture taken at Mr Fink's. This time she was to be a pre-Raphaelite damsel. The photograph became one of Arthur's favourites and he had several copies made; he kept one in a locket, hidden in an inner pocket of his jacket. The cape Hannah wore was probably hired from the studio, and her hair had grown since the photograph of her in mannish clothes was taken. Hannah would have been shy when shown this likeness of her as a 'lady', a bohemian type. (Plate 5) She was embarrassed to hear how Arthur's friend, Dante Gabriel Rossetti, had reacted to it. Munby and two friends had breakfasted with the recently bereaved artist (his wife Elizabeth

Siddal had died of a laudanum overdose in February). The widower 'seemed to have recovered outwardly at least, to the loss of his wife'. Proudly Arthur wrote: 'Rossetti this morning to my delight, dwelt with admiration upon the portrait of my darling – little suspecting who she was. "It is a beautiful face," he said, "a remarkable face indeed," and he was anxious to get a copy.' 'I should like to know that lady,' he told Arthur.[56]

Arthur saw Rossetti the following evening at a supper party at the artist's new rooms at 59 Lincoln's Inn Fields which were 'lofty and immense . . . which R adorned with antique furniture and with his own masterly drawings'. Through his host, Arthur had met Algernon Charles Swinburne, but this did not become a close friendship: Swinburne was, according to Munby, 'an intolerable little prig'. Also present were Rossetti's brother William; the translator Charles Bagot-Cayley; Arthur's barrister friend Whitley Stokes; the artist Ford Madox Brown; and William Ralston, a Russian translator and friend of Arthur's from Trinity days. Arthur and Ralston returned to Fig Tree Court for a smoke and were joined by a lawyer friend who reported on his evening dining with the author of the best-selling *Vanity Fair*, William Makepeace Thackeray.[57]

Earlier that day Arthur had been offered pictures of nude women in a small photographer's shop in Bloomsbury. He had been visiting Mudie's Circulating Library and on his way home to the Temple he had stopped to buy

> a beautiful view of the Haunted House at Hampstead. The man, who was young and well drest, wanted to show me various photographs of nude female figures. Producing one of a young woman *entirely* naked, 'This, Sir,' said he 'is Miss Peacock, the Academy Model!' . . . I did not look at the others, except one, which struck me by the strange

contrast exhibited: for it was a picture of two very respectable looking damsels, fully clothed, but holding up their dresses in a grossly indecent manner. I enquired how persons of such modest aspect came to sit to a photographer in such a fashion.

The photographer told Arthur that most of the 'damsels' were milliners, and ballet dancers who were free during the day. They arrived at his studio sometimes as early as six o'clock on a Sunday morning, which was his busiest day for this type of 'artistic work'. Excited by this potential new customer's interest, the young man added: ' "Give them something to drink, and they don't mind how they are taken, nor in what postures, however degrading." ' The trade in such pictures did not shock Arthur, wondering if it was 'only the exceptional morality of a great city'.

Two nights later there was a farewell dinner for Whitley Stokes who was leaving for India. After a

simple and unpretending supper we had punch brought on, and sat smoking and discoursing in little groups – earnestly enough, but with little jollity; for everyone felt that a friend was going away. Stokes, Rossetti, Swinburne and I had a good deal of talk about old French literature, with which, in spite of his priggishness, Swinburne seems to have a considerable acquaintance, though not always of a reputable kind.[58]

Arthur gave Stokes *The Opium Eater* by Thomas de Quincy, and Rossetti read poems by François Villon from a book he presented to the traveller. Arthur noted that Villon was a thief and a pimp who was only saved from the gallows by his poetic genius.[59] Swinburne, notorious for 'drink and bawdry', was a friend of Richard Monckton-Milnes, who was created Lord Houghton in 1863. He was a Member of Parliament, a poet, and biographer of John Keats: his wife was an artist. Monckton-Milnes was an avid collector of erotica: his collection, some of it smuggled into the country from Europe in diplomatic bags, was only exceeded by that of Henry Spencer Ashbee, who may have been the author of the pornographic epic tale *My Secret Life* by 'Walter'. Arthur had been introduced to the raffish politician in 1859.[60] Monckton-Milnes and Swinburne both enjoyed flagellation and wrote about it at length: the former was probably the author of the poem *The Rodiad*; Swinburne's *The Flogging Book* was not published in his own lifetime.[61]

In July Arthur placed a classified advertisement in the *Daily Telegraph* to find work for Harriet Langdon: 'Needle-work, or housework, where she would not be much seen, wanted by a tall, healthy, young woman aged twenty-nine, *whose face is very much disfigured*.'[62] Four people responded but would not see her when they heard of the severity of her condition. One sweltering day in late July Arthur took Harriet to have her portrait taken. They met at Charing Cross Station, she swathed in her thick black veils, and set off by boat to Westminster, to the studio of Joseph Sargood in Bridge Road. If it had not been for the lupus Arthur imagined he could have found her attractive; 'with her tall slight figure and neat dress, she might have passed for a comely young woman'. Despite being warned, Sargood stared, remarking to Arthur what a 'dreadful object she was'.[63] This photograph has not survived.

Next door to the Royal Free Hospital was the factory of Eley Brothers, 'patentees of waterproof percussion caps, wire cartridges and manufacturers of sporting and military ammu-nition'.[64] After Harriet was discharged from the hospital Arthur took her to meet the forewoman at Eley's, who pitied her and promised to see 'whether such an object could with some concealment be admitted among the girls of the factory'. After some thought, 'because they will not have her hideous face among the women at the factory', Eley's offered Harriet piece-work, making shot-bags at her sister's home, earning three shillings a gross.[65] But within two months Eley's stopped giving Harriet work and all Arthur's schemes had failed. He despaired of what was to become of her.

In August the Fosters were due for another holiday, so Hannah suggested asking her 'missis' if she could have time off so that she could go away with him: 'she made her next inquiry more timidly, it is a strange one. "I couldn't go with you drest in my servant's things – we couldn't be together: and of course I couldn't go like a lady . . . and so I thought I could go with you in men's clothes."' He confessed to his diary, though not to her, that the same idea had crossed his mind, but he talked her out of it. He looked again at Fink's photograph of her with short hair, a man's suit, collar and tie, and ruefully decided against the experiment:

> Her nature is so genuine, and in spite of her rough life, so womanly, that I doubt if she could play such a part: and I would not have her learn to act and to conceal. Besides, is it safe? possible? right? I promised however to think it over.[66]

With the Fosters out of the way, Hannah and Arthur went back to Fink's for a portrait of her as his 'faithful drudge and slave'. 'The phlegmatic little German was their photographer of choice: Munby must have trusted him to be discreet. (Plate 6) Hannah sits cross-legged on the floor at her master's feet, the toe of his boot intruding into the shot. She is looking at him beseechingly: her 'navvy strap' and slave chain are visible. 'She slipped from behind a screen where she covered her hair and removed all her clothes except a pair of cotton drawers, and blacked herself. She curtsied to Mr Fink and 'begged him "not to mind seeing me like this, sir"'. Another photograph, which has not survived, was of Hannah crouching and tugging at the chain with one hand, like a dog on a lead. Arthur had directed her to crouch and look forlorn while he glared down at her 'like a tyrant ... it is a record of her in her noblest guise'. This was one of his favourite pictures, hidden behind a more conventional image in a travelling frame which he carried round in his breast pocket.

At the end of the session Arthur took Hannah to Fig Tree Court where she begged him to allow her to stay for two nights. He agreed but remembered the temptation of the last time they had slept under the same roof. As soon as they were safely inside his chambers, Hannah wanted to carry on the drama which had started in the studio, and proposed to strip off and sweep the chimney. Neither of them tells what happened next. Arthur found it hard to keep their romance celibate, especially 'when the hour came and she said her prayers between my knees. I was able to kiss her with due self-control as she lay alone in my spare bed and smiled "Good night Massa"'.

The following day they went to Southend, travelling third class, where he tried to blend in with people of her class. But the situation became awkward when they had tea in a public house in Shoeburyness and 'everywhere people stared at us being together, and addressed me with respect, while they spoke bluntly to her as an equal'. He was glad to return to London: her visit had been enjoyable, but frustrating for him:

> pure she came, and pure she went; and for her the visit was one of simple affection merely and enjoyment. But for me it was very different: and I scarcely knew how far it is right thus to strain one's own endurance, and allow her to cheapen, though from love, her maidenly reserve of charms and permit oneself to discount the quiet freedom of domestic life, because her humble and obscure position makes it possible for me to do it.[67]

While the Fosters were away, Hannah set to work cleaning the house and summoned Arthur to see her 'in her dirt', their favourite state. When they met at dusk she was agitated that she was not as dirty as she would have liked. Her appearance was unusual for a lover's tryst:

> a creature with face and arms as black as a coal heaver's, and dingy servant's cap and apron all begrimed and sodden . . . her boots and petticoats were soaked with mopping and scouring . . . 'Don't I stink of dirt?' and she seemed disappointed when I confessed that *that* charm was absent. . . . Her Don Quixote, when he kissed her in the midst of her squalor did not ignore the facts but accepted and rejoiced in them. . . . She has overcome the vanities and weakness of woman's nature and learnt to choose and absolutely delight in the vilest lot, because thereby she can find expression for her love as (as she thinks) give pleasure to her 'master'.[68]

Arthur knew he was taking advantage of the class differences between them, but this was the basis of their love. The risk-taking behaviour increased when Hannah insisted on spending the night with him more often whenever her employers were away, and even when Mrs Mitchell, the chambers' housekeeper, was there. Whenever the doorbell rang Hannah was happy to crawl under his bed and 'lie still like a mouse, till the [front] room is clear'.

While certain days were devoted to certain tasks, Monday being wash day, the rhythm of servitude was much the same: cleaning, scrubbing, fetching and carrying, grate-cleaning and fire-lighting, emptying of slops, and more of the same. Fifteen-hour days were usual, with small meal breaks. Many servants had poor food, often living on left-overs from their employers' meals. Hannah attributed her rough-and-ready table manners to a life in service:

When I was a scullion the footmen used to make game o' me cause I licked the plates as come down from the [dining] room. I always did it. I licked the bits off 'em and them footmen despised me for it. 'Why, you're like a dog!' they said. But I didn't mind it; it didn't seem to matter what I did . . . I used to have my meals anyhow and at odd times, and in my dirt, just at the corner of a poor kitchen table. . . . An' so I come to like that, and I always do it now. . . . I don't reckon to have no manners, only my own.[69]

The monotony of daily life meant that Hannah's visits to the Temple were imbued with great importance. The time she spent with Arthur was always electric, sometimes fraught. In late September they had a close shave when Arthur's father arrived earlier than planned at Fig Tree Court while Hannah was telling her Massa how she had cleaned the privy, 'the vilest and most unmentionable of her weekly drudgeries. Quickly my poor child had to be hidden away as usual, willingly enough, and then to be dismissed, with a secret kiss to find her way back alone.'[70]

As well as the demands placed on him by his secret romance, Arthur was worried about Harriet Langdon and her bleak future. On one of his visits at her sister's home, he was so moved by her plight that when they said goodbye he kissed her forehead, 'for reverence and because it was the only part of her countenance that was not diseased and loathsome'.[71] Curiously, it was more comfortable for Arthur to walk out with a heavily veiled Harriet, a woman who was clearly hiding something, than it was to walk openly with Hannah. Arthur and Harriet certainly looked an odd couple and attracted second looks, but Hannah had to endure far worse when she was out with her sweetheart.

On 24 October Arthur determined to buy Hannah a new

bonnet from a haberdasher's shop near her place of work. She accompanied him with extreme reluctance: she did not want a new bonnet and anticipated her own embarrassment resulting from his stubbornness:

> I made her take my arm . . . and we walked up and down the back streets . . . and then we went to Paddington Green where much against her will I made her go in to a little shop with me. . . . The shop-girl knew not what to make of our conjuncture; and indeed it was an experiment on my part, and as such a failure . . . the shop-girl tittered, saying 'Sir' to me but affecting a chill superiority to her; and wondering when she tried on the bonnet I chose, a black straw of plain old-fashioned shape, and they saw her short-cropped hair.[72]

Christmas 1862 saw Arthur returning to his family as usual, and Hannah working. They frequently dashed across London to see each other in the weeks leading up to his departure: she would clean his rooms, prepare meals and wait on him at table (despite his pleas she would never sit down and eat with him). Bizarrely, Hannah used her hands and even her face to remove the dust from some dirty wooden boxes: 'she rubbed her cheeks on the boxes till her features were black with dust'.[73]

Over Christmas servants had ways of enjoying themselves and making their own entertainment. They might be given some wine, and, with judicious juggling by the cook, substantial left-overs for a festive meal below stairs. Relatives, friends and sweethearts were smuggled down the area steps into the basement, hidden in the kitchen and entertained, kept out of sight. And guests could stay overnight, in secret, sharing a bed in the attics. Hannah's diaries describe the sometimes anarchic life beyond the green baize doors which kept the master and mistress's lives separate from their servants. Tolerant employers

like the Jacksons and the Fosters did not mind these arrangements so long as the work was done.[74]

When Arthur returned to London in early January, Hannah told him about being kissed by George, a visitor to the
kitchen, who was twenty-two years old and a long-lost nephew
of Sarah, the head servant. Being a 'country lad', he appealed
to Hannah and was clearly taken with her; he suggested a kiss
under the mistletoe which she decorously declined, but she
agreed to walk with him to the gate, where she shook hands
and asked him to return soon. The following day he was back,
accompanied by his sweetheart who he insisted was his sister.
Hannah was unperturbed by the confusion and enjoyed the
attention he lavished on her, following her round and helping
her to wash up, joking and laughing. He asked for a kiss and
she obliged: ' "Give us a kiss Hannah," and he kissed me on
the lips and me him. I liked him cause he's a nice country
chap.' George flourished the mistletoe several more times that
day and Hannah agreed to have tea with him in the room
where he lodged and go to a pantomime. Arthur was surprised
by Hannah's 'artlessness' and refused to be provoked to
jealousy, preferring to believe, as an anthropologist, that this
was 'a salient instance of the freedom of manners which her
class enjoys'. If Hannah had hoped to rouse Arthur to
passionate jealousy she failed, but her behaviour reminded
him that he must not neglect his sweetheart. Two days later,
on 10 January 1863, Arthur took Hannah to see an Italian
opera at a music-hall in the Edgware Road, travelling by the
new Metropolitan Line underground railway between Paddington, nor far from the Fosters' house, and Farringdon, a
short walk from Fleet Street and the Temple. He and 30,000
other passengers crossed London on that 'historic day'.[75]

Hannah and Arthur enjoyed reading about situations
which paralleled their own: stories of 'misalliances' were
popular in Victorian society. Accounts of handsome toffs

seducing their young servants were commonplace, and there was an appetite for stories about marrying out of one's own class. The upper classes had the pleasure of tut-tutting such errant behaviour; the middle classes likewise; and the working classes could join the debate from both ends, being sanctimonious like their social superiors, or railing against the suffocating yoke of class. 'The Great Montagu Case' was a hot story in January 1863 and Hannah gave Arthur the details. Lord Robert Montagu had seen Betsy Wade, a maid, on her hands and knees scrubbing in the street, and they had ended up getting married. Arthur remembered Montagu from Trinity College: he was interested by the kitchen version of a story that he had heard in his own scandalized circle. Arthur's sensitivity about that misalliance would surface in his diary from time to time. In early 1863 he had heard about the lord and the servant over the teacups of his family and friends:

> Now I happen to have heard lately the views by Society of this fatal deed: I have heard from ladies of the shocking degradation of poor Lord Montagu and of his hopeless exclusion from family and friends by reason of this inexplicable depravity and have of course expressed my deepest sympathy and horror.[76]

From January, Hannah felt bowed down not by her work but by Arthur's demands that she write about it. Munby found the 'difficulty Hannah finds in writing down daily the few monotonous facts of her kitchen life incredible. She cannot get herself to take a pen into her unaccustomed hand.' After much cajoling and pleading, he tried to change her attitudes by banning her from visiting him. She, strong-willed, turned up anyway and he did not have the heart to turn her away.[77]

The tedium of her daily life was numbing but he wanted to read page after page of description of domestic work. The following is an account of a typical Saturday at 22 Carlton Villas:

> Lighted the fires and blacked the parlour grate. Cleaned the hearth and five pairs of boots. Swept and dusted the room and the hall. Cleaned the steps on my knees and laid the cloth and got the breakfast up. Cleared and washed up and filled the skuttles and made the fires up. Cleaned the knives and got the dinner ready. Cleared the things away and laid the kitchen cloth. After dinner I took the carpets up and shook 'em. Cleaned the kitchen tables and floor and laid the carpet down and had my tea in my dirt and then I took the furniture out and swept the passage. Washed my hands and arms and made pies. . . . I got the supper ready after I'd washed up and cleaned the scullery on my knees. I didn't finish till eleven and then I'd to wash myself and had to do some mending. Besides I was boiling a ham for breakfast and that wasn't done till twelve. . . . And then I skinned it and to bed.[78]

Hannah would undress in the kitchen which was much warmer than her attic bedroom, and 'because I did not want Eliza [a servant] to see my chains and padlock round my neck'.[79] She wrote of her disappointment when Arthur visited her and complained that she was not 'black enough' for him. The captive boredom that she and the other servants felt is conveyed when she recorded that she had cleaned seventy-four pairs of boots in January and had visited Massa five times. On her Sunday afternoon visits she not only washed his feet but licked his boots. She liked the taste of boot polish and horseshit. She would kneel on the floor between his knees and they would 'pet' before she left.[80] Once in a while he would cut her hair before they petted. Hannah was also asked to describe her dreams: for years she had a recurring one of herself as a dog:

I was at Massa's. I was on the floor and he was showing me a book when some gentleman walked into the room, and looked astonished to see me there – I asked Massa what I was to do and he said 'Lie still,' but I crept round the table somehow and lay curled up like a dog under the window and Massa was talking to the gentleman and he didn't seem to notice me, nor hardly know I was a girl lying there, and I was glad of that.[81]

In early March Hannah sent Arthur pages of her diary describing how she had taken the dream sequence further and actually behaved like a dog in disgrace:

I took the matting out and shook it. Swept the passage and took the things out of the hole under the stairs Mary uses for dustpans and brushes. It's a dark hole and about two yards long and very low. I crawled on my hands and knees and lay curled up in the dirt for a minute or so and then I got the hard brush and swept the walls down. The cobwebs and dust fell all over me and I had to poke my nose out of the door like a dog's out of a kennel. Then I swept the floor of it and got my pail and cleaned it out and put the things back in their place.[82]

When Hannah visited she would call Arthur 'Sir', curtsey to him and tell him about her life as if he were a stranger, talking of being a slave, why she wore chains and the strap and 'the rest of it'. Then she would serve his meals, heat the coals for hot water to wash his feet, clean his boots and make his cigars while he read improving literature to her.[83]

On 21 March, now eighteen months into his friendship with Harriet Langdon, Arthur returned to the Royal Free Hospital and asked the doctors about a mask for her. He also wrote letters to benevolent institutions and started to wage a campaign to get her a pension from the Royal Home for Incurables – opened in 1854 and chaired by Charles Dickens

– which would succeed at the second attempt in the summer of 1864. He had placards made urging 'Vote for Harriet Langdon: A Case of Great Disfigurement'. The best mask, which cost £10, was too expensive, however. The outlook was grim: Harriet's condition was currently stable, but likely to get worse: her sister was growing impatient with her prolonged stay in their tiny home and Arthur felt under pressure to do more. No one could guarantee that her medicine would continue to be free and Harriet did not want to return to Ilfracombe as a pauper. After all, he had brought her to London. There was some resentment felt by both Harriet and her sister at the changes in their lives he had engineered. Arthur could sound despairing:

> her sister who was in the room and who is evidently tired of having that hideous object constantly about her and dependent, spoke out with the brutal frankness of her class, when I suggested washing or some such employment. 'Nobody will have her, Sir, nobody could bear to see her about with a face like *that*!'[84]

At the end of March 1863, Hannah and her fellow servants, Sarah and Mary, were sent to Brighton to prepare the house the Fosters rented. Although the enforced absence from Arthur made her anxious, she looked forward to the time she would spend on the beach with the Fosters' young children. In the first month she was there she cleaned 138 pairs of boots, the most ever, and she was proud of this.[85] There was a chance meeting with two male servants, Bill, a groom, and Ralph, a footman, whom she knew from her days working for Lord Stradbroke at Henham Hall. Ralph was 'glad to see me and offer me his arm': she had blossomed in the intervening eight years. Introducing Hannah to his sweetheart, who was cook at his place, did not prevent Bill from visiting her at Royal Crescent several times and taking her for walks along the beach, sometimes in the moonlight. There were also stolen kisses, all described in her diary for Arthur. It was easy and uncomplicated: Hannah introduced Bill and Ralph to her brother Dick who had decided to visit her for four days in Brighton, and took lodgings close to where she worked. Hannah's descriptions of the time she spent with her brother and her two friends were of warmth and happiness: having drinks in local taverns, being introduced to dashing young lancers Bill knew: meals with servant friends, and friends of friends, in their employers' kitchens, more like a working holiday than work. Hannah was too busy to miss Arthur much: the place, the weather and the company all conspired to make her life sweeter.

Arthur did not visit Hannah in Brighton this year. Most weekends while she was away he rambled around the country-side, recording working women, visiting Teddington where the Reverend Borland lived, Chislehurst, Acton, St Albans and Epsom.[86] Hannah expressed no anxiety about his absence. In early May he spent the weekend with a friend in a cottage in Ripley, Surrey, and wondered if such a place could offer a safe haven for him and his sweetheart: 'it almost seemed as if in such a nook one might work out the long sad problem, how to live with Hannah and do justice to her love and my own'.[87] On Sunday, 20 May, Arthur set off to acquire a photograph of a gipsy for his collection. Twenty-year-old Abie Reynolds and her family were spending the summer at the Welsh Harp, a reservoir in the west of London. Arthur found Abie and her mother and sister in a field where a photographer's studio was also located. He was bewitched by her beauty at first sight, and for two summers she led him a merry dance. Abie was

in stature five feet eight or nine inches; a figure that was commanding, in height and breadth of shoulder, but whose symmetry and youthful lissomness made it seem most feminine: a wild and artless grace of manner and movement that gave a new charm to everything she did . . . her face was wonderfully striking . . . and a bright frank smile, most unlike that of a Romany; but her large eyes were black and brilliant hazel, and her complexion . . . was a deep olive brown.

She was a natural model and after some talk, lubricated with a small tip, during which she told him her father was a horse-dealer and offered to tell his fortune, Arthur asked her to have her photograph taken, for which he paid a further shilling. She was certainly picturesque:

she wore no crinoline . . . stout boots and best of all her head-dress was simply a black wideawake [bonnet] poised sideways over her eyes to shade them from the sun. Beneath it her shining black hair hung loosely . . . her hands which she tossed freely and gracefully about, were as large as a man's and were even browner than her face: but they were soft within, and beautifully shaped . . . she stood up before the camera in a pose of easy outline that could scarcely be bettered.[88]

The picture was developed on the spot but was of poor quality and not worth keeping, and Arthur resolved to return the following week and have it taken again. He reckoned himself a connoisseur, having seen many gipsies but never one like Abie. He was disappointed that she would not agree to be photographed on his second visit: he gave her more money and departed, arranging to see her on the following Sunday, his third trip, and collect the awaited photograph. On the third visit there was still no picture; Abie and the photographer blamed each other. Arthur gave up for the time being.

Meanwhile, Hannah woke up in the early hours of her thirtieth birthday in Brighton, disturbed by a dream of being found hiding under Massa's bed in her dirty work clothes by

Mrs Mitchell: 'so I thought I'd better do something to show
I was a servant and so I set on and scrubbed a dirty floor and
stairs for it seemed as if she thought I was a thief'.[89] Hannah
had been missing the secret life that she shared with Munby.
She jumped out of bed, lit the fires, cleaned five pairs of boots
and got the breakfast ready, 'packed and corded my box and
put it in the hall ready to go. Went over the inventory with
the landlady. Washed the breakfast things up in the scullery
. . . said goodbye to neighbours [servants].' The Fosters travelled on their own, the children with Hannah and the other
servants.

There was a warm welcome at Carlton Villas and letters
from Arthur asking her to go and see him if she could, and
good wishes from her sisters Ellen and Polly. Hannah went
up to the parlour to thank Mrs Foster for her birthday present
of fabric to make herself a frock, and was given permission to
go out that evening. She dashed to the Temple.

> We clasped for a good while and then I took my shawl
> off and he looked at my arms and said they looked fatter
> than he'd ever seen 'em and he said how nice and brown
> and red my face was an' all that and he looked to see
> me again in my green shawl and black bonnet. I got the
> dinner ready and lit the fire. Took Massa's boots off after
> I'd licked 'em of my own accord. Washed his feet and
> then made a few cigars. . . . And Massa talked to me of
> my thirtieth birthday and that nicely and we petted a bit
> and Massa told me to kneel wi' him by the table wi' my
> arm around him and he prayed for himself and for me.
> We said the Lord's Prayer together and then got up. . . .
> Massa came wi' me to the 'bus and I got home by half
> past ten.

A few days later Hannah was back at Fig Tree Court where
Arthur recorded 'her dimensions'. He complimented her that

she was 'jolly and fat' and wondered if she could pick him up, which she promptly did: 'I lifted him up easy and carried him and then he lifted me and said I was heavy.' Hannah weighed 11 stone (154 pounds); she was 5 feet 7¾ inches tall; 28 inches round the waist; the bicep of her right arm was 13¼ inches round, bigger than Arthur's, and a little bigger than her neck.

On the last day of May they met covertly at the top of Chancery Lane and walked off separately to the Temple. Arthur heard the gatekeeper speak roughly to Hannah and refuse entry when she would not say who she was visiting. She became upset and returned to Kilburn, and Arthur stood by unable, or rather afraid, to intervene. This altercation made her 'feel lower in heart':

> I've bin a servant now twenty years or more. Always the lowest kind, but I think different about it now a good deal more than I did ten years afore I knew Massa. He has taught me though it's bin difficult to learn thoroughly the beauty of being nothing but a common drudge and to bear being despised by others what don't have to work the same way . . . but I could not change from being Massa's slave for anything else I know off. I've bin a slave nine years and worn the chains and padlocks six years.[90]

On 18 July Arthur took Hannah to Fink's studio for three more likenesses to be taken. They have not survived. She travelled by omnibus 'in her dirt', her wet and dirty clothes hidden by a dress worn over them. For the first picture she stood next to Arthur wearing her bonnet and shawl; for the second she removed her clean dress and stood leaning against a broom, the third was a head-and-shoulders shot. Fink told Mr Munby that he thought Hannah was looking 'much coarser than before'.[91]

A few days later, Arthur took stock of his pupil's progress:

his programme was not just about drudgery; from the beginning he bought Hannah books of 'improving literature' and aimed to add to the basic education Shifnal's charity school had provided. Hannah read as much as she could, though never enough for her impatient teacher who seemed unable to accept that there were huge constraints on her time. Although he encouraged her to work hard, he also despaired of her preference for cleaning and scrubbing to reading and writing. The struggle between Hannah's further education and her salvation through hard work worried Arthur throughout the 1860s. Reviewing his experiment, he explained her life as he had planned it:

> She was to try . . . and become and *has* become a noble and gentle woman, not only without the aid of technical help but in spite of ignorance and lowly isolation, and *by means* of that very toil and servile labour which is supposed to make a woman contemptible and vulgar. Physical degradation was to be the channel and even the source of spiritual beauty. It had often been so among religious women of old, but with an English maid servant, how would it be? After the motive is everything . . . but love and self-sacrifice have glorified all her drudgery and in proving her capacity for them it has made itself and herself tenfold dearer. Some day I may perhaps be able to do justice to her devotedness and to my own scheme of training her.[92]

At the end of July Hannah and her brother Dick went to Shifnal for a ten-day holiday: Arthur gave her a list of dos and don'ts, but his express wish was for her to 'bring back some type of charity garb she wore when she got her humbler schooling as a child'. Although she visited her old school in Aston Street and met old schoolfriends, she could not find such a relic and there was no mention of it on her return.

This was her first visit to Shropshire since Christmas 1854. Hannah and Dick arrived when market-day was in full swing: 'it all looked so green and the town seemed so small and looked so strange after such a many years away.' For the next ten days they went from cottage to cottage, catching up on years of family news, spending a hugger-mugger night with their brother Jim, his wife Eliza and daughter Emily and son William Henry at their cottage in Oakengates:

> We came to Jim's [wheelwright's] shop. He was very hard at work building him a new cottage. We knew his wife who stared at us, seemingly not to know us quite: so we passed on to Jim at the shop door. He knewed us and was pleased to see us and after that Eliza came up and kissed us . . . She showed us some cartwheels she'd painted for Jim . . . he makes them things and barrows and all that.[93]

Halfway through her holiday Hannah felt restless: she was homesick for Arthur and missed her work:

> I am already getting tired of being away from my reg'lar work and been out and about so at different places wi' no boots to clean but my own and then it's no use o'cleaning here the country's so black and dirty and my legs and skirts are black too.[94]

On Friday, 7 August Hannah and Dick returned to London and on the journey home Hannah realized where her heart and future lay:

> Started away at half past eleven after kissing Polly [her sister] and looking round on Shiffnal [sic] and thinking such deep thoughts about it and still glad to get away for no place seems *home* but London now. Sisters nor brothers, nor my relations are like a mother or father to anyone and Massa is all to me now.[95]

While Hannah was travelling back from Shropshire, Arthur was visiting an old friend from his studies at the Bar, Richard Doddridge Blackmore. Poor health had forced Blackmore to abandon his legal career in 1858 and he started a market-gardening business in Teddington, Middlesex. During the 1860s his poems and novels were published: in 1869 his romantic novel *Lorna Doone* would become a best-seller, some editions of which were dedicated to Arthur.[96] Munby often visited the Blackmores and loved hearing about the pitched battles fought by the English and Irish female labourers they employed every summer. He may have been tempted to tell his friend about Hannah, but he never did.

Hannah and Arthur's reunion on 9 August was not a total success. She told him about her visit to her old school, remembering the roads from which she had shovelled horse manure for her father's vegetables, and telling him of the pit wenches and the other working women she had seen. She had longed to see him again and was hurt when Arthur blamed her for a disagreement she had with a collier wench, and it

> put me out and vex'd me so that I couldn't help showing it and he said I shuffled round the room like anything but a good slave and so I did I know but I was aggravated and forgot myself for the time. I was sorry after though but I didn't say so and Massa was kind so we got on all right and I did my usual work.[97]

Arthur's account suggests that he was more displeased with her than she realized, or cared to admit. His middle-class sensibilities are exposed:

> So Hannah having waxed fat, must kick a little for once. We had a bit of temper tonight. I blamed her for one of those little proofs of defective delicacy – proofs which betray the one vulnerable point of my training of her . . .

I soon brought her round while she stood panting under my hand with mingled passion and repentance. I assumed the requisite sternness and rebuked her as a master. . . . She came round and in due time the appointed sign was laid upon my lips.[98]

The situation calmed when Hannah washed his feet and petted him and they discussed his plans to visit her family in Shifnal, incognito. The upset was the first recorded in her writings, and in his diaries: a tension remained for the rest of the year.

A week after Hannah's return Arthur went to the Midlands to see the women in the nail-making industry, and the pit women of Shropshire. On 15 August he went to Shifnal, and using the reminiscences she had shared with him, explored the town in Hannah's footsteps. He went to St Andrew's church and spoke to her uncle Owen Owen, the parish clerk, who showed him around. Arthur did not mention the 'memorable old countryman's niece, and tipped him a shilling. He enjoyed meeting Hannah's Cullwick and Owen relatives and imagining her being with them the previous week, not telling them that she was his secret sweetheart.[99]

By the middle of September Hannah was exasperated by Arthur's demands and told him in the pages of her diary of her frustrations, mostly petty ones. She was happy with the Fosters: like the Jacksons, they were generous to their servants and tolerant of the entertainment of family and friends in the kitchen. But she was not eating properly and perhaps drinking too much on an empty stomach. Beer had been rarely mentioned by Hannah until now, and it may have fuelled her resentment:

I never eat my dinner cause it's half cold and I wait till half past two for it and I've not always time . . . and my beer is chief food. I buy my own and pay four shillings and six pence for a cask of four and a half gallons and that lasts me three weeks, and I have two shillings a week allowed me.[100]

One of Arthur's ways of disciplining Hannah for causing a row was to play at master and servant. One day in October they discussed what had gone wrong the previous week and she apologized for it and

> then I was good again and so Massa told me to black my face ... So I did and got the dinner and cleaned boots and washed up the things and Massa's feet with it [her face] black and Massa seemed pleased with it so but said my hands wasn't looking so red and coarse as they did on Sunday when he read them verses to me.[101]

Two days later, when 22 Carlton Villas was empty, Hannah engaged in a ritual which she enjoyed and Arthur loved hearing about: sweeping the kitchen chimney, naked but for a duster on her head and a pair of boots. When she emerged from the chimney she

> lay on the hearth in the soot a minute or two thinking, and I wished rather that Massa could see me, I then got the looking-glass and looked at myself and I was certainly a fright and hideous all over, at least I should seem so to anybody but Massa.[102]

At the end of 1863, Hannah reviewed her year in a voice that was calm but critical: the visit to Shropshire had clarified that 'home' was here, with the Fosters, or anywhere so long as it was near to Massa. She knew that she had aged, partly because of her short hair which was 'like a man's ... except in the front'. The other servants annoyed her by their lack of interest in learning, and their comments about her shabby dress and slave chains. Hannah ended the year disappointed to have cleaned only 937 pairs of boots.[103]

In January 1864 Arthur saw 'Queen Kitty' clanking down Lancaster Place, her milk-pails swinging from the yoke across her powerful shoulders. He rejoiced in her strength, ascribing a morality to her wearing only working livery and making no concessions to fashion. He failed to grasp that Kitty's poverty made even a nod in the direction of fashion unaffordable, and naively wrote that her motives were pure and simple, not financially driven:

> She has been wet through hundreds of times: she has never had an umbrella or an illness in her life. Parasols, veils, gloves, crinoline: she has lived so long among the grandest of developments of such things, and throughout her youth too; and yet she knows no more of them than a savage, and no more thinks of any one of them in relation to herself, than if she had never seen it ... I protest my respect for such a woman is immense; she has been tried in the furnace of London, and not found wanting in her rustic homeliness at all.

Arthur was in awe of her strength and agility that she could carry such unwieldy apparatus and not spill a drop, even when she was being teased by a baker who 'with playful gallantry gave her a farewell dig in the ribs with his fist, but, bless you, the blow never shook one fibre of our Kitty's massive frame. She only smiled at that delicate compliment and disappeared down an area steps.'[104]

One morning Arthur was upset by a vivid and poignant dream. It started with him and a guide standing at the foot of a steep, snowy mountain. They tried to climb it but were unable to find any footholds and were forced to turn back and attend a dinner party where he talked to a servant who looked and dressed like Hannah. The master of the house, wearing Quaker dress, approached Arthur and Hannah and she tried to hide under the table. Arthur prevented her from doing so but she was reprimanded for being in the parlour, and talking with a gentleman. She trembled and remained silent: Arthur intervened and told his host not to admonish her: '"Do not blame her, nor me: I must apologize for being in your house, but I mean no harm, I am honestly your servant's sweetheart."' Their host said: '"It is impossible, come with me and explain and you [Hannah], you go to your kitchen."' Arthur boldly refused to tolerate her being dismissed: '"No, where I go, she goes; but I will tell you and tell you all."' They all trooped off to the dining room, Arthur seated and his sweetheart on the floor beside him, 'leaning her cheek on my knee'. Then Arthur told their story:

> I told him of my love for her, and hers for me, of the cruel discipline by which I had educated her, of the degradation which had purified her spirit and how all that she has done and suffered for me had (as I knew it would) increased my love tenfold.

As if to re-enact one of their love rituals, while Arthur talked Hannah disappeared from his side to hide under the sofa. The partygoers were startled to see her emerge and crouch,

> her face pressed against the floor, between her outstretched arms, she moved forwards towards me, crawling on all fours, from along the ground as if she would abase herself to the utmost. I knew what was in her heart. I trembled with indignation at myself for letting her lie low, with love and intense delight at the loveliness of her humility. She crept up to my feet and flung her lips upon them and would have licked my boot. . . . Her humiliation is glorious, my lordliness is tyrannical and base. I know it and rejoice in her triumph over me.

Arthur disengaged her from his feet, lifted her up and embraced her, and said to her master: ' "*Now* do you think she loves me? Do you think I owe her any love?" ' The master told Arthur to ' "take her, I understand it all now" '. They adjourned to prayers: Arthur's arm around her shoulder and her cheek on his shoulder. Everyone, ladies, gentlemen and servants 'stared and jibed and tittered to see us so'. Arthur remembered feeling proud when he had told of his love for her, and having humbled himself for her sake. He also noted the horror of the ladies when he announced he wanted to marry Hannah, who screamed out: ' "Sir you cannot love her." ' He yelled back defiantly, ' "I do" ' and kissed her forehead, whereupon Hannah fainted and fell backwards, cutting her head on the floor. Confusion reigned: the host called for a doctor and Arthur carried Hannah to her attic room, up dark and winding stairs, 'kissing her cold cheek, waiting and praying that help might come'. Time passed and Arthur returned to find out how she was, but the host and the doctor said: ' "Don't you know? She is dead." ' Arthur wept 'with the passion of one whose life and all has passed away for ever'. He woke from the dream sobbing 'like a child and all my pillow was wet with tears'. He wept 'hysterically and uncontrollably' back to sleep.[105]

Arthur was still shaken by this dream when Hannah told him she had been dismissed by the Fosters. His reaction was mixed with feelings of guilt:

And now worn with overwork, and upset with this little tragedy, she sits and weeps and opens her heart half hysterically about it all, now as never before it comes how clearly she has caught my meaning and made her daily drudgery a bond between us and not a bar.[106]

Hannah would have been happy to have carried on working at the Fosters', but their patience with her strange, scruffy appearance snapped and she was dismissed on 2 March 1864, but with an excellent character. Her refusal to clean herself before she answered the bells brought the situation to a head. She was a hard worker, doing the work of two servants, but they were puzzled at her carelessness of her own appearance. Mrs Foster told her when she cleared away the breakfast dishes:

> 'Hannah, your Master and me think you'd better leave and get a place where you've no waiting to do.' I looked surprised and she says: 'You're a good hardworking servant, and we like you, but that strap on your wrist, your Master can't bear to see it, nor your arms all naked and blacked sometimes and you so dirty.'[107]

Hannah's lack of comprehension of the Fosters' feelings shows how far she and Arthur had descended into their mad love. The sticking-point was the wrist-strap: 'I couldn't *leave* that off when it's a sign that I'm a drudge and belong to Massa. But after all I was glad to be sent away for been so dirty, so then Massa may know I *am* dirty.' On 8 March Mrs Foster gave Hannah her wages and a photograph of their six children, and told her she was welcome to visit them at any time.

Hannah's first night 'out of place' was spent with a woman called Biddy who ran errands for the Fosters. At such short notice she had been unable to go to the Smiths in Clerkenwell. She was grateful for Biddy's offer of a bed but her night had been bleak: snow had come into the room through a broken window.[108] The following day Hannah's brother Dick carried her things to the home of Ann Crook, a servant friend in Kilburn who was married and expecting a baby and who had offered her a mattress on the floor. Next day she did some jobs for Ann, washing, cleaning and errands, and walked to Clerkenwell to arrange lodgings with Mrs Smith, and then on to see Arthur. Hannah had a cold and a cough, and was hurt by his reaction:

> But my throat and cold was so bad I couldn't talk and o' course Massa wanted to know all about my leaving and asked me a lot o' questions directly and I couldn't answer 'em nicely, so he thought I was ill-tempered and then he got cross although I said I wasn't naughty and he sent me home by myself.[109]

Arthur felt guilty and responsible for Hannah's predicament, but he could not offer her the practical help she needed. For the next two weeks she spent odd nights with the Smiths and a night or two sleeping on Ann Crook's floor. Arthur took her to see *Leah* at the Adelphi, but it was not a time of joy: 'Massa liked the play but he never spoke hardly all the while. We came to Chancery Lane and said good night and I walked to Mrs Smith's.'[110] A week later she was allowed to spend the night with him at Fig Tree Court, where she did the cooking and cleaning, and he suggested that she go to Margate and find 'outdoor work'.[111]

On Good Friday, 25 March 1864, Hannah left London for Margate. It was a frosty, foggy day, and she cut a sorry figure as she walked from her friend Tilly's lodgings in Paddington, carrying her luggage in bundles to Victoria station. She was nervous of working with strangers, but Arthur had convinced her that for health reasons – the sea air would do her good – Margate was the place. Their last evening together was tearful:

> But I was very down about it all. . . . And I lay on the hearth rug and cried a bit, but Master sat down by me and kissed and comforted me and said how gladly he

would keep me there always if he could, and told me how my home is with him wherever I go and so I got better.[112]

On arrival in Margate, Hannah met a 'respectable-looking old woman', Mrs Hook, who gave her lodgings for two nights. But she proved to be an odd and 'fussy old body' and asked Hannah to leave, suggesting she stay with her friend, Mrs Eastlands. The price of lodgings only covered the cost of a night's sleep and a few pieces of coal for a fire: food and tea were extra. To her dismay, Hannah's small amount of money was dwindling fast, and she asked Mrs Eastlands if she could work in part-payment for the room. Hannah was unable to find any 'outdoor work' such as picking stones in the fields, but found a place through a servant's registry as a maid of all work with the Misses Knight who ran a lodging-house for ladies at 20 Union Crescent. Starting work on Saturday, 9 April, Hannah was paid 4 shillings a week, 2 pence a day beer allowance, and as a perquisite was allowed to sell the fat off the meat, and the bones to a local rag-and-bone shop. Hannah liked Miss Julia Knight immediately, recognizing her as a lady in spite of her plain, well-worn clothes.[113] The Knight sisters, one of whom had been bedridden for seven years, lived in reduced circumstances, and ran a seasonal and precarious business. Hannah's predecessor, Eliza, a young drudge, had not been conscientious, and in the kitchen:

It was dark with not much fire, and a little dirty table and the chairs to sit on, and the other one stands broken. . . . I looked in the cupboards and all seemed higgledy-piggledy and the candlestick I had in my hand was all over grease. I found some blacking brushes and a pot all dry so I see there'd bin no boots cleaned lately. And the sink, oh it was in a mess.[114]

Hannah slept in a room next to the basement kitchen which was just as squalid: 'it was terribly dirty and my bed was anything but soft and a straw bolster and no pillow.' The following morning she was woken early by flea bites, and started to scrub her way through the house. Miss Knight helped with the easier tasks such as making tea for her sister, and filling hot-water bottles, leaving the serious work for her undaunted maid. Back in a familiar routine, Hannah's mood soared, and her time in Margate was exhausting but happy:

> I waited on them and the lodgers and filled my time up wi' cleaning the house down and the windows and I took the blinds all down and washed 'em and starched 'em and put 'em up again, and liked being alone in the kitchen, and my work and the air at Margate. And I used to go to church and could write freely and nicely that I felt quite happy . . . And lots o' nice jobs and the lowest work I did the while for there was lots o' fresh lodgers came through the summer – carrying luggage up and down, laying carpets as the ladies wanted 'em and one proud one stood over me as I swept and was crawling on the floor once. Instead o' showing me wi' her hand, she kicked me wi' her foot and pointed. I dare say she thought I should feel hurt and vex'd wi' her but I didn't. I was glad she thought me humble enough without kicking me again.[115]

The Knight sisters were fascinated by Hannah's appearance, while recognizing that she was doing the work of two servants. They were grateful for her cheerful willingness, and Hannah was relieved that her dirtiness was not an issue.[116] But for a misunderstanding with Miss Julia about throwing away cinders, which resulted in Hannah being dismissed and reinstated, the summer at Margate went swimmingly. On her weekly afternoons off she explored the town which was 'much frequented as a watering-place on account of the salubrity of its air'.[117]

On 14 May Arthur resumed his quest for that elusive picture of Abie Reynolds and returned to The Welsh Harp. He was delighted to find her there: her family had wintered in Bushey and were back, this time with one of Abie's brothers. Arthur noticed that she was

> brown . . . buxom and lithe as ever . . . the maiden had a black wideawake [hat] and a frock a few shades browner than her skin . . . she looked round and recognized me and came forward and said 'How do you do, Sir?' in her soft and measured artless-seeming way, and offered me a large well-shaped dusky hand.

A tense scene followed when Arthur asked her about the photograph which he had paid for but not received. Abie's brother, 'a man of horsey look with a shabby cutaway jacket and tight trousers and close shaved face, a compound of a betting man and a horse-stealing gipsy', intervened. Their mother also joined in 'whining' and between them, Abie and her family ran rings round him as they tried to bully more money out of the hapless collector:

> the jealousy of the savage over his women arose in the brother and he and Madame showed symptoms of loss of temper. It couldn't be allowed, not for five pounds: true the girl had consented last year, but she didn't know then that it was not 'feasible', 'didn't know the result in it,' said Mother Reynolds in her strange speech.[118]

As Abie 'glided off' she told Arthur, ' "Oh no, Sir really! you don't know, we gipsies are so different to other people." ' He cut his losses and gave up hope of adding Abie's picture to his collection.

Hannah celebrated her thirty-first birthday in Margate,

waking up that morning from a familiar dream. She told her diary that:

> I dreamt as I saw a lady stoop on her knees and lick her husband's boots cause he was going away for a while and so I thought surely if she does such a thing for love I needn't think it too much in licking Massa's boots. I shall do it the more. I thought of when I went to him as I used to of a Sunday and knelt down and licked his boots so many times and so joyfully that Massa wondered what it meant.[119]

Later that day, at Arthur's instruction, Hannah had her photograph taken by Mr Usher. In order to achieve the picture Arthur wanted of her as 'one of the lowest things I could be on my thirty-first birthday' she did all the muckiest jobs and made herself as dirty as she could beforehand, putting on her carpet-apron, bonnet and shawl before she left. Hannah called in to a public house for half a pint of beer on her way to the studio: it was a rough-and-ready place and the barmaid did not flinch at Hannah's appearance, pouring her beer into a pewter tankard that a workman had just drunk from.

It was ten years since Arthur and Hannah had met: her sleeves were rolled up, biceps and wrist-strap displayed as she sat pretending to clean the boots, props supplied by the studio. She wore her carpet-apron as a badge of pride and looked confidently into the lens of the camera. The other picture taken that day seemed sulky, arms folded defensively as she stood impatient for the session to end and to return to real work. But Arthur and Hannah were disappointed with Usher's work: she did not look dirty enough for their discerning taste.

The following day Arthur discovered his most unwholesome women's work to date: trotter-scrapers who worked for William Healy Brier, the 'horn, bone and plasterer's hair merchant' at 44 Crucifix Lane in Bermondsey.[120] He stumbled across the story when he started talking to a 'tall hulking wench of eighteen rolling along like a sailor; but with a simple modest countenance' without a bonnet or shawl, and wearing a 'soiled ragged gown and boots to match; having her arms bare and her throat wrapped up in flannel for she was very hoarse'.[121] When Arthur asked her what she did for a living she told him: '"Sir, *I scrapes trotters*."' He found the answer 'so comic and the speaker so serious that I had hardly forbore to laugh; but perceiving that this was a "find", I went on to ask particulars.' She pointed out 'the works, a group of low wooden buildings standing suspiciously all alone', and soon they were joined by another trotter-scraper, who was:

> in appearance most forlorn, and repulsive: for her ragged frock under which was a broken hoop [for a crinoline]; and her bare arms were splashed all over with lime, and with yellow dirt of an unknown kind; and she shuffled along in an unlaced pair of men's ankle boots, which were old and foul and wrinkled.

Arthur noticed that she was a 'stout buxom lass, rosy and healthy, with wavy black hair, bright eyes and pleasant sprightly face'. He gave her the soubriquet 'the belle of the boneworks', delighted to find such a specimen. She was one of fifty women who worked for Mr Brier, who earned between 2 and 3 shillings a week:

> 'We scrapes not only trotters, but also bullocks' feet, sir, and horses' feet. We scrapes the hair off 'em and steep 'em in lime and prepares the hoof. We makes a place in the lime for ourselves to sit down in: it do burn one's clothes and we had to wear these old boots.'

Arthur asked archly, '"Is it nice work?"' to which she replied, '"Well, Sir, it's nice for 'em as likes it."' He found the women's wages pitiful but was more concerned at the effect it had on their femininity, destroying: 'all grace and form and character'. Arthur shuddered to think of sitting among heaps of offal all day, 'cleaning and scraping the gory and half putrid feet which had been cut off the carcasses of sheep, horse and bullocks'. He was amazed that the women he spoke to were not 'gross or unsexed'.

The obvious 'unwomanliness' of mudlarking was another occupation that attracted Arthur, and one summer Saturday in June as he strolled along the river front past Old Jamaica Wharf, he remembered the mudlarkers who had caught his eye ten years ago. He recalled how the dirty young girls, sometimes accompanied by their mothers, crawled out of the darkness between the barges, wading up to their knees in the black mud. His memories of one were still vivid:

> who had been crouching in the mire, suddenly appeared out of it and ran across the beach and into the river to wash herself. She was barefoot of course, and her skirt was held up high between her legs . . . and as she washed the black from her limbs, it became obvious that she had been in mud *up to her hips*, and that her arms also, with which she raked up the waste coal, was steeped in the mire up to her shoulder.[122]

Arthur had spotted this girl another time up to her knees in mud 'with her bare thighs visible over it. She was hewing away, with a pick-axe at a bilgewater bung in the side of a coal barge, until she got it out and let the foul liquid squirt through the hole upon her limbs.' Mary Casey, a tall, twenty-five-year-old Irish mudlarker, was reckoned the boldest and deepest wader of them all. On the shoreline she and her friends 'would deliberately walk along, naked from the thigh down', and once Arthur saw her caught by the tide when she had to 'scale the side of a muck-barge and creep on hands and knees up the wooden shoot [sic] whereby it was being laden'. Many times he had seen her 'sunk to the waist in the fetid black ooze, and from her, standing afar off by the reason of her evil odour, I learnt her name and some details of her work.'

Arthur called the mudlarkers 'miry mermaids'. One of his favourite memories is of seeing them hanging round the coal barges, like pigeons, hoping the colliers would throw scraps of bread and cheese to them as they stood waist-deep in water. They 'would wade away, munching with one hand and holding up their skirts with the other'.

The day after his nostalgic walk on the river-front, Arthur visited Hannah in Margate. She had been expecting him and noticed him hovering outside, and went to draw water from the pump in the street:

> And Massa saw me pump the water and he looked pleased as well as I did and we spoke and I brought the water in and Massa followed me in soon after. I was so pleased to see him and after we had clasped and kissed, I knelt down . . . and Massa kissed me again.[123]

This was dangerous behaviour, which they enjoyed. Hannah used her diary to tell Arthur when he disappointed her: on this visit – the first time she had seen him in two months – he had fallen asleep under a secluded cliff for an hour, reducing their already short time together. It was all a rush at the end; he quickly cut her hair and they hurried back to the town, saying a furtive goodbye. For his part Arthur enjoyed the day-trip hugely and was glad to have seen the place where Hannah worked: 'a place of dully respectable dwellings . . . of mostly second- or third-rate lodgings'.[124] He felt rejuvenated at having seen her in her 'close white cap, short frock of lilac cotton, coarse sackcloth apron and strong boots' and called her 'the noblest and sweetest natured woman

... in the world'. Arthur described them returning to their own worlds 'each in their own contrasted but coalescing sphere'. Two days later, when writing to her, he deliberately misspelt her name as 'Hannah Cullender' and used cheap notepaper so as not to arouse Miss Knight's suspicions about who her maid's corrrespondent might be.

During the summer Arthur took Harriet Langdon to exhibitions and sightseeing trips round London. On 24 June she braved the omnibus on her own and travelled to Fig Tree Court where Munby offered her some wine, examined her face and listened to her news. They discussed the first photograph taken of her and planned another. Her second experience of having her picture taken was a disaster. Despite warning the photographer:

> when she raised her thick veil [he] was so horrorstruck at the hideousness of her face that he hastily laid down the plate and *ran away* declining he could not do it, could not bear to look at her – and to my grief the poor girl heard it. 'Her face is like a death's head,' he cried.[125]

Eventually her picture was taken by another photographer on the premises. This was later destroyed by Arthur, though there are pen-and-ink drawings by him of Harriet Langdon.

A couple of months after this distressing scene, Arthur had a riding accident while on holiday in York: his horse stopped suddenly and he was thrown.[126] His head was gashed and he suffered from concussion for some months, requiring convalescence away from London. His employers at the Commission were tolerant of his lengthy absence. Apart from the dizzying headaches and periodic depression caused by his head injury, the autumn of 1864 and the first half of 1865 were a good time for him: distance from Harriet Langdon gave him some respite from worrying about her and her future, and the chance to travel and enjoy his hobby.

As the summer season drew to an end, Hannah had to think of her next move. Arthur had visited her again at the beginning of August, but the hot weather made her thirsty and she was drinking more beer which she paid for from her fat and bone 'perk'. She was distraught by the news of his riding accident. At the end of September they started to plan her return to London, due in mid-October. She told him how 'I thought I should like to tramp all or pretty nearly all the way to London', over seventy miles away.[127] When she heard from him that he would be convalescing away from London, she abandoned her plan to tramp all the way and left Margate on 2 November, having worked for Mrs Eastlands for a fortnight after leaving Union Crescent.

Six weeks after his accident, on doctor's orders, Arthur travelled with his parents, sister Caroline and two servants to take the waters at Scarborough's spa. While he was there he went for bracing walks, sometimes with his father, mostly on his own to Filey and Flamborough. The limestone cliffs at Flamborough Head were stunning:

> purely white, [and] extend in range from five to six miles and in many places rise to an elevation of three hundred feet perpendicularly from the sea. At the base are several caverns, worn by the action of the waves, or formed by some extraordinary convulsion of nature.[128]

In 1861 the population of Flamborough was 1,300, and most were involved in fishing and fish-curing. Arthur was captivated by the place, the thousands of seabirds, but most of all by the women who worked in the fishing industry, gathering different types of bait for the fishing pursued at various times of the year. To him the 'flither lasses' were an enigma: they were strong and brave, climbing the cliff face to gather gulls' eggs for food and 'flithers' (limpets) for fish bait. He called them 'noble and rugged creatures, scorned of by

men, but loved by me as passionately as I love the grand
country where they dwell'.[129] Arthur bought several photographs of them, sometimes taken in the studio of Walter
Fisher of Murray Street, Filey, and sometimes on the beach
at the bottom of the cliff which was the women's hunting
ground. He made friends with half a dozen 'flither lasses'; a
special favourite was Molly Nettleton, for whom he bought
pairs of second-hand boots and a new, stronger rope for her
cliff-climbing.

Hannah left Margate with two bundles, armed with 'a
capital character' from Miss Knight, in a state of limbo. She
was returning to London, but not to Massa, and was faced
with the prospect of finding the right sort of work near
enough to Fig Tree Court to visit him there. She walked along
the coast road to Canterbury, some fifteen miles away: it was
a sunny day and even though her heavy boots made her feet
sore, her spirits were lifted by the weather and the scenery.
The road was more or less deserted, but the few villagers she
saw on the way 'looked so strange at me so wi' my bags, one
on my back and t'other hanging on front and my stick in
hand'. At Canterbury she caught a train to Chatham and
spent two nights with Harriet, a young girl who had helped
out for a short time when the Knights' house was full with
fourteen lodgers. Hannah was stared at when she went for a
walk with Harriet who told her that they had 'never seen
anyone dressed like me in Chatham, nor wi' such a red face
as mine and wi' no veil'.[130]

Hannah was delighted to return to London and find herself
in the bosom of the Smith family in Clerkenwell again. Their
warm welcome went some way to making Arthur's absence
bearable. She visited her brother Dick and sister Ellen, went
to the local church of St James with Emma Smith, visited her
friend Ann Crook who had had her baby, and took tea with
the servants at Carlton Villas where she heard that Mr Foster

had been ill.[131] During her three-week stay she did sewing, cooking and cleaning for Mrs Smith who 'was so kind' to her. Those days were cut short by a 'cross letter' from Arthur telling her to leave Mrs Smith's lodgings immediately and move into the Servants' Home in St Clement's Lane off the Strand. He had written to the matron, Miss Wilmot, and arranged for Hannah to stay there and he was annoyed she had not acted accordingly. Hannah was happy at the Smiths', and having stayed at the hostel before was in no hurry to return. Reading that he was not due to return until Monday, Hannah decided to disobey Arthur and spend the weekend with her friends.[132]

On Monday, 28 November, tearful and carrying her bundles, she left the Smiths and walked to the Home, dreading being there. There were 'a lot o' strange girls and people' milling about, and her room was

> big wi' five beds in, very cold looking and bare floored and smelt I thought closeish, but I was come and must make the best o' it. I got a cup o' cocoa among the others down in the kitchen and they seemed to be all sorts and ages o' respectable working folks, but very different to any I'd bin wi' before.[133]

Hannah was glad when it was time to walk to King's Cross station to meet Arthur from the York train, and she travelled with him to the Temple, heaving his luggage into the hansom cab, behaving as a servant and saying little. She analysed her confused feelings after their reunion:

> Massa was kind and I was glad to see him for many a reason. I seemed to be quite alone before and hated to be in the streets. There seemed such a confusion o' noise to me after the quiet o' Margate and that been out o' place altogether makes one quite low spirited.

They had a good evening together enjoying some of their favourite rituals, her cooking for him, foot-washing, petting and prayers.

The following day Hannah withdrew some money from her savings to lend to Mrs Smith and delivered it, her anxiety growing at her lack of employment. Staying at the hostel was monotonous – she was glad when daylight came as the mattress was hard, and she ached as she trudged the streets looking for work – and was relieved by staying with servant friends in St John's Wood whose master and mistress were away. Plagued with tooth-ache and worried, Hannah visited Arthur where he disciplined her about some errant behaviour:

> washed Massa's feet and made cigarettes . . . and he talked to me about what I'd done to show my love and about me not been kind and gentle to him as I might be and all that till it was time for me to go.[134]

Eventually Hannah received some replies at the Servants' Home to the advertisement that Arthur had written and she had placed in the *Daily Telegraph* and the *Clerkenwell Times*: 'As charwoman, or any rough sort of work by a strong woman aged 31. Cleans boots, knives or windows. Can be hired by the day or job.'[135] Proximity to Arthur was the deciding factor and on 8 December Hannah went to work as a charwoman and cook for one shilling and three pence a day at Mrs Gillon's in Avenue Road in Regent's Park. She lived in and received 'victuals and beer'. Hannah was mystified by the living arrangements, and was not sure that the master and the mistress, the mother of a two-year-old child, were really married. Her anxieties about her new employers proved to be well founded and they behaved badly when they ended her employment, refusing to pay her for the nine days she had worked for them. She bundled up her things and walked through the freezing night to Clerkenwell and a warm welcome from the solid and dependable Smiths.[136]

Hannah wrote to her sisters Ellen and Polly asking them to spend Christmas with her at Clerkenwell. Hannah and Arthur's last evening together before he left for York was blissful:

> We had a nice long time together and I did lots of nice things after I'd washed Massa's feet. I helped to pack and got the portmanteau and the other cases out and dusted 'em. And after all was done we petted and then Massa talked to me very seriously about all the years we'd loved one another and how it was pure and sacred but deeper now than at the beginning for we had grown more into *one* like from being together in heart and yet I was still a servant and Massa still in *his* place. I sat on the floor between Massa's knees and I said not much but felt grateful and delighted with the thoughts of the last ten years and more as I told Massa I should be happy if it was the same all my life.[137]

On Christmas Day, Hannah and Polly went to St James's church, just off Clerkenwell Green, then had a hearty dinner of turkey and pudding, after which they went to another service at the Temple church, and by omnibus to see their sister Ellen, at 3 Percy Place, off Clapham Road, where she was nursemaid to the family of Jeremiah Pilcher. The Cullwick sisters had a jolly time in the nursery with the children, singing hymns and carols and enjoying wine and cake sent up to them by Ellen's master.[138]

On 27 December Hannah left London for her next place as general servant and cook to Mr and Mrs Caulfield of Clone House, 3 Upper Maze Hill, St Leonard's-on-Sea, Sussex. Desperate for work, and unsettled because Arthur would be spending months away from London convalescing, she decided on this place which paid £18 a year. Arriving in the dark, Hannah was timid, finding the street 'dismal, quiet and strange'. Inside, the house 'seemed so very grand' but the Caulfields were friendly, and invited her to have some tea with them. She had a cup of tea but was too nervous to eat the cake or any of the slices of mutton Mrs Caulfield cut for her. After settling into the servants' attic bedroom Hannah joined the household for prayers and went to bed 'feeling tired and strange'.[139] There was a charwoman, Mrs Gardener, the lady's maid, Mrs Mogford, Sarah, the housemaid, and a man came to clean the boots and knives.

Hannah's days included answering the front-door bell until one o'clock in the afternoon: this was new to her and it made her nervous: 'I'd to show the gentlemen and ladies into the drawing room and . . . say who they was – all that and so new to me and I felt terribly awkward and timid after it.'[140] After three days Hannah started to settle into her new situation and wrote to Arthur, which cheered her up. The last entry in her diary for 1864 shows Hannah grateful that her new 'missis' was so kind, but disoriented by the changes of the past twelve months:

> And after all it's the wisest to be content wherever one is placed. And I know it's for my own good, so I *am* content, but it *is* a trial to me to be so far off Massa and not to be able to have them few hours of a Sunday evenings as I used to have. . . . The number of boots will be less than usual for this year and fewer next I doubt. I am sorry to give up my old work but o' course I shall do it when I can, and I'm sorry I've to look smarter in a morning cause it's troublesome to me.[141]

Hannah was low-spirited during the first three months of 1865: her normally cheerful mood hardly lifted above a feeling of dull resignation. She was missing Arthur and it dawned on her that she would not be able to return to London until he had convalesced fully. Sensing Hannah's depression, her mistress sent her and Mrs Mogford (who was said to be consumptive and not allowed to answer the front door to avoid breathing in any cold air) for a treat in a carriage to Hastings to see 'General' Tom Thumb, the American midget, and his tiny wife. Hannah was amused with 'Mr and Mrs Thumb and the baby looked nearly as big as themselves. I thought the little lady was very proud and the little general rather vulgar in manner. I bought a card of the little pair for a shilling.'[142]

Clone House was detached, and quite new: in the 1860s Upper Maze Hill was a cliff road surrounded by green fields, breathtaking views and few other houses. Hannah walked across open fields to reach the butcher and greengrocer and when the wind was in the right quarter she could hear the organ being played at a nearby church. She learned what a smart town she was living in, that 'there seems to be none about here but gentry, and a few smartly dressed servants' and this added to her sense of alienation. Hannah's avowedly sensible dress, with no concessions to fashion or femininity, often seemed out of place and this darkened her mood.[143]

Even though it was not such a 'hard place' at the Caulfields' as, say, at the Fosters', Hannah found it difficult to keep up her diary:

> I've found no time for writing my diary nor letters as I should like. Every day and every hour seems to bring the same work over and over again. Still in many respects this is a very good place and I oughtn't to be so dissatisfied. Yet I feel anything but happy and going out only seems to make me feel more alone. All strange and so different to me – they are all that one sees walking about so that after all the *work* passes the time away the pleasantest.[144]

Arthur received a Valentine's card from Hannah. Inside was an imprint of her blackened hand. The day she posted it she had cleaned five fireplaces, lit the kitchen fire and made breakfast for the Caulfields, and bread, butter and tea for herself and the other servants. Sweeping, beating mats and cleaning upstairs was followed by cleaning and dusting Mrs Mogford's bedroom, and then making the picture of her hand:

> I got the oil and black lead in the scullery and the paper and I blacked my hand o'er it and laid it on the paper. It came out broad and thick and I thought o' a verse and wrote it on the paper and this is it:
>
> > 'Massa, you'll know what is meant
> > By this black thing of a hand
> > And as its lines deepen and fingers get bent
> > So love in my heart for its owner withstand.'[145]

Hannah ran to the nearby pillar-box and posted it, and sent cards to her sisters. She was excited at the thought of what the post would bring in the morning. Mrs Mogford received two cards, Sarah got one, but Arthur's did not arrive until the following day.

In April the Caulfields left for a two-month holiday, taking the unpopular Mogford with them. Hannah and the other servants looked forward to the freedoms they could enjoy while their employers were away. There was plenty to be done, spring-cleaning for example, but they could devise their own timetable and come and go as they wished. It was a joy to break the stifling routines and do as they pleased, when they pleased: 'they drove off and we was delighted at been left alone'.[146] There was also the chance to save or spend some extra money – their board wages – a subsistence paid when employers were away and servants had to find their own meals. There was a frenzy of cleaning and scrubbing to get the work done so as to allow themselves an illicit holiday.

Hannah made her special preparations for the arrival of the chimney sweep, probably Jeremiah Freelove, of 5 Market Street, St Leonard's. Elizabeth, a new housemaid, was curious at Hannah having a bath in the kitchen before the sweep had been, but Hannah fobbed her off with an excuse and, satisfied Elizabeth was asleep upstairs,

> took the matting out and moved the fender. Swept the cinders up and then undressed me and put on an apron over my head and my back where I couldn't reach to wash and an old pair of boots on as the grate was warm. There's a good space behind the grate and I got on a stool and up the chimney out o' sight. The soot was thick all round and soft and warm and I lay in it and fetched a shower or two down wi' my arms and it trickled over me like a bath. I stopped in the chimney and thought about Massa and how he'd enjoy seen [sic] me when I got down. It seemed quite cold out o' the chimney and I got into the water and washed me. It took me a good while to get clean and the water I made thick and black.[147]

Two days later Hannah sent Arthur these pages from her diary and a posy of flowers tied with her hair. In early May, halfway through the Caulfields' holiday, Hannah wrote to Mogford to ask their mistress for permission to go to London for a few days. Mrs Caulfield agreed, and Hannah, mindful of burglars, arranged for someone to come and stay in the house the nights she was away. Eight months after his accident Arthur's headaches and concussion were still a problem and he was not well enough to visit her. They had been apart for five months and she was desperate to see him.

Carrying her bundle, a posy of flowers and a pot of ferns, Hannah walked to the station to catch a train to London. To save carrying too much, she wore her new violet frock over her working clothes. It was a glorious morning. she left her things with the porter and walked down to the beach until it was time for her train. A little dog followed her: 'I thought that little dog was like me following Massa as I often have done since he noticed me in the street.' When she arrived at the Temple in the afternoon she had to reconnoitre to judge when it was safe to knock at his door.

> We had a long kiss . . . I licked his boots once of my own accord and took my top frock off and wrapped it up and hid it and my bonnet and the other things away. Then Massa looked at my hands and came and put 'em alongside his. Mine was brown and looked hardworking by his and after that Massa told me to lift him up and I did it quite easy and I carried him round the room. And then I had to hide myself while the servant brought in Massa's beef tea. Massa's got a writing table with drawers each side and a kind of bridge in the middle where the legs go under. So he had filled one end in with a shawl over the backs of the chairs. I couldn't get in head-first and hide but I found I could get in wi' getting in backwards. So I got in and was quite out o' sight with my back up again the table and my head hanging down like a sheep's. It was very cramping to stop there long and made my head ache else the degradation I of course didn't care for cause Massa says he was sorry but couldn't help it.[148]

Hannah stayed with the Smiths for three nights, spending as much time as she dared at Fig Tree Court. Arthur was feeling much better, rejuvenated by her visit, and on 15 May they met at Charing Cross station and travelled back to Sussex. They parted at St Leonard's; Arthur stayed two nights at an hotel in Hastings. Their days together were happy, spent walking openly arm-in-arm along the clifftops and through the streets of Hastings: they were more confident than usual and Arthur brazened it out, even when 'people and children stared'.[149] When Arthur left he was not embarrassed to kiss Hannah in front of people of his own class and the station porters. She was flustered by his tight embrace and long kisses: 'I was half ashamed but much pleased too wi' Massa for it.'

When Hannah returned to Clone House she confided her feelings to her diary, and thereby Arthur. The eleventh anniversary of their encounter in Oxford Street was looming and:

> I was pleased that I'd bin to London for I enjoyed it extremely tho' I was wi' Massa so very little and Massa seems better again today an' I never knew him bin so much wi' me neither which I was pleased at – but I've got so used to the other way that altho' it must needs be unpleasant I don't fret about it and Massa says it makes him unhappy. If it does o' course I am sorry for him more than I pity myself for *I* don't want to be thought his *equal* anywhere, only it's so unsociable to walk apart and yet together – belonging and seeming *not* to belong to one another. It is worse than if I was a *real* dog for then Massa might not be ashamed to own me, but now I can only *hope* that when Massa gets old and I get old all those years off what the world thinks'll wear off. If not I think I couldn't bear it. But I am *his slave* and *he* is my *master* freely given and freely received only for *love* and while I have the chains on I am sure nothing can part us and that is the same to us as marriage is to other folks.[150]

A week later Arthur was on the Isle of Wight. He hero-worshipped Alfred Tennyson who was elected Poet Laureate in 1850 and would become a reluctant peer in 1884. Arthur yearned to meet the great man: for many years he had to make do with meeting people who knew him. Arthur's first glimpse of him was on the morning of 23 May 1865 as he walked past Tennyson's home, 'Farringford', on the Isle of Wight; later that day Arthur travelled on the same boat as

Tennyson and his wife Emily, crossing the Solent, but was too nervous to approach the poet. To our modern sensibilities Arthur's description is that of a devoted fan:

> On board with us went Tennyson and his wife ... T about 5 feet 8, largely made, hands big and muscular: wore odd careless dress, tall wideawake [hat], camlet cloak, loose trousers, frock coat and open shirtfront – no gloves. Long wild curling hair: beard thin on cheeks, full and wild round lips and chin. Complexion sallow, finely cut aquiline nose, veined: mouth grave and subtle in expression, face deeply lined: eyes hidden by blue spectacles. Voice deep and slow: gait stooping and heavy, almost aged. I watched him talking with a fat parson: round him other parsons, tourists, sailors; and his face supreme in manliness and mental power.[151]

On 9 June Hannah's master and mistress returned from their holiday. A few days later Mrs Caulfield noticed a deterioration in Hannah's personal appearance and gently asked her to be clean when she attended evening prayers. Hannah had not bothered to change out of her dirty clothes into a clean frock for the lighter duties of the afternoon and evening.[152]

On 28 August Hannah received bad news from Shropshire: her nephew Willie, Jim and Eliza's five-year-old son, had died of measles. She was shocked: 'I couldn't help crying out and been very sorry for he was a sturdy, healthy-looking little chap when I saw him. But I thought again he's better off – for now he'll be a little angel spirit.'[153] Three weeks later the couple's ten-month-old-baby, James, also died of measles: and within a month, Eliza was dead of 'phthisis', tuberculosis of the lungs.

*

Arthur Munby was an eligible bachelor, a man about town: several women were attracted to him, and hoped to become Mrs Arthur Munby. Although he was not well salaried, he was interesting and considered good-looking; some of his poetry had been published and he could expect to inherit a sizeable sum when his ageing parents died. As he settled into his safe career, his parents must have wondered why their eldest son showed no signs of marrying.

Arthur always enjoyed the company of women and occasionally had hopeless crushes on wives of his acquaintances: he was a regular visitor to the Chelsea home of Theodore Martin, the biographer of Prince Albert, eagerly seizing any opportunity to be in the presence of Mrs Martin, the acclaimed actress Helen Faucit. She was eleven years older than Arthur, beautiful and sympathetic. George Eliot said she was 'the most poetic woman I have seen for a long time', and William Thackeray declared her to be 'one of the sweetest women in Christendom'. While he could fantasize about Mrs Martin, however, the real love of his life was at the opposite end of the class spectrum.[154]

Arthur formed muddled attachments with two women from backgrounds similar to his own, Sarah Carter and Julie Bovet. Their hopes for marriage were raised and dashed, while Arthur agonized and finally decided that 'his Hannah' was the only woman to whom he could devote his life, causing Sarah heartache; Julie (of whom more in Chapter 5) was too sophisticated for this.

Arthur first mentioned Sarah Carter in September 1865. He had fallen in love with the hamlet of Pyrford, near Ripley in Surrey, and had spent weekends that summer as a paying guest of Sarah's mother at Wheeler's Farm. The house of which he became so fond was a 'grey old gabled farm, with a quaint little garden in front'.[155] Arthur liked the local church which 'stood in a nest of trees, small with a short wooded spire'. The farmhouse and church had gorgeous views of the ruined Newark Abbey and meadows.[156] Arthur discovered that Mrs Carter, a Canadian by birth, was the widow of a tenant-farmer whose death had caused financial problems for his wife and three daughters, Sarah, Susannah and Alice, and son Eddy. Now living in reduced circumstances, Mrs Carter was grateful for any monies she could earn in a genteel way and was particularly concerned about her daughters' futures. She was decribed by Arthur as ladylike and placid – the model of a Victorian middle-class mother. Largely recovered from his riding accident, Arthur spent long weekends in 1865 exploring the countryside around Wheeler's Farm, using it as a bolt-hole to escape from the heat of London in summer.

His first description of Sarah is as a pre-Raphaelite: his friend Rossetti might have used the scene in a painting: 'I shook hands with fair Sarah, who sat in the broad old window seat with the morning light playing on her curly clustered amber hair and on her sober pearl grey gown.' Then he walked in a warm glow from the farmhouse to Woking station and caught the train back to London.[157] Arthur played the Victorian paterfamilias as he kissed little Alice and Eddy goodbye in the garden where they were playing with their rabbit. As he walked away, he reflected on the cosy times of recent weeks in the company of such a 'simple, graceful, God-fearing family'. He admired them for not being too proud to serve him as a guest. They were not

> ashamed to cook and clean and wait on me, yet cultivated, artlessly refined in taste, in dress: knowing nothing of the world and its ways, yet loving the best things – music and books and flowers. And so we talked and sang and made friends: and charming as Pyrford has been, the constant presence of their gentle life has made it more so.

Thus the Carters became a second family for Arthur Munby. At Wheeler's Farm at the weekends he was the man of the house. His frequent visits, during which he sang and played the piano, accompanied the family to church and helped Sarah sell copies of the *British Workman* and *Children's Friend* in the parish, may have given hope that romance was in the air. Lulled by domestic bliss in Arcadia, Arthur was attracted to Sarah, and this impaired his judgement for two summers.

CHAPTER FIVE

'Out of Place'

Do you know, have you ever heard tell,
Why a wave rises out of the sea?
Ah, then you may guess pretty well
Why you are so precious to me!
Do you know why the wave at its height
Curls over, and breaks into foam?
Then you know why I loved you at sight,
And gave you my heart and my home!
Do you know why the moon's face allures
And governs the strength of the tides?
Then you'll see in a moment how yours
Drew me – and a hundred besides!
Ah, folly! You ask me for what
Did I choose you as soon as I saw –
Would you have me give reasons for that
Which itself is both reason and law?
Ah, love! When I've skill to explain
Why the seas or the heavens are blue,
Then at length I shall *not* try in vain
To fathom my passion for you.[1]

'Seaside Questions' is a tender evocation of Arthur's secret love for Hannah, from his *Verses Old and New* of autumn 1865, a collection of sixty poems and his first for a dozen years. Arthur told his diary, 'It will fail of course.' It sold only 100 copies in the first two months, but after a good review in the *Athenaeum* Mr Mudie ordered it for his Circulating Library.

At the same time as Arthur's second collection was published, Hannah was enjoying a new ritual that he had suggested: 'Massa told me of something to do the first thing when I awoke in the morning and so I'm doing it if Elizabeth [with whom she shared a bed] is asleep.' On 4 October, at five o'clock in the morning:

> it wasn't *quite* light, so I got out o' bed quietly and crept under the bed and there I lay for ten minutes and thought that perhaps Massa was awake too and thinkin' o' me and what I was doin' just then. I thought how different he was to me, instead o' gettin' up early to get ready to do the breakfast for the other servants and for the parlour folks as I was, *he* was no doubt in a nice room and could be till his hot water was brought and that wi' plenty o' time to dress himself and read or anything till he went down.[2]

On 14 November Arthur went to a 'conversation party' at the home of Mrs Barbara Leigh Smith Bodichon, a major figure in the founding of Girton College, Cambridge, and a leading light of the women's suffrage movement. Given his interest in working women, it is surprising that he did not get involved in the campaign whose aim was to get women the vote on the same terms as men: Bodichon and others argued that only political representation would redress the many inequalities between men's and women's lives. Six months later Arthur's opinion was still lukewarm, even after 'the buxom Madame Bodichon' button-holed him at a soirée about her current petition to Parliament: all he had to say to his diary was: 'let them vote by all means, if they will also work'. Always attracted to powerful women, Arthur was dazzled more by Mrs Bodichon's looks than by the content of her conversation, and flattered by the attention she had paid him that evening when she 'was in great request'.[3] A fierce champion of women being allowed to do work regarded as 'men's work', he had a poor opinion of women as public speakers: when he attended a meeting of the great and the good in women's suffrage circles four years later he would still be surprised at their abilities:

> I had thought it would seem strange but it seemed quite natural, to see that gentle earnest ladylike woman [Mrs Taylor, a friend and co-founder of the Pen and Pencil Society] acting as chairman of a public meeting, and to see other ladies standing up on the platform and making speeches. There was nothing 'bold' or unfeminine in their words or manner and the two best speeches I heard ... were made by women: Miss Helen Taylor, who did the rhetoric ably and Mrs Fawcett [Millicent Garrett Fawcett], who was logical and calm.[4]

The year 1866 brought reports of the Cullwicks in Shropshire. On 9 January Hannah's Aunt Elizabeth was buried in Shifnal. During the summer came better news: Jim was to be married to Elizabeth 'Lizzie' Beetlestone, née Cullwick. She was a widow and his first cousin, the daughter of their Uncle John. The Victorians did not object to marrying first cousins, indeed it was quite a common practice. Lizzie was older than Jim and childless. He mourned his wife and two sons and was struggling to look after his little girl, Emily, and run his business.

Arthur went to a soirée given by his colourful acquaintance Richard Monckton-Milnes at 16 Upper Brook Street, Mayfair. Since 1863 he had been known as Lord Houghton: his appetite for life was undimmed by his elevation to the peerage. They talked of Swinburne's excessive drinking and sexual escapades and the conversation turned, as it so often did with this host, to his favourite subject, pornography:

> he produced out of a secret drawer R. Payne Knight's *Worship of Priapus*, a book full of antique obscenities ...

then he discoursed ... how the ancient world was based upon it, saw nothing unnatural in it ... how Grote had said to him that on this account it *is impossible* to draw a true picture of Greek life. ... And then he went on to speak of other subjects more loathsome still. ... There is nothing noble in Lord Houghton's face: it is sly, sensuous, and potentially wicked. After sitting two hours with him, and drinking brandy and seltzer (which he insisted on our doing) we left.[5]

Arthur visited Hannah in St Leonard's the day after her thirty-third birthday, going by excursion train from Charing Cross. The Caulfields and the other servants were out when he arrived and Hannah told him that 'she *must* show the house and her own doings'. The grates she cleaned, the stairs and the passage she scrubbed on her hands and knees were pointed out with pride. It was a poignant moment for him to see her sitting alone in the kitchen and he was moved by the sight of her 'rosy and healthful, neatly drest in clean white cap and apron, clean cotton frock, that showed her strong working arms and hands'.[6] Hannah and Arthur left the house discreetly and walked across the clifftops down to the sea. At the first Martello tower they turned inland and trudged across the marshy flats to Hollington for a service in the picturesque church in a hazel wood. The church was full and a number of stragglers and servants listened to the service outside. Arthur and Hannah heard the hymns standing in the churchyard by a tomb of an old friend of Arthur's family. It was a happy day and Arthur returned to London restored by the time he had spent with Hannah.

Soon after his visit Hannah had two photographs taken by Francis Ross Wells of Hastings, in unusually clean work clothes, and in her Sunday best.[7] The picture of her in working dress with her sleeves rolled up showed her biceps to the maximum effect. The wrist-strap was eye-catching, on the hand from which a carpet-brush dangled.

Arthur's circle was widening: he saw his chums from Trinity; fellow students from the Bar; and fellow teachers at the Working Men's and Working Women's Colleges. He had entered the world of social reform and had friends and acquaintances who were Christian Socialists. There was the Reverend Charles Kingsley, author of *Alton Locke* (1850) and *The Water Babies* (1863); the Reverend Frederick Denison Maurice, founder and first principal of the Men's College; and the Reverend Frederick James Furnivall, founding editor of *The New English Dictionary*. In 1866 Munby joined the Pen and Pencil Club at the invitation of Mr and Mrs P. A. Taylor. Often calling himself a member of the 'Aubrey House Set' (the Taylors' home), he made friends with the poet Austin Dobson, who helped him get his poems published, and who was Arthur's obituarist in *The Times* of 1910.

During the summer of 1866 Arthur visited Sarah Carter and her family at Pyrford. His visits added to their hopes: his eyes would fill with tears when he arrived from London and found them at tea, Sarah playing the piano and a sunset on the horizon. It was all so perfect for him:

sweet Sarah, ladyborn, but bred as a slighter rustic, her hands are bonny, as those of a farmer's daughter. Long, shapely hands, but thicker and larger than a lady's; with a russet apple texture and a warm apricot hue *which were well seen as they moved on the white piano keys. I went into the garden glowing with the moonlight.*[8]

Arthur decided that Hannah should leave St Leonard's-on-Sea and return to London in December. The job with the Caulfields had been a good one, her highest-paid thus far, but the two-year separation troubled the couple. Hannah

was sorry to leave and always believed that Mrs Caulfield
was

> the best missis I ever had. When her used to show her
> friends over the house, or coom in the kitchen, her always
> made 'em notice *me*; she used to point to me and say
> to the ladies, 'This is our Hannah' quite civil and nice,
> and they smiled and nodded at me and I made 'em a
> curtsey.[9]

Arthur was back at Wheeler's Farm again two weeks before
Christmas, arriving at the farmhouse overwhelmed by the
starry night he had walked through from the station, to be
greeted by a cosy scene in the parlour: a white tablecloth, a
bouquet of fresh roses, and after tea 'sweet Sarah plays the
Christmas carols I have brought and we sing together'.[10] Then
followed her French lesson with him, Arthur enchanted by
the way she leaned on the piano, reading the exercise to him,
'with bright eyes and cheeks pursed her pretty lips, at my
bidding, to get the "ou's" and the "u's"; and laughed with
wonder at my unheard-of skill in pronouncing'. Mother
Sarah's sister and Susannah sat sewing close by. Doubtless
they wondered what the New Year would bring.

Hannah celebrated Christmas with the Smiths in Clerkenwell. Arthur had proposed she 'tramp' back to London as she
had started to do in 1864, perhaps stop off on the way and
work in the hop gardens to aid his research. But Hannah
returned to London as speedily as she could. She refused to
go to the Servants' Home again; staying with the Smiths
lessened some of her worries: 'December is a wretched month
to be out o' place.'[11] Hannah and Arthur's first evening
together was joyous: cooking, cleaning, serving and:

> doing what I am always pleased to do for him, that is
> washing his feet by the fire, me sitting on the brass on the

hearth – Massa in the armchair leaning back enjoying the
warm water and seeing me. I think he must have missed
it these two years as much as I have, for it's a pleasure
to me, as well as a useful and humble little service that
I never can tire of, especially as I know Massa likes it and
loves me too.[12]

After a week's holiday, Hannah walked to the Bazaar in
Soho Square to look for a place at the Registry of Servants.[13]
She paid a fee of two shillings and sixpence, the rate for
'lower' servants – cooks and other 'upper' servants paid five
shillings. Hannah took part in the morning prayer service:
job-seekers were given religious tracts to read and then taken
upstairs to 'sit in the room where the ladies come in to look
at us'. Hannah was picked out and quizzed by a Mrs Milne,
who offered her a place as a general servant. She talked it over
with Arthur who thought the house was too far from the
Temple, and then he discovered Mr Milne was a solicitor with
chambers in the Temple, and this was too risky. Hannah 'was
obliged to write and give it up'.
    Hannah returned to the Bazaar and seized on the first lady,
a Mrs Bishop, who showed interest in her. The address was
39 Craven Street, off the Strand, very close to Arthur. Hannah
knew immediately that Mrs Bishop was not a lady, but did
not mind that: 'I thought it was perhaps the better as she
wouldn't be so fussy to know who I went out to see as my
other missis had been.'[14]
    Hannah's new place was a rough-and-ready lodging-house,
not an eating-house as Mrs Bishop had said. She would be
working in the kitchen, but was also to clean the hall and
doorsteps, and when there were few lodgers she would help
with the cleaning upstairs. The wages were good – £16 a year
and beer money and tea – and although the work was of the
roughest kind, having every Sunday evening off and being so

close to Arthur blinded Hannah to her intuition to refuse the offer. She struggled to put her disapproval of the way Mrs Bishop and her partner, Mrs Andrews, cheated their customers to the back of her mind. Hannah was not allowed to have visitors, even female servant friends, and came to feel she had lowered herself 'to the very bottom of service' by taking this job: her last lodging-house place had been entirely different because 'Miss Knight [in Margate] is a real *lady*'.

Mrs Bishop was 'vulgar and not an Englishwoman, but French' who was married to an Englishman who left home early in the morning on horseback. Hannah was a little afraid of Mrs Bishop. But she comforted herself that such low work would be part of the programme that her master had devised for her. She reasoned, 'still I thought if only I could work hard and low, and be near Massa and see him comfortably I shouldn't care how low I was.'

In the scullery 'all under the tables was inches thick of solid muck and the passage and stairs too, and so dark in every place I could see to do nothing without a light'. It was a subterranean existence: any errands were done by 'the other little servant'. The kitchen was in a deep basement and the 'area' was 'latticed over in front and one could scarcely see without gas'. The only fresh air Hannah got was when she shook the mats in the street and cleaned the steps in the morning. She detested the job but soldiered on, hoping that her perseverance would please her Massa, but she felt demeaned by working in such a place:

I could see myself cleaning the doorsteps of a vulgar London lodging house in a street full of nothing but the same thing, and the servants of the next one looking as common and vulgar and low as the houses and them who kept them ... I did feel vex'd to be put on a level wi' them as it were – and I soon found that my missis was really vulgar and couldn't understand *me* nor my willingness to oblige her and to work all I could.[15]

When she was told, ' "I think you don't seem settled or comfortable here Hannah, therefore you'd better go," ' she agreed and said, ' "No, ma'am, I really am not." ' By the time she left Craven Street Hannah looked 'a regular drudge', almost too rough even for Arthur. After telling her to visit him 'in her dirt', he was shocked by the deterioration in her appearance: 'I walked up the Strand wi' my dirty frock and striped apron and my old bonnet and hands and arms and face begrim'd wi' dirt, so that once I think he really pitied me, and never wished me thrown out [of work] again so soon.'[16]

In early 1867 Arthur's relationship with Harriet Langdon had become volatile: from descriptions of his visits to give her her monthly allowance it is obvious that she was in love with him. In London she only saw her sister, brother-in-law and Mr Munby. Arthur was good-looking in a whiskery sort of way, certainly attractive to women, and Harriet would daydream about him. In February, harsh words of criticism of Harriet are recorded by Arthur: 'she has a rude, narrow nature' which makes it 'hard to deal with her'. On a visit to Paris he had bought her a false nose and top lip, but this did not please her. It was not enough:

she 'thinks she shall go mad' . . . I am the only friend she has near; she would so gladly hear from me or see me oftener. She disdains pity, yet says 'you neglect me – you don't feel for my wretched lowly condition' and the tears run down that formless scarlet surface which should be a human countenance.

Arthur was annoyed that she criticized his gift: at first it would not stay stuck to her face. She broke down and cried:

'"I think of my ugliness, but I should have been *handsome* only for this disfigurement. I know it, everyone says so."' As she cried he wondered 'what can that vast shapeless mouth, that ghastly hole betwixt the cheeks, express of the masked soul within?' Arthur feared for his own future and worried about the consequences of his own actions:

> Doubtless she might have been both human and hand-some, her large eyes, her hair, her elegant figure show that. And with such a loathly [sic] horror for a face who would not pity and bear with her? Still she threatens to reward my help by becoming a kind of Frankenstein monster, exacting sympathy from me in proportion as she feels herself cut off from it elsewhere.[17]

On 14 February Arthur received a Valentine from Hannah. She chose a card with 'a big black dog with a chain around its neck, lying on a box'. Hannah chose it thinking, '"That's me."' The shopkeeper let her have it for half price, telling her, '"I see you're a poor servant so you may have that one for sixpence."'[18]

A few days later Harriet visited Arthur at his chambers wearing the nose he had bought: 'it was a pretty retroussé one with an upper lip attached to it, and was readily gummed down on to her face, it fitted her exactly.' Her petulance exasperated Arthur and he 'almost vowed she should not come again'.

By March Arthur was beset with worry about Hannah's search for a place. Relieved to have left Mrs Bishop, she tried for a job with a clergyman's family and interviewed well. All seemed set until her prospective employer discovered that her last job had been at a lodging-house. She nearly went to work as a kitchen-maid in a lunatic asylum in Hampshire. Neither she nor Arthur really wanted her to move so far away but Hannah thought,

Well, beggars canna be choosers and I must get a place somewhere an' I should like to be near Massa, but when I am in London, it's difficult to get to him, people *will* wonder and suspect me o' going where I should not.

Arthur suggested she return to Margate and work for the Misses Knight for the summer. He argued that the change and the sea air would do her good. Hannah drew lots for what she should do: she wrote and asked for the job in Margate. At the end of March, she walked from Clerkenwell to Ludgate Hill station with a bag full of working clothes and set off for Margate with a happy heart. She and Arthur bade each other a tender farewell when they were positive about her plans. He was:

> pleased when I come to Margate for he knows I am well there, and fully in good spirits, for I am a real happy maid of all work then, without restraint, working as hard as I like, and serving a real lady who enjoys seeing me at work and understands and appreciates my big caps and aprons.[19]

When Hannah arrived at the Knights' new place she received a warm welcome from Miss Julia, and started to clean and polish and get the place ready for the visitors. A young servant, Mary, gave her some tea: they were to share a truckle-bed in the kitchen which was packed away during the day. After they divided up the workload, they told each other something of their lives and Hannah enjoyed hearing about Mary's sweetheart, wishing she could talk about Arthur.

Hannah had taken a cut in wages to be at the Knights'. Although theirs was a lodging-house, Hannah felt that her reputation as a servant was enhanced by working for ladies. The visitors were slow to arrive that spring and summer: the sisters worried. Hannah sensed their concern and on an afternoon off she scrubbed her face and hands and went out soliciting for lodgers in the town:

> I didn't tell the missis, cause she wouldn't like it being a *lady*, though poor . . . I went out in my apron and plaid shawl and walked about and when I saw people I thought looking for lodgings, I spoke to them and said there was good apartments at seventeen Athelstan Road if they wanted any, and I was servant there if they'd please let me show them to the house. I hardly liked doing so, but it was entirely from feeling for the missis. Some spoke shortly to me and others not at all, so I thought it wasn't prudent and that lodgers would come in time.[20]

Arthur spent the Whitsun weekend at the Knights'. Hannah had concocted the plan and he was delighted. The prospect of sleeping under the same roof and sharing their delicious secret got them both excited. She knew there was room and they planned that he would call and ask if there were any rooms free:

> I was all anxiety to hear the front door bell ring at six o'clock in the evening [Saturday]. I was at work in the garden and Mary had to leave to go out, but I succeeded so far to keep her wi' me till the bell rang and she says, 'Can't you answer that, Hannah, as I've got my bonnet on?' I said, 'I'm not fit wi' these black hands, besides it might be people for lodgings . . . you must take your things off.'[21]

Mary let Arthur into the dining room and went out to find Miss Julia to 'speak to the gentleman'. Hannah was proud when Mary rushed down to tell her that their visitor was ' "*such* a swell with a beard and mustachios and missis has took him up to see the rooms".' Hannah was told by Miss Julia, ' "a gentleman has come to stay in the next room for a

night or two, and he wants some dinner, so *you* go in and tell
him what you can get and I'll put the sheets out for airing."'
Hannah was amused to see Miss Julia flustered by Arthur's
arrival and went to see the new guest:

> I knocked once and walked in and there was Massa! I
> made him a curtsey and said, 'Yes, Sir' pretty loud and
> then put the door to but o' course didn't shut it, and then
> I . . . went up and he kissed me quickly then spoke louder
> about his dinner, giving me half a sovereign to get what I
> thought best.

Hannah hurried to the shops for his dinner, which she
cooked, and Mary waited on him. After she was sure that
Mary was out and Miss Julia was upstairs in her room,
Hannah went into Arthur's room and

> had a petting wi' Massa and talked about things. It was
> delightfully amusing altogether, for our having such a
> grand lodger at Margate was quite a new thing that even
> the missis seemed pleased, for she said, 'He's *quite* a
> gentleman.'

Arthur was the only guest, receiving all their attention.
Hannah slipped into his room for a goodnight kiss: he could
hear Hannah and Mary talking and laughing in bed in the
kitchen. The next morning Mary woke him up and Hannah
bustled into his room to clean the grate and light the fire. She
made sure she was 'in her dirt' before she entered the room: 'I
had a dirty face and my arms was black too . . . I wore my
striped apron and Massa sat up in bed to look at me do my
work, and when I'd done, he called me to him for a kiss.'²²
With Miss Julia at church and Mary out, and the other Miss
Knight confined to her bedroom, Hannah was alone with her
sweetheart. She showed him the kitchen and scullery and they
arranged to meet later in the day. They walked along the cliffs

way beyond the town: Hannah could not disguise that she was a servant as she only had her working clothes with her, but they strolled along as sweethearts. At dusk they returned, Hannah arriving first, asking airily if 'the *gentleman* was come in yet'. The next morning more of the same: Hannah cleaning his grate, and kissing him 'in her dirt'. She was given most of Whit Monday off and they returned to their secluded spot and made their goodbyes there. Hannah hurried back to carry his bags to the front door, receiving a shilling tip from him. Although she knew there was no alternative, the role play could hurt:

> I made him a curtsey and said 'Good bye, Sir,' all the time wishing he had called me 'Hannah' as well, and not said goodbye in such a proud way either, but I knew how lovingly we had parted a few minutes before and I could forgive the other. If the missis hadn't followed me down I should have sat down and had a little melancholy as well as happy thoughts to myself about him.

Hannah relished the irony of Miss Julia asking her whether she thought he was 'very good looking'. '"Yes, ma'am, what little I've seen of him."'[23]

The day after he returned to London, having first sought Mrs Carter's permission, Arthur took Sarah and her brother Eddy to the Royal Academy Summer Exhibition. An old friend from Trinity, Cuyler Anderson, and Mademoiselle Julie Bovet, a sophisticated Swiss miss Arthur had met in May 1866, and who once had designs on him, were to join them. Julie had intrigued him, he found her 'very bright and pleasant', but she was not his type.[24] By the summer of 1867 he had made his feelings clear, and she cheerfully transferred her hopes of romance into a solid friendship. Arthur had been delighted to meet her friend Giuseppe Mazzini, the Italian patriot and republican, one night at the opera.[25] Julie Bovet,

widely travelled and fashionably dressed, was in marked contrast to the young girl who was to join them: Arthur had
confided his sometimes rapturous feelings for Sarah to her.
Sarah seemed to show no nerves at the occasion: Arthur was
charmed by her naivety and lack of guile. The difference
between the two women was great and one wonders, knowing
a little of Bovet's waspish wit, how she really felt about this
country girl about whom she enthused:

> They were such a contrast too: Miss Bovet, a cultivated
> lady, drest elegantly in perfect taste, in costly silks of
> fashionable cut; and Sarah, a lady too, yet only a poor and
> rustic maiden in attire. She wore her plain round hat of
> black straw, and it is far from new; her jacket-cloak of
> common dark cloth, well worn and without any orna-
> ment; she actually had on her black and blue striped
> gown, the same in which I saw her weeding the garden.
> Then her gloves; large thick gloves of brown leather, often
> mended, yet neat; and her plain unfashionable veil of
> black net through which you saw her large blue eyes
> sparkling and her rounded cheeks flushing with unwonted
> pleasure.[26]

The visit was a success and Arthur took Sarah, Eddy, Julie
and Anderson to tea at Fig Tree Court. Sarah had glided
round the exhibition 'as serenely as a Homeric goddess' and
sat in his rooms 'in a sort of virginal dignity'. For Arthur she
showed 'transparent innocence' when she accepted the offer
of going into his bedroom 'to wash her hands and smooth her
golden hair'.

That evening Arthur escorted Sarah and Eddy home to
Pyrford and stayed the night. The following morning was the
beginning of the end of Sarah's hopes. Arthur found her in
the garden at seven o'clock, she had been too excited to sleep

and had been up for hours. She was 'radiant and smiling' as she dropped a bombshell:

'I did not thank you half enough yesterday, I don't know *when* I have enjoyed anything so much!' And she meant it. There is no affectation in such a character as hers. Then she said brazenly, with a quick timorous laugh, looking at me, as if she had determined to humiliate herself by saying it and was rejoicing in the humiliation, *I cleaned your boots this morning Mr Munby . . .*' She told me . . . that she had done for me the lowest work of a servant, had made herself a shoeblack, to do me service.

Sarah had no idea of the effect this would have on Arthur. She had cleaned off the cow dung he had slipped in the night before: he was disturbed and 'simply transported to the very limits of self control: but not, thank heaven, beyond them'. As he walked to the station his mind was filled with Hannah and his betrayal of her and the hurt he was to inflict on Sarah. He was shaken out of his country reverie of the past two years: 'a horror of great darkness was upon me. What if between this dear innocent soul and mine, there is a danger of too close an attraction? Music and French lessons, must they be repressed? Pyrford itself – but that does not bear thinking of. This is a great evil that I have seen under the sun.'

Shortly after Arthur left Margate, Mr Skates, a musician, rented rooms at the Misses Knight for his wife and five children. He worked at Spier and Pond's 'Hall by the Sea', and Hannah made friends with the three boys and two girls, giving Miss Alice piggybacks in the garden. When Mrs Skates and four of the children returned to London, leaving Alice with her father, Hannah looked after the girl when he was playing at the 'dancing rooms'. Mr Skates and Hannah became quite close: he asked her for a likeness, gave her tickets to see him perform, and offered her a job in London: 'he said

how much he should like me to live wi' them for I did things
so well and I should have a good home, only they could afford
to keep but *one* servant, so I was pleased at his wanting me
even if I could hardly afford to take the place'. Hannah
reasoned that though their house in Regent's Park was further
away from Fig Tree Court than she would have liked, she
believed they would treat her 'kindly' and that they might be
good employers because 'they weren't exactly gentlefolks . . .
and not be so fussy as to where I was gone to or if I was half
an hour late of a Sunday night'. She agreed to go to their
house when she left Margate.[27]

Arthur wanted to extricate himself from his entanglement
with Sarah Carter but was afraid of hurting her feelings. He
continued to visit at the weekends: several times his nerve failed
and he did not tell Sarah they had no future together. For the
first time in his life Arthur was on the brink of a relationship
on more or less equal terms, not a shameful liaison conducted
in subterfuge. His lack of experience and confused feelings had
caused the situation to get out of hand: his love of the rural
idyll had blinded him to what had been obvious to everyone
else. Eventually, on 5 August, he told Mrs Carter that he could
not marry her daughter, and then walked Sarah and Alice to
Pyrford church. For the first time he held Sarah's hand as they
sat in church: 'thinking of what was to come, regrets and
longings uncontrollable came over me and shaking my very
self-control, that sweet yearning face sitting by me.'[28]

After the service, he sent Alice home and took Sarah to sit
in the church porch: 'and there in that beloved place, now
tenfold sad and dear, I spent with that darling, two hours of
bitter and sacred love, as ever I shall have or have had in this
world.'

Arthur left for London at seven o'clock the next morning,
kissed his host and the children goodbye and left a note for
Sarah. As he walked away he took a last look at the 'rose-

covered white walls, and the lichened roof, and the little window of her room ... I walked out of dreamland, out of the Eden which I may see again, but never as I saw it until now.'[29]

Sarah Carter was the most significant other woman in Arthur Munby's life. Hannah was perfect for him: they had made each other for each other. Sarah came second. Given the psycho-sexual dynamic of Arthur and Hannah's life, they excluded the rest of the world. If Arthur had not fallen in love with Hannah, Sarah Carter would have been perfect, all that he hoped to find in a woman: big hands, rustic beauty, hard work and submission. Although poor she was genteel, nearer to him in class terms: she was a 'lady' he could have taken home to meet his parents; her family were pious and had been monied. But there was a but, and that was Hannah. The summer of 1867 shook Arthur and reminded him that their love was unique.

He had recently received more evidence of Hannah as a slave to his love: she had sent him pictures she had taken by James Stodart whose studio was at 5 Cecil Street in Margate. (Plate 15) Hannah made several visits here and got to know the Stodarts quite well: he asked her to come and be their servant but she declined the offer. She was disappointed with the usual poses of her 'in her dirt', fearing that she did not look dirty enough, but Mr Stodart was pleased with the results, displaying one in his shop window. He appreciated her as a model, wanting 'to take me again in other ways ... one to be done as Magdalene'. Seeking Arthur's permission, she returned for another likeness with her hair down and wearing only a white skirt and her slave chain:

I had to strip off my servant's things to my shift, what I hardly liked, but still I knew that there was no *harm* in that, and Mr Stodart was a serious sort o' man and we neither of us laughed or smiled over it – he took me in a kneeling position as if praying, with my hair down my back and looking up.[30]

The embarrassing moment came when he asked her to remove the chain. She blushed and told him she could not as she did not have the key. Stodart remarked: '"Ah, there's some mystery about that then."' It is likely that the picture of Hannah as a Magdalene was seen by other eyes: many photographers did a roaring trade in under-the-counter 'artistic poses'.

On 14 September Arthur plucked up courage and went to Margate for the weekend to tell Hannah of the muddle he had got into with Sarah Carter, and also Julie Bovet. He set off in an ill-humour: the train 'was crowded with cockneys' and Arthur blamed his fellow passengers for his sinking mood. He was delighted and nervous on arrival: he and Hannah went to see the photograph of her in working clothes in James Stodart's window. This calmed his nerves, and after more walking and smalltalk they 'went down to the sands in the moonlight, and talked over the sad story of Pyrford'.[31] He explained his friendship with Sarah Carter and told Hannah more about the time he had stayed with Julie Bovet's family in Switzerland. His relief was palpable. Hannah handled the 'confession' with aplomb: she was not perturbed by the news; she did not fear these women.

Arthur's trip to Paris that summer had yielded what he hoped would be a better nose and lip for Harriet Langdon. Three days after his stressful visit to Hannah, he proudly handed Harriet her present. The nose and lip had been 'coloured to suit her scarlet face, but not deep enough'. Arthur's patience was at breaking-point when she put it on and complained that it was not pretty enough: '"I do not like this new nose half so well as my old one, it doesn't suit my

face, *it's not like me; it's a man's nose.*" [32] Despite feeling
provoked, Arthur stood by Harriet and continued to help her.
His parents were proud of their son's work for such a
deserving case, and contributed too: his mother and sister's
old gowns were given to Harriet, which she unpicked and
remade to her own size, and Arthur's shirts were recycled.
When he took her money and parcels of bread and tea, he
noticed that everything she wore had been provided by his
family. In 1868 she would leave London to live in Kingston-
upon-Thames where Arthur continued to visit her. [33] There is
a footnote in his diary noting Harriet's death in 1881 at Cardiff
aged forty-eight.

During this tumultuous summer Arthur started another
hobby, a distraction from the complications of his emotional
life. He started to write down the epitaphs of faithful servants
on headstones in churchyards, which he eventually edited and
had privately printed in 1891 by Reeves and Turner: *Faithful
Servants: Being Epitaphs and Obituaries Recording their Names
and Services*. Usually servants were buried without headstones,
which were beyond the reach of the working class. The
servants whose memorials Arthur published had earned theirs
by years of long service for employers who were well heeled,
God-fearing and gracious enough to commemorate a loyal
member of their household.

On 26 October, after a tearful goodbye to Miss Julia,
Hannah left Margate and caught the train to London. She
started her search for a place by visiting the Skateses. Although
they were expecting her, Hannah was told that the master was
in Ireland and the mistress was out: only the children were at
home. When she saw that 'every place showed such signs of
disorder and uncertainty of comfort, I thought I had better
give it up, so I left my respects for Mrs Skates, but not my
directions [address]'. [34]

The following day, Hannah signed on at the Servants'

Registry where she met a prospective employer who 'seemed anxious to have me, but was very fussy and particular about how she liked the dishes sent up. The thing I liked was that they was six months in London and six in the country and took the servants with them.' Hannah agreed to go and look at the house the following day but declined the job when she heard, ' "There's one thing that Mr — will not allow and that is staying out after church time on weekdays." ' She replied: ' "I don't like been compelled to go to church and to feel I dare not stop out if I wanted to one evening a week." ' When Hannah left the house she jumped for joy. Servants had to weigh up new situations very quickly, balancing the advantages and disadvantages of a new place. Hannah never wanted to be an 'upper servant': she would have preferred always to remain a 'lower servant' and, but for the low wages, would have remained one all her life: 'The feeling is dreadful – been stuck in a drawing room and having a fussy fine lady talking to you. I'd liefer [rather] work for eight pounds a year wi' comfort – on'y you don't feel satisfied wi' that cause you canna lay by for a rainy day out o' it.'

Hannah's visit to the Soho Bazaar was successful. She was engaged by Mrs Redmayne as a general servant at 25 Gloucester Gardens, a short walk from Paddington station, earning £20 a year. She was not needed immediately and was pleased to be able to 'give herself a holiday' at Mrs Smith's until she took up her new place in January 1868. Hannah's first impression of Mrs Redmayne was good: 'I liked the manner . . . she didn't talk so proudly and . . . the master was a linen draper. I wasn't so much afraid o' the place altogether and there was no restrictions about Sunday or church going.'[35]

Before Christmas, Hannah prepared her box to take to the Redmaynes, deciding what to ask Mrs Smith to store. She sorted out her clothes and photographs, and certainly took the pictures of her taken by the famous Swede Oscar Gustaf

Rejlander, whose studio in Camden Town she and Arthur had visited. Born in 1813, he was a portrait painter who turned to photography, becoming a leading 'art photographer' in the 1860s.[36] Hannah's likeness was taken by him when he was at the height of his powers, eight years before his death in 1875. Arthur, who would have known Rejlander's images of working life, commissioned the 'blunt but pleasant man' to take five pictures of Hannah in working clothes, indoors and out-doors.[37] Hannah and Arthur liked the image of her sweeping the back-yard showed off her prized possessions: strong hands, powerful biceps and wrist-strap.

One crisp Saturday afternoon in March 1868, Arthur went to watch Hannah scrub Mr and Mrs Redmayne's steps. On the way he noticed other servants working, but none with the manic enthusiasm of Hannah.

> She was cleaning the steps and pavement . . . kneeling on all fours on the wet flags with her pails and her pot of whitewash beside her earnestly scrubbing away. A large and strong young woman . . . she was drest like a drudge and looked like one, a large old fashioned servant's cap, coarse sacking apron, stout boots [his old ones] and a very plain frock of lavender cotton without sleeves. Her bare arms were ruddy like a peasant girl's and muscular . . . her face too was dusty and was rosy with rustic health – coarsened by weather and work, but the aquiline features were fine and the expression of this strong rough wench's countenance was gentle and most sweet.[38]

When Hannah saw Arthur she scrubbed, swilled and crawled harder; she looked up and turned her face to him and 'moved her lips without speaking and looked as if she would smile but dared not'. There were too many people around and there was no chance to speak: he turned and went on his way.

Hannah's time at Gloucester Gardens was brief: Giles

Redmayne's work took him abroad and all the servants were given notice. Hannah was disgruntled at having to leave after just three months.[39]

On 16 May 1868, she walked nervously around Norfolk Square, Paddington, to the house of Mr and Mrs Sanders.[40] It was an imposing house and her new job was as cook, an 'upper servant', earning £22 a year. In recognition of her age, thirty-five, and seniority in the household, she was to be addressed as 'Mrs Cullwick'. There were several women servants and a 'big man', Gower the footman, a sign of a well-heeled household. Arthur and her servant friend Mary Dunn had to coax Hannah to take this job: her exaggerated sense of humility made her uneasy about seeking promotion:

> I felt unequal to being anything like an 'upper'. Not as I was afraid o' the cooking, but from me always been under and never hoping nor wishing to think myself as highest nor the lowest servant in the house it was awkward and contrary.

Hannah settled in, asking the servants to call her Hannah instead of Mrs Cullwick. Finding herself under-occupied, she cleaned the front-door steps and shook the mats for Ann the kitchenmaid. She agreed to leave London and work for the newly-wed Sanderses on the Isle of Wight when they moved there. This was a long way from Massa, but Hannah wanted stability and continuity in her working life. Life at the Sanderses' house seemed to be going well until Hannah fell foul of Gower and the situation unravelled.

One afternoon in the kitchen, Hannah, engaging in some rumbustious kitchen frolic, picked up Gower and carried him round. His ego was hurt. All the servants' curiosity was aroused by her frequent writing at the kitchen table. They were keen to know to whom she wrote and what she was writing. One Sunday afternoon, Arthur was walking up and down in front of the house waiting for Hannah to come out when he was noticed by Gower, who had been footman to Arthur's uncle, Lieutenant Colonel Pearson, who lived at 46 Hyde Park Square. Gower's pride had been hurt by Hannah and he bribed the butcher's boy, whom Hannah paid to take her letters to the pillar-box when she was busy, to show him the name on the envelope. Gower and Harriet the housemaid went to Mr Sanders and told him about Hannah and her gentleman friend:

'what they said I don't know exactly, but making out that I was living dishonestly and so I was surprised and grievously hurt when I was sent for to see the Master and he at once gave me notice to leave. I asked him *why*. And he said, 'It is a painful thing to talk of, and I am sorry for Mrs Sanders likes you so much in the kitchen.' And he didn't seem to like to tell me what it was about and I wished to right myself if I could, so I ask'd him what was the reason for my having to leave. So he said, 'You are keeping company with a gentleman. Gower has told me as *truth*.'

Hannah was shocked and hurt that Mr and Mrs Sanders would have a bad opinion of her and Arthur. Tearful, she told her master:

'Yes, Sir, it *is* true. I have for a great many years and he's a gentleman in every sense of the word, even as you are . . . and if you think a bit, and know how I've worked for my living as a servant, and had settled to go to the Isle of Wight with you – right away from him, you'll know there is nor ever was anything wicked or wrong in him.'

Mr Sanders assured Hannah that he believed her to be honest, but that he could no longer take her with them to their new home as he would feel she was in a 'false position'.

He then reassured her that he and his wife did not think of her as 'wicked or foolish'.

The following morning Mrs Sanders came down to the kitchen to give Hannah her orders for the day and cried, saying how sorry she was that Hannah was leaving, and that she would always respect her and wish her well. Hannah was comforted, but felt drained. The experiment of moving up the servant hierarchy had not worked: the work was not menial enough to suit her; she had not enjoyed the kitchen politics and the resentment expressed by those servants below her. Mr and Mrs Sanders were her eighth employers in as many years and

> I was got so tired of changing places and also o' that continual worry o' writing to Massa and in fear lest anybody should know who I wrote to and yet finding it so hard to keep the secret, that I begin to feel so long loving was irksome, especially at not being equals.[41]

Hannah vowed never to work where there were prying eyes. She hoped that her next job would be as a general servant where she was the only one in the kitchen and the work suited her humble disposition:

> I dislike the thought o' being over anybody and ordering things, not only cause I'd rather do the work myself but for fear anyone should think me set up or *proud*. No, I've long resolved in my own mind and felt that for freedom and true lowliness there's nothing like being a maid of all work – no one can think you set up or proud in that, and I'd liefer be despised than cause spite or envy from my fellow servants; and I would liefer do all the scrubbing both out o' doors and in, wearing my thick striped apron, peasant's bonnet, short frock and thick boots – having black arms and hands and face too if it happens wi' soot or dust, than I'd be prim or clean in the kitchen looking

on anyone else doing the work I've bin used to these thirty years. And as I would say to Massa, 'I was *born to serve* and *not* to order' and I hope I shall always keep the same humble spirit – that of liking to serve others, and obeying instead of commanding.[42]

In the middle of July 1868 Hannah went to work as a general servant for Mrs Henderson at 25 Sunderland Terrace, in Westbourne Park. She had heard about the position from the Sanderses' greengrocer's wife two weeks before she was dismissed, and sensing trouble was brewing, she arranged to meet Mrs Henderson. She dressed carefully, wearing her old black bonnet and white apron, with a black shawl over Massa's favourite old dress from her mother dating from the 1830s. There was only one other servant, Emily the housemaid, and a page boy, Walter, who ran errands and cleaned the boots and knives. As she waited in the dining room for Mrs Henderson, Hannah studied the pictures on the walls which reassured her that they were a good family. Her prospective new mistress was sixty-six years old, a colonel's widow who had been born in the East Indies: two daughters, Eliza and Margaret, who lived at home, had been born in Calcutta. Miss Eliza asked Hannah the usual questions: where she had lived, why she was leaving her present place, what wages she wanted and what kind of a cook she was. As directed by Mr Sanders, she was to tell Mrs Henderson she was leaving because the family were moving to the Isle of Wight. Mr Sanders offered to see any ladies who wanted to know her 'character'. This offer was appreciated by Hannah as 'very kind and manly of him and wise too, as ladies are more apt to let out *little* things which might prove great hindrances', and so he did. But Mrs Henderson was not available and Hannah was sent away to return another day when she was interviewed by Miss Margaret, who acted as housekeeper.

Hannah formed a poor impression of her when she spoke 'vulgarly and spitefully', and on hearing Hannah's surname remarked: '"I never heard such a funny name in all my life."' After checking Hannah's character, Miss Margaret offered her the job with a wage of £21 a year, providing her own beer and tea.

The house was newly built and small and evidently did not suit the Hendersons who planned to move to a bigger house. Most of their possessions were in packing cases, ready to leave as soon as the right house became available. Hannah was received warmly by Emily and shown to her own attic room. She learned that Mrs Henderson's husband had died recently. Hannah found her mistress to be:

> a simple and unaffected lady . . . very fidgetty and funny
> about everything – very exact in the books and a perfect
> lady by birth and in manners, only very plain and very
> fond of knowing all that was done, and especially where
> a servant went to and if she went to church or no of a
> Sunday – that was a matter of greatest importance.[43]

Of the two unmarried daughters, Miss Margaret was the hardest to please: grieving the death of their father, she was also disappointed in love. Although she had been acerbic with Hannah on their first meeting, Hannah was surprised at the timid way she conducted herself as housekeeper: she was 'quiet . . . too much so for the orders, almost as you couldn't understand her and it was rather tiresome, but I saw that she couldn't help it somehow and I bore it as patiently as I could'.

In September the Hendersons, and their servants Hannah, Emily and Walter, moved to their new house at 20 Gloucester Crescent, Westbourne Park. Much of the extra work was done enthusiastically by Hannah, and Mrs Henderson let her know she considered herself very fortunate to get a servant who could cook nicely and be such a good cleaner too.

Arthur's visit to York in October 1868 made a trip to Molly Nettleton and her friends irresistible. He describes her at Brail Head:

and there looking down, I saw the new rope [that he had bought her] . . . Molly's treasure, hanging from the stake and going down the whole height of the cliff, to the broad platform of table rock at the bottom . . . two girls appeared near the foot of the cliff, striding and stooping among the wet seaweed. Both were breeched up to the knee: the tall one with the long legs was evidently Molly. At that height one could not hear their voices: but I saw them clamber up the base of the rock, and there Molly seized the rope, tried it with her own weight, and begin to mount. Hand over hand, sticking her toes into the crevices of the cliff, she went up as easily as one might walk upstairs; and having climbed some fifty feet, she turned round, and with her back to the cliff worked her way along a level ledge that just supported her heels, to an overhanging point. Then, stooping forward as coolly as possible she handed up her full basket and her fellow's, which the girl below first tied to the rope-end. When the baskets came up she loosened them, and hoisted them up, with one hand, upon a broader ledge, above her head: then grasping the rope again, she climbed up to it, and sat down. . . . The rope knotted to the fixed stake was trembling . . . and very soon the crown of Molly's lilac hood bonnet appeared above the lower ledge of the slope thence, holding the basket on one hand and tugging at the rope with the other, she soon climbed up to the stake, grasped my offered hand, and flung herself down beside me . . . panting for breath and still smiling.[44]

The stereoscopic photograph of Molly with her fellow 'flither lasses' (Plate 10) – she is on the far left – gives a hint of the drama of their work. Behind them tower the steep cliffs which they climbed, often in cold and blustery weather, wearing warm clothes padded for protection from the cliff-face, not the easiest garb in which to climb 300 feet. Working as a team here was based on trust and comradeship. Arthur's friendship with Molly was genuine: in 1871, hearing she was married to George White, a farm labourer, he visited her new home and gave her a wedding present of half-a-crown and wished the couple well. Arthur's many acts of kindness to working women suggest he regarded them as an extended family and not just cases to collect.

By Christmas, the Hendersons were able to receive calls in their new home from their neighbours, Madame Louise Lucet, a professor of music, and the Misses Neale and Randall. There was a stricter regime of prayers than Hannah was used to: twice daily in the dining and drawing room. Being close to the railway line, there was more cleaning to do. So Hannah settled into

> the life of a drudge again, and as the cold weather come on my hands got red and coarse and grenered [ingrained] ... the lines in my hands filled with blacklead and ... tho' it was a gentleman's family, it was a rough place for me, having all the rough and dirty work to do.[45]

Also, Hannah's working days could be lengthened if Miss Margaret or Miss Eliza went out in the evenings. She would have to escort them home, and unless a hansom cab was ordered, she was obliged to walk several paces behind as etiquette demanded.

On New Year's Day 1870, Hannah reflected on her time with the Hendersons. She had often wondered where she would be on the first day of this decade, to which she attached great significance. She was thirty-six years old and mindful of the future. Hannah recorded her overall contentment with her work and her employers. Walter, once the lad, now the

1. A pencil sketch of Arthur Joseph Munby in 1848, aged twenty.

2. Hannah Cullwick in her 'Sunday best' in 1853, aged twenty, while working as a scullion at Pitchford Hall in Shropshire.

PRINCESS'S ※ THEATRE.
OXFORD STREET.
UNDER THE MANAGEMENT OF
Mr. CHARLES KEAN,
No. 3, TORRINGTON SQUARE.
LORD BYRON'S TRAGEDY OF
SARDANAPALUS
WILL BE REPEATED
This Evening, To-Morrow (Thursday) and on Friday, Saturday, and Monday Next.

☞ The Free List will be Suspended on the Nights of "Sardanapalus."

In the production of Lord Byron's tragedy of "Sardanapalus," I have availed myself of the wonderful discoveries made within the last few years, by Layard, Botta, and others, on the site of the ancient Nineveh. It was during the latest excavations, made by Mr. Layard, in the south-east palace of the Mount of Nimroud, that our illustrious countryman arrived at the conclusion that this interesting structure was the work of the son of Esar-haddon, who was himself the son of Sennacherib, so famous in sacred history. Although, says Mr. Layard, no part of the history of this son of Esar-haddon was no other than the Sardanapalus, who, conquered by the Medes and Babylonians, under Cyaxares (B.C. 706), made one funeral pile of his palace, his wealth, and his wives.

To render visible to the eye, in connexion with Lord Byron's drama, the costume, architecture, and customs of the ancient Assyrian people, verified by the bas-reliefs, which, after having been buried for nearly three thousand years, have in our own day been brought to light, was an object that might well inspire the enthusiasm of one who has learnt that scenic illustration, if it have the weight of authority, may adorn and add dignity to the noble works of genius.

I have humbly endeavoured to convey to the stage an accurate portraiture and a living picture of an age long since past away, but once as famous as our own country for its civilisation and power; and more intimately associated with the destructive wars of the Jewish race than any other people. No pains have been spared to present to the eye the gorgeous and striking scenery, that has been so unexpectedly dug from the very bowels of the earth. The sculptures now in the British Museum have been rigidly followed; and where recent discovery has failed to give authority for minor detail, I have, wherever it has been possible, borrowed designs from surrounding nations, flourishing at the same epoch. In decoration of every kind, whether scenic or otherwise, I have diligently sought for truth; and it is with some pride and satisfaction I am enabled to announce that a verdict of approval has been received from the judge most competent to speak with authority upon the surpassingly interesting subject with which I have had to deal.

It is hardly necessary to remind the reader that Assyria and the country beyond the two rivers, the Tigris and the Euphrates, constituted, "if not actually the cradle of mankind, at all events the theatre on which the descendants of Noah performed their first conspicuous part. The plains of Shinar witnessed not only the defeat of that presumptuous enterprise which scattered them abroad upon the face of the earth, but also the exploits of the 'mighty Hunter,' and the triumph of his ambition, in the establishment of the first monarchy recorded either by sacred or profane writers." "More than two thousand years (says a modern writer, in recording the marvellous results of French and English discovery on the Assyrian plains) had Nineveh lain in its unknown grave, when a wandering English scholar and a French savant, urged by a noble inspiration, sought the seat of the once powerful empire, and, searching till they found the dead city, threw off its shroud of sand and ruin, and revealed once more to an astonished and curious world, the temples, the palaces, and the idols, the representations of war, and the triumphs of peaceful art of the ancient Nineveh. The Nineveh of scripture—the Nineveh of the oldest historians—the Nineveh, twin sister of Babylon, glorying in a civilisation of pomp and power, all traces of which were believed to be gone—the Nineveh in which the captive tribes of Israel had laboured and wept, was, after a sleep of twenty centuries, again brought to light. The long lost was found—the dead palaces were exhumed—the strange huge sculptures were dug out and their inscriptions deciphered. The proofs of ancient splendour were again beheld by living eyes, and, by the skill of the draughtsman and the pen of the antiquarian traveller, made known to the world. Patience and industry rescued from the earth these treasures of a long gone people, giving proof of a great civilisation existing in the earliest stages of the history of the human race."

It is a note-worthy fact that, until the present moment, it has been impossible to render Lord Byron's tragedy of "Sardanapalus" upon the stage with proper dramatic effect, because, until now, we have known nothing of Assyrian architecture and costume. It is also worthy of remark that, interesting as the rescued bas-reliefs which have furnished such information are, they could not find dramatic illustration but for the existence of this very Tragedy that has reference to the period of which they treat. I consider myself fortunate in having been permitted to link together the momentous discoveries of one respected Englishman with the poetic labours of another.

☞ Lord Byron having closely followed the history of Sardanapalus, as given by Diodorus Siculus, who has erroneously placed the site of the ancient Nineveh on the banks of the Euphrates, I have ventured to alter the text wherever this mistake is made, and have given the city its proper position on the river Tigris.

CHARLES KEAN.

This Evening, WEDNESDAY, JUNE 29th, 1853,
Will be presented a Petite Comedy, in One Act, entitled, The

DAY AFTER
THE
WEDDING

Colonel Freelove,	— — —	Mr. WALTER LACY
Lord Rivers,	—	Mr. G. EVERETT,
James.	Mr. F. SAKER,	Groom, Mr. WILSON,
Lady Elizabeth Freelove,	— —	Mrs. WALTER LACY
Mrs. Davies,	—	Mrs. W. DALY

After which, (commencing about a Quarter before 8 o'clock) LORD BYRON'S Tragedy of

SARDANAPALUS,
KING OF ASSYRIA.
(CONSIDERABLY ABRIDGED FOR STAGE REPRESENTATION.)

The Costume and Architecture throughout the Play selected from Layard's Discoveries of the Monuments of Nineveh.

The Scenery Painted under the Direction of Mr. GRIEVE.

The Overture and Music composed for the occasion, by Mr. J. L. HATTON.

The Dances and Action	by Mr. OSCAR BYRN.
The Dresses by	Mrs. and Miss HOGGINS.
The Machinery	by Mr. G. HODSDON.
The Properties by	Mr. BRUNTON.
Perruquier.	Mr. ASPLIN. of No. 13, New Bond Street.

Sardanapalus, (King of Nineveh and Assyria)	Mr. CHARLES KEAN
Arbaces. (the Mede who aspired to the Throne)	Mr. G. EVERETT,
Beleses, (a Chaldean and Soothsayer)	Mr. GRAHAM
Salemenes, (the King's Brother-in-Law)	Mr. RYDER,
Altada.	Mr. ROLLESTON,
Pania, (Assyrian Officers	Mr. J. F. CATHCART
Sfero, of the Palace)	Mr. PAULO
Zames,	Mr. BRAZIER
Officers,	Mr. DALY and Mr. TERRY,
Balea, (a Courtier)	Mr. J. COLLETT,
Herald — Mr. F. COOKE,	Cupbearer, Mr. COLL...
Zarina, (the Queen)	Miss HEATH,
Myrrha, (an Ionian Female Slave)	Mrs. CHARLES KEAN

Guards, Archers Nobles, Musicians, Standard Bearers.
Dancing Girls, &c. &c.

3. Playbill for Lord Byron's *Sardanapalus* performed at the Princess's Theatre, Oxford Street, London in the summer of 1853.

4. Arthur Munby's self-portrait made in 1860 at the beginning of his career at the Ecclesiastical Commission.

5. The picture of Hannah so admired by Munby's friend Dante Gabriel Rossetti, 1862.

6. Hannah posed for her 'chimney sweep' photograph in 1862, aged twenty-nine. She wore the slave-collar and wrist-strap for more than twenty years as a sign of Munby's ownership of her. She was at his feet, one of which is just visible. Arthur took the picture everywhere with him hidden behind a photograph of her dressed up as a lady.

7. Hannah sits between thur's knees on the floor of ilip Fink's studio in Oxford Street in 1857.

8. Munby asked this Irish 'dust-wench' to pose for him at a studio in Lambeth in March 1860.

9. 'Pit broo wenches' at Shevington Colliery, near Wigan, in 1863.

10. 'Flither lasses' prised limpets off the rocks for bait at Flamborough Head 1 Yorkshire. Munby's end Molly Nettleton is on the left, c. 1860.

11. The exotic acrobat Mademoiselle Senyah, (Elizabeth Haynes) in 1868.

12. Hannah's 'grannered hands' photographed by Fink in 1860. Munby collected the dirty palm prints of Hannah and other working women.

13. On 13 February 1861, Fink photographed Hannah's short-lived androgynous look. At her suggestion, she cut her hair and practised wearing Arthur's clothe hoping to pass herself off as his val But is was too nerve-racking and l insisted they abandon the idea.

14. Hannah uncomfortably dress up as a lady while working at boarding house in Margate in 18

In 1867 James Stodart of Margate took his 'magdalen' photograph of Hannah wearing the slave-collar to which only Arthur had the key: 'I had to strip off my vant's things to my shift, what I hardly liked, but still I knew that there was no *harm* in that, and Mr Stodart was a serious sort o' man and neither of us laughed or smiled over it . . .'

16. The entrance to Munby's, and for four years Hannah's, home in Fig Tree Court. The chimney-pot for number six is on the far right.

17. Arthur Munby photographed for the frontispiece of his collection of poetry *Vestigia Retrorsum* in 1891.

18. The last picture of Hannah in 1902, aged sixty-nine.

footman, had errands to run and this gave her extra work when he was out. Her diary suggests some irritability:

> So when Walter is out I have to answer the doors or parlour bells and do anything there is to be done – sometimes to change the plates at dinner what I don't like doing cause I don't think I'm fit to go in the room and wait on the ladies. . . . I've got the two dining rooms and the back room, the hall and the front steps, the water closet upstairs and the privy out at the back, the passage and the larder and nine cupboards – the closet and the kitchen windows I clean and the dining room window, blinds and sills, two copper scuttles and scoops and four grates and the fire irons to keep clean. I've no boots to clean as they're only ladies' boots here it doesn't matter much. . . . I have the cooking to do and all the dirty plates, dishes and saucepans to wash up, the tins and covers to clean, the coals to dig and carry upstairs, the carpets, rugs and doormats to shake and a good deal o' paint work to clean . . . the kitchen and scullery floors to do on my knees and I wash all my own clothes, and the kitchen cloths.[46]

A few days later there is an insight into the dynamic of Hannah and Arthur: 'I am as ignorant as a child and more but that doesn't matter if I'm a child in *heart* Massa says. And I can talk even to him hardly except about my work an' that.'[47] Hannah often related to Munby as if she was an errant child and he punished her as if she was. On the morning of 5 March, she received a note from Arthur saying he was unwell. It was not her evening off but she wanted to give him some pills. She had missed the post which would be delivered the same evening, so after she had sent the Hendersons' dinner up at six o'clock and was washing up she thought:

why if I make haste I might pop in a train to get to
Massa's and back by our suppertime. I *should* so like
to – so I got done and washed me. Put my red frock
and white apron on and my cloak and bonnet and got
in time for the eight o'clock train. I got to Massa's by
half past eight. Found the door open which I was glad
to see, else I must put the letter [containing the pills] in
the box and come away. I knocked and Massa come and
was surprised to see me and I was so glad I found him
in and I felt so well and jolly pleased too to go to Massa
so unexpected and *he* looked pleased to see me which I
was glad of and we petted a few minutes and talked
lively as long as I could stop. I got back to the station at
nine o' clock and reached here by half past . . . I got our
supper ready. Cleared away. To prayers and to bed by
eleven o' clock.[48]

Hannah ran from the station and slipped into the basement
kitchen breathless, her absence undetected. A couple of days
after this dash across London, Hannah received a letter from
Arthur, parts of which made her happy, and others guilty: 'I
got a nice long letter from my master – but it made me rather
unhappy for it showed how much he had suffered on my
account.'[49] The next time they met Hannah was cool towards
Arthur and he did not like it, and while telling her how much
he loved her, he also made his feelings about her moodiness
clear. She wrote:

I felt bothered at been [sic] so late and altogether I wasn't
very pleasant at first so as Massa said I chilled him. I
didn't wish to do *that* if I did but I couldn't help it.
We had a most pleasant evening and enjoyed it very
much. Massa talked to me freely and I did rather more
than usual to him, for it was like forced to come out
when I found that Massa had felt so much for me and

loved me so that he couldn't bear the thought of losing me any more than I could bear to lose him so I promised to be good and not sulk again. I got the dinner and washed Massa's feet and did as much as the time would let and I got back by half past ten feeling oh *so happy*.[50]

In the late nineteenth century there were a quarter of a million horses at work on the streets of the capital. The streets, roads, pavements and steps were caked with horse manure: these moments in Hannah's daily routine may surprise the modern hygienic reader:

Took the ashes out and swept and dusted. Cleaned the copper scuttle and filled it with coal. Carried it upstairs – I was black by then and I wiped my hand across my nose and mouth to black me some more and wi' my striped apron and bonnet on I went up to sweep the hall and steps and do the sign what I promised Master I'd do about eight o' clock or before. So after I'd swept and shook the doormat well I laid it on the causeway and I knelt on the flags and brushed the mat well wi' a hard brush on both sides and then I rubbed my face on it and put my lips again' it and I thought how I was one o' the lowest drudges as could be – but Massa loved me and I loved my work, but for itself and also for Massa's sake and I felt so happy.[51]

Passers-by stared at Hannah in disbelief and some made remarks out loud, others were appalled and walked past as if she did not exist. She was the subject of gossip amongst the fraternity of servants who worked in the Crescent.

In April, Arthur's worries about his future, her future and their future, triggered a soul-searching which filled their letters from Gloucester Crescent to Fig Tree Court and back again

with pain and anger. The origin of the upset was when
Hannah looked around at servants and ladies and could not
help but:

> wonder very much how could Massa *love* such a one as
> me. It has took seventeen years to make me understand
> it and even now I am soon ready to think he does *not*
> entirely, for all I've had such proof of it. Is it a want of
> simplicity I wonder, or from a knowledge of my extreme
> lowness and ignorance and the difference between me and
> a lady. Perhaps both. But if it's for want of a trustful *spirit*
> I wish I could get over it for it often makes me rude and
> sulky to Massa when I ought to be gentle and nice . . .
> but my love for my master is too deep and fixed for me
> for that obstinacy to last long.[52]

On Sunday, 8 May Hannah's mood was lowered because
'her belly ached' and she 'hadn't felt well all day'. Perhaps
period pains were the cause, and though Arthur gave her some
brandy, she was unhappy with his lack of attentiveness,
thinking him 'a bit selfish and cared more for his little bird
than for me'. Before she left she washed his feet, and went
home feeling 'rather dull and unhappy' and knowing that she
had 'behaved badly instead of as I ought and I knew it all the
while but I couldn't help it somehow'.[53] The following day,
Arthur sent her a 'kind note' asking how she was but, still
feeling unwell, her reply was critical, contrite, frustrated and
loving:

> My dearest Massa
>   I am so much pleased to think that you wrote to me
> today . . . I *was* cool and indifferent last night to you, I
> felt so, but it was cause I felt so weak and in pain and
> more especially cause *you* seemed so cool and as if you
> were *averse* to me and had that feeling of 'dislike' what
> you spoke of once. I *ought* to behave nicely and with tact

at such times I know, but sometimes I can't – my spirits won't let me – for all I know I'm only a slave and might be very humble and meek, but *I* think if a man dislikes a woman it's no use to her trying to make him so I *never* shall. It isn't that I'm careless about you disliking me or no – far from it – but every year that you live alone, I can see that it makes you more selfish and as if no one can do anything right for you. I am *sorry* to see it cause that above all other things would make me afraid to be with you always either as a servant or anything else – for I should never feel that I gave you satisfaction or was the least bit precious. Don't you be vex'd now, Massa, at me saying this – I don't want to vex you – I should like to be all the comfort possible and I'm quite sure I love you as much as you love me.[54]

Hannah was inclined to move on from their differences and was taken aback by Arthur's doggedness in keeping the conflict simmering. On 10 May she received a letter from him and fired one back in response: he had objected to her calling him 'a selfish old bachelor' and would not let the matter rest. All was well by her visit to him on Friday, 13 May when 'Massa wasn't a bit cross with me'. She was unable to be with him on her birthday as the Hendersons were entertaining guests, but she was happy with his card and 'very pretty present'.

During the summer Arthur continued to court Hannah as if they were social equals, but people stared and made cruel remarks. Hannah dreaded the times when he suggested they go out together in daylight, preferring to spend time together in private. But Arthur could sometimes insist on walking arm-in-arm and kissing her goodbye even when she wore her working clothes. Thrilled by the public show of his love, she was also mortified by the reaction of others when they 'stared – so that it made me feel nearly half-ashamed'.

Hannah's arrival at Fig Tree Court always had to be carefully choreographed: there were signs and signals to follow, and the light evenings of the summer months presented dangers of being discovered. If Arthur was out, she would have to hang around trying to be invisible. On 12 June a difficult two weeks began. When he arrived late she found it hard to

> get over the vexation of losing so much time and all my fear o' bin spoken to, that I was almost rude to Massa and said I would give up comin', but my master was so nice and made me good again and I showed my strength with carrying him round the room and then into the other room and then Massa kissed me and said whatever he did I should still be his slave.[55]

On 16 June Hannah was feeling wretched: the day before she had received a letter which made 'me feel bad again . . . and very miserable'. She went to bed worrying if she would see Arthur on Sunday. Bravely she laid her cards on the table and told him through her diary:

> This upset going on so long *is* so very wearying and tiresome – nothing makes me feel so weak and bad as it does – till I could wish that my sweetheart was a dustman or a coal heaver, better than one so different to me if that would make it better.[56]

Towards the end of that day, Hannah had received a note from Arthur which prompted her to tell him she was on the verge of ending their relationship. Her reply was a confusion of masochistic love and pleasure and rejection of the pain it was causing:

> My *dearest* Massa
>   For such you'll ever be to me I *hope* but I must say my patience is well nigh exhausted and I *cannot* come to you

any more till I know your mind and whether you are master of yourself as well as of me. I was thoroughly humiliated on Tuesday and ashamed of having wrote that letter to you in the morning . . . and the while I was thinking very hard thoughts of you and made my mind up *not* to come to you again I took the hair [locks of her own hair] away so as you mayn't find it there – *that's* what made me nearly faint – the thought o' doing all that and wishing you goodbye perhaps for the last time and that I should ask you to keep the plants alive as long as you can for my sake.

The remainder of the letter refuted some of the points he had made, and she painted a picture of their love which she feared was one-sided:

you speak of *my* love as if you had *none*. It's painfully delightful to suffer so much for love. I will not be unhappy . . . what is it I've pledged myself to be to you – your slave? Well then I must come to you if you send for me on Monday or Tuesday whichever my missis can spare me best – but I must have an understanding for I canna bear all the uncertainty any longer. I must post this letter or no – yes I must – you please forgive me if it's wrong and may God forgive *you* for trying the life and soul out of a low mean drudge.[57]

There was a reconciliation. On Sunday, 19 June, Hannah rushed through her chores to reach the Temple by half past six. She waited for Arthur by the fountain in the gardens feeling conspicuous. It was a flying visit: there was little time for anything more than having his feet washed, his clothes mended and his tea made, as he had to catch a train. Restoring the balance of power which had become so unstable, Arthur insisted that she follow him to the station. There were no hansom cabs and she had to run after him:

I knew it'd be awkward and didn't want to go but Massa
made me follow him to Waterloo Bridge and the people
stared to see him beckoning me on. I was *glad* he made
me go but I was annoyed too, cause of having to run in
and out o' folks.[58]

Hannah returned to her favourite theme: her dirtiness.
Boosted by the strength she had gained in their recent
altercations, she chastized him for his criticisms of her appearance. Describing how she had swept the rooms, shaken the
mats and scoured the flags and steps, so that her

> hands and arms looked so red and big and my face was all
> sweatin' and red too. I thought, 'Well, if Massa seed me
> *now* I'm sure he wouldna have any cause to complain. *But
> you on'y see when I'm washed* and not at work. . . . So I
> wish you'd leave off complaining and not be so *hard* wi'
> me. *There's nothing I like better nor a good bout o' cleaning.'*

She ended by telling him that her happiness depended on
him loving her, as long as she was confident of his feelings she
would be 'happy and can work and write with a good heart.
The least thought different to that takes all my spirits away
and you don't know how different it is to feel sure that you
do.'[59]

Arthur added a new element to their repertoire in July. He
needed to see her dirty, and wanted to know everything about
how she looked and behaved when her chores had made her
black and sweaty. So she would change out of her working
clothes, put on a clean frock and take her dirty clothes in a
bundle and put them on again in his chambers. Hannah
would re-enact that morning's cleaning dramas and improvise
the voices of the ladies with whom she had interacted, exulting
in her lowly state. Arthur directed and she starred in her own
one-woman show:

I took my striped apron and dirty frock and Massa told me to wipe the dusty boxes on my face and arms to show him how I looked in the morning, for I said how the ladies called and I opened the door looking such a drudge – and how I took the [calling] card from the lady with the corner of my apron cause my hands was so dirty and how I curtsied to her and spoke respectably as I could to make up for I *did* feel rather ashamed.[60]

That autumn there was a bizarre row and flurry of cross letters about a bonnet that Hannah did not want. There was also little harmony below stairs between her and the Hendersons' other servants. Eventually order was restored when she blacked her face for him one evening during a hurried visit to Fig Tree Court:

He was so nice and kind and I soon got right. After we'd petted a bit, Massa asked me if I should like my face blacked and I said yes, so I got the black lead and oil out and I knelt twixt his knees and he brushed my face all over with it until I was a negress like I was the first time in the little room where I lodged and Massa came to see me. I blacked the grate and brushed and cleaned round the chimney piece. Washed the window sill ... washed Massa's feet and rubbed 'em and then I washed the black off me and wiped me.[61]

Before Arthur left London to spend Christmas with his parents, he and Hannah met in the Edgware Road to buy a pair of stout boots for Molly Nettleton. Hannah did not fear this friendship: she was the instigator of the shopping trip. Molly and Hannah were roughly the same size and she tried on a pair of second-hand pair of milkmaid's boots, modelled them for Arthur who waited outside, and paid with the five shillings and sixpence he had given her.[62]

With a resolve to be less anxious, on 7 January 1871

Hannah rushed to the Temple to see Arthur for the first time in nearly three weeks. It was a good time: they celebrated the New Year with kisses, she licked his boots and polished them. On many visits to Fig Tree Court she nursed him: their roles were reversed and she was the mother and he the child: 'Massa was very kind. I sat in the chair and nursed him for nigh on half an hour. Massa sits on me, feet and all on my knees, though he thought I couldn't bear [the weight of him] but I said, "Oh sir, I can." '[63]

On 1 March, Arthur was summoned by telegram when his mother had a stroke: on his return to London Hannah visited him as soon as she could. He was charmed by the reminiscences Hannah had sent him while he was at his mother's sick-bed of her life as a scullion at Woodcote in Shropshire. To prove a point she

> took Massa's boots off, and socks, and it was so wet and sludgy they was wet through and I licked some o' the dirt off just to show Massa that I was as good, and humble as ever. After I'd washed the dinner things up and that I did his feet and washed 'em as usual.[64]

On 3 May Arthur told Hannah that he would be going to a cousin's funeral the following day at St Mary's Church, at nearby Paddington Green, and asked her either to come, or be cleaning the steps when he travelled to the church via Gloucester Crescent. Hannah, eager to please, hovered on the steps looking out for him as long as she dared without incurring the wrath of Miss Margaret. Then, between cooking the parlour breakfast and clearing away, she put on her bonnet and ran to the church where she peeped inside but could not see him. Afraid to wait as there was work in the kitchen, she ran back to the house where Miss Margaret wanted to change the luncheon pudding. Once this was sorted out, on went the bonnet again and she run round again and the service had begun, and I could see Massa. I was still in my dirt with striped apron on but there was lots o' people in the church I thought wouldn't notice me, so I got up nearer and stared at the side benches where I thought Massa could see me and it was so solemn and the singing so beautiful and I thought Massa was looking so calm and nice and humble too, that I felt myself really too low and not half nor quarter good enough for him to love – *but I felt thankful I was his servant* and slave and I felt I'd not done wrong kneeling to lick the dirt off his boots so often and I felt very humble and very happy when it was nearly over and they was going out and went round and stood in the crowd to see Massa get in the coach and I was in time and I *looked* at him and he looked at me, so I understood it that he was pleased to see me there. Then I rushed back to my work thinking of it all I felt a bit overcome and had to sit down and rest ... at half past twelve *I put my striped apron on and cleaned the front steps in hopes that Massa'd come by and see me on my knees.*[65]

The death of his cousin Julius jolted Arthur's feelings of inertia. His grief was overtaken by the sadness of his own circumstances: seventeen years had gone by and he and Hannah were still not fully together: 'O humble and wistful face, how long shall it be thus with you and me? Here is another death and our mutual life is not yet begun!'[66]

On 10 May there was a row with Miss Margaret and Hannah was dismissed. Miss Margaret had given orders for the meals for the day and Hannah decided not to ask her permission to go out in the evening because 'the last time I did she scrupled and said she would ask Mrs Henderson, but never gave me any answer'. So when Miss Margaret was out, Hannah tidied her hair and clothes and went to see Mrs Henderson in the parlour. On the understanding that the tea would be prepared and everything done, Hannah was allowed to go out, and she returned to the kitchen happy at the prospect of seeing Arthur and relieved that 'the asking part was over, what I always *do* dislike' and finished her work. Soon after Miss Margaret called her into the store-room and asked if tomorrow evening would do instead. Hannah guessed this would happen and told her firmly:

'*No, ma'am* it won't,' at once cause I knew Massa wouldn't be in and this was the only day he could see me, and besides it was too late for me to send him word and I wouldn't disappoint *him* anyhow if I could help it, so perhaps I was a bit hasty. Well, Miss Margaret said, '*Why* won't tomorrow do?' and looked rather proud.

An unseemly row followed when Hannah was reprimanded for 'making appointments without knowing whether you can be spared' and was told that Miss Margaret was the best judge of her workload. Hannah begged to differ: 'No, ma'am, you canna tell about my work so well as I can.' She told Arthur, through her diary: 'I suppose she saw a little temper in me, the same as I saw in her, for she said: "*Hannah, you forget your place*," to which I hotly replied: "*No, ma'am, I don't*," but it puts me out after I've got leave to be stopped for nothing.' Miss Margaret, taken aback at Hannah's attitude, warned her that '"things can't go on like this"', to which Hannah firmly answered, '"No, ma'am, they can't."' Hannah stomped back to the kitchen feeling 'very angry and vex'd', and a short while later Mrs Henderson summoned her to the dining room and scolded her for being 'so insolent to Miss Margaret and thought it was best for her and me to part'. Hannah agreed and added cheekily: '"I hope you'll stick to it and not ask me to stop on as you did before, for I've a hard place o' work, but that *I like*. It's what I have to bear from Miss Margaret what *I don't* like and she is very mean in the housekeeping."'

Hannah left the room pleased to have given vent to her feelings, but was troubled by the consequences of the row. She wanted to leave and felt she was justified in her remarks, but began to feel haunted by the prospect of an uncertain future:

> I felt very much annoyed, but not sorry for I felt that for a good many reasons it would be a good thing, having never been in the country [Shifnal] for three years and never dare ax for a holiday and Missis never going away for a night or day ever, so as to give one time to clean or turn round for a bit o' sewing and that. Still the disagreeable feelings of throwing oneself out of place and searching for a new one come up and made it unpleasant, and I'd rather not have to tell Massa tho' it was chiefly through him.[67]

Hannah finished her chores and went to the Temple and told a worried Arthur what had happened. He was sympathetic and guilty that he had been the cause. Later that evening he wrote her a letter in a different tone which she received the next morning: Arthur was upset by Hannah's 'naughtiness' – her rude remarks to Miss Margaret. Before his letter arrived Hannah went into morning prayers and was pleased to note that Miss Margaret smiled at her, so she 'dropped her a curtsey', and Hannah could tell that 'she was all right after what had happened yesterday same as I was'. Judging by the body language, good relations with the Hendersons seemed to have been restored, Hannah noted, still pleased that she 'had spoke up'. To her dismay, Arthur's letter told her that she had been insolent and that 'he was sorry I should be thought so'. Hannah was frustrated with his change of heart: 'he doesn't know all I have to bear, nor how hard it is to be always meek and indeed I don't think it's right to be quiet when there's need to speak up.' She averred that while she was not wrong she had been 'certainly a bit hasty'.[68] When Hannah visited him at the Temple three days later she was reprimanded again, ostensibly for not replying to his letter. Her heavy workload and lack of time were ignored. Hannah was indignant and did not take his words well:

> and Massa thought I was naughty. As I was nursing him he gave me a talking to about it and my behaviour to Miss Margaret the other day. I was very tired and I felt rebellious rather as if I'd been *played* with and annoyed too, though I didn't care for having had warning to leave. Therefore I couldn't bear for Massa to take their part against me and I told Massa how it was to feel *a great wench and strong as I am, as I could crush a weakling like Miss Margaret wi' one hand* (tho' o' course I wouldn't) and she must know that for her to trifle about going out, when I'd got leave to and *play* wi' me as if I was a child and unkindly too, especially when it was to see Massa – I *must* o' spoke up it'd bin a degree o' cowardice to have took it so quietly when I meant otherwise and I *wasn't* rude nor insolent. I only spoke up plain and so if I leave through it I don't care and if I stop in again, either way I'm sure it'll be for my good.[69]

Eventually calm returned and the difference with the Hendersons was put to one side, though not forgotten.

One Sunday at the end of June, when Arthur was sitting on Hannah's lap, they talked about how dirty she looked in her daily work. Although he had encouraged her to see her hard labour and blackened face and body as a badge of honour, he worried that she had gone too far down that path, and that it would be difficult to rein in this enthusiasm. Arthur was afraid that her behaviour would become permanent, that she would not be able to pass as a 'lady' in disguise and they would never be able to be seen together in society.

Timidly he broached the subject: ' "Oh dear, if you're not fit to be seen by ladies as a *servant* however shall us two be seen together?" ' Hannah's attitude was held to from this time onwards:

> I don't *want* anyone to see us. I *like* the life I lead – working here and going to Massa when I can of a Sunday and a chance to clean of a weekday when I can get leave now and then – oftener of course if I could – better even than a married life, for I never feel as if I *could* make my mind up to that, it's too much like being a *woman*. Still I do think it's hard that the world should so interfere and mar one's happiness if it chances to know of love twixt two different in station like we are. . . . So let it be, only I don't wish the world to see me anything else nor a servant, but Massa's love I couldn't do without.[70]

At the end of July Hannah's banter with a carpenter who was working in the house turned into romantic interest on his part. Over the years she had received several invitations to 'walk out', including proposals of marriage. The carpenter was attracted to her earthiness, her physicality and

> made such flattering and winning speeches like, and he leant on the table till I was quite tickled and couldn't help laughing at him. I said, 'Please be quiet, I don't under-stand all that,' and told him how old I was but he didn't seem to believe it and asked me if he should come on Sunday to go out with me. I said, 'Oh certainly,' but it was only my fun.

Several times he tried to kiss her but she rejected him, and when his work in the house finished they shook hands and parted on friendly terms. Hannah was honest in her dealings with people and these tales of flirtations were told in a spirit of frankness, rather than trying to make Arthur jealous. Her surprise in the carpenter's interest in her shows how the emotional upheavals of 1871 had taken their toll on her confidence:

> There was something so absurd to the man seeming to like me that I was more amused than anything else and *it's so unusual for anyone to praise me in my dirt* except Massa that I never look for it. *Indeed I always take it for granted that I'm looked down on and despised.*[71]

On 10 August, Clara Manshardt, a new parlourmaid, arrived at Gloucester Crescent. Helping her up to the attic bedroom next to her own, Hannah liked the young German woman straightaway. She discovered that Clara had only been in service for four months and that she had left her last place because the work was too hard and the cook too ill-tempered. Hannah hoped they would be friends. Clara's arrival coincided with Arthur's long summer holiday. Hannah's diary reveals her to be a little infatuated: Clara taught her some German, they sometimes slept together and shared the same bath:

> Locked up after I'd made the arrowroot and gruel and to bed. Clara and me had a bath in my attic. She borrowed Miss Margaret's bath (as she is away) and we'd such a nice wash, but Clara prefers cold water . . . She rubbed me all dry and made me so comfortable.[72]

Hannah's intimacy with Clara and her sister Bertha reminded her of the closeness she had enjoyed with her own family. Loving Arthur had led to sacrifices: most of the time her sisters and extended family were ignored. She was philosophical that she and Arthur shared a powerful and painful destiny:

> and so I feel safest . . . when I'm at my regular work in service. When I was young I remember my whole mind used to be on going out or seeing my sisters or aunts, or anything belonging to the home – that was afore I knew

Massa – then was a new interest and what was much deeper and with it all sorts of joys and troubles and so it's lasted all this while – a mixture of pleasure and pain and after all who in this life is without both *and it's a settled delight to me knowing I am Massa's own servant and slave*, however difficult it is to feel he is really mine.[73]

Within six weeks of her arrival the Hendersons were showing displeasure with their new maid who thought she was 'a cut above' and too good to be a servant. Clara, who said she was unused to service, disliked being reprimanded when her work was not up to scratch and was 'very hasty in her temper and speaks out what she thinks'. Hannah was sad when Clara was dismissed, seeing none of her faults other than being 'careless and giddy but a good person . . . and I think she likes me very much'.[74] Clara was granted a reprieve and allowed to stay, but incurred Mrs Henderson's wrath when she was told that Hannah and Clara slept in the same bed.[75] The Hendersons gave Clara another warning and told her to sleep in her own bed in her own attic. During the period leading up to Christmas, relations between Hannah and Arthur were good and many 'pleasant' visits are recorded. His feet were washed and rubbed, his boots were licked and he was 'nursed like a baby'. Clara's growing influence upon Hannah may have unsettled Arthur and caused him some anxiety about how close a confidante she was.

Hannah looked forward to Christmas: her sisters would be staying with the Smiths: Mrs Smith was now eighty and lame, her daughter was forty-eight: they combined the roles of grandmother, mother and elder sister which Hannah, Ellen and Polly had missed. Arthur would be in York, and she looked forward to introducing Clara to her sisters and being shown the 'German way of decorating for Christmas'.

On Christmas morning, Clara was up at five, banging and

hammering in the kitchen. All were banned from entering until she had finished and was ready for them to see her handiwork and receive the gifts she had brought them. Hannah had a sense of foreboding about Clara's Christmas decorations and music.

> It was certainly very gay looking and pretty coloured paper cut and done in festoons all round the top of the kitchen and holly trimmings round the lower part. One side of the kitchen hung a picture of Jesus and the Wise Men, Joseph and Mary, and the oxen there too in the stall. Then under the picture was a table spread with presents for each of us, and nuts and biscuits and oranges too – in the middle was the box o' music playing and a dozen coloured candles burning. All very pleasing and gay to the senses but with it all I felt afraid it was too much for Missis to hear and Miss Margaret to see, for the Missis wouldn't allow us sixpence worth of holly and had none themselves. I didn't like to tell Clara but I felt that it was hardly safe and that I was sorry after the trouble she'd took with it and spent so much money. So I said nothing, but that it was very pretty and kind of her to do it.[76]

Instead of going to church as Mrs Henderson had told her to do, Hannah went to Clerkenwell to see the Smiths and her sisters, arranging for Polly to visit her the next day. She would hide Polly from the Hendersons when Miss Margaret came down to the kitchen. They all sang the German songs that Clara taught them, and some hymns and carols. Hannah was also feeling guilty that she had put Arthur before her own family:

> I've *done all* I can for both my sisters and Dick too, and would so still, but since they've grown up and gone away from me and I've had Massa to love and think about he certainly is first and chief and then I think he's so far

above us all and cannot and will not acknowledge them at all and me only when we're not seen. That after all it seems selfish and unsisterly of me to neglect them in the least.[77]

The first day of 1872 saw Hannah in a nervous mood: she was afraid that things were coming to a head between herself, Clara and the Hendersons for a number of reasons. She was sure that Clara's wilful attitude would not be tolerated much longer: she had had two warnings and her disobedience about letting 'the music box play all hours' and her 'random and careless behaviour' frightened Hannah. And Clara's extravagance at Christmas bothered her as she set much store on frugality and saving for the future. Hannah wrote as if she had been bewitched by the flighty parloumaid: 'But Clara calls me "Hannah dear" and will sleep with me and is so winning and determined to do as she likes that it's no use me talking to her. Only I *do* tell her of her faults if there's a chance the same as if she was a sister, but without any loving words.'[78]

After eighteen years Arthur's demands for lengthy descriptions of her humility in public, and in the privacy of his chambers, were insatiable, and Hannah obliged. It was important that she record the first day of each new year, to set a standard for the days and months to come. Hannah, who was superstitious, noted that Mr Smith, the grocer, had been the first man to enter the house after midnight: not good luck, she feared, as he had 'reddish hair'. The first 'foot-fall' into the house was supposed to be a dark-haired man, so Hannah added this to her unease about what the future would bring. Happily, some men stared at her scrubbing as they walked by, and she heard one say, 'What a dirty creature.' Hannah was delighted: now her Massa had evidence of her 'being low'.

On 6 January Hannah's brother Dick came to say that he

had lost his saddlery tools and a large quantity of leather in a fire at his lodgings in Shoreditch. Hannah worried more about her young brother than any of her other siblings, fearing he was kind and vulnerable:

> I felt sorry for him, cause I knew it was cause he was trying to help wi' their goods instead o' minding his own things and tho' they was insured, turned round on him and wouldn't help him a bit ... I felt sad and prayed heartily that God *would* help us through – poor orphans as we was left and still are at the mercy of strangers for a home, so whatever I may save I feel poor and unable to do what I should like to do either for myself or them.[79]

Two days later Mrs Henderson dismissed Hannah for the third and final time. Miss Margaret had agreed to her request to go out to see Arthur in the evening, but said that her mother wanted to see Hannah before she left. With the information that Hannah and Clara were deliberately disobeying her and still sleeping together, the noise of Clara's musical box jangling in her head, and Hannah's nocturnal visits to see heaven knows who, Mrs Henderson was determined to have her say:

> 'Hannah, I don't feel satisfied about your going out. I think you'd better leave me.' I says, 'Very well, ma'am.' She says, 'I heard a sermon last night which made me feel that my servants' souls are in my charge and I must say I can't understand about you. I should like to know more of your history.'

In the politest way Hannah told her to mind her own business and refused to answer any of Mrs Henderson's probing questions, other than to say that her sweeetheart was a Christian man, and that she was ' "pure and he is honourable, so I don't care what people think of me" '. Hannah backed out of the room, as servants did when leaving their superiors, 'vex'd yet glad to leave', and took the chance to move to Clerkenwell. The Smiths were now both lame, and needed Hannah's help around the house. It was with relief that Hannah went to the Temple where Arthur listened to her account with a mixture of concern and guilt:

> He was sorry and very much surprised at what I told him but I said, 'Don't be sorry – it'll all turn out for the best.' But however, it must be a trouble and it's happened a good many times through the same thing – that is from my loving Massa – one so much unequal to me so as I canna tell about him. But I know as there's no harm in it. I don't really care and as I've got on so far I may go on further. . . . Massa was kind and nice through the evening and seemed to feel for me especially as he said it was chiefly through my loving him.[80]

Afer Christmas, Arthur had returned to London determined to re-order Hannah's place in his life, and he decided to tell his friend from Trinity, Henry James, about her. On 24 January the two men went back to Arthur's chambers for a smoke after they had dined out, and reminisced about their student days. Arthur showed him 'that lovely picture of my darling' and his friend was impressed: '"It is indeed a fine face, a remarkable face."'[81] Later that day Hannah visited Arthur and was proud, and worried, to hear that he 'has shown my likeness to a gentleman friend of his and had almost told him about me'. Hannah was glad because it showed that 'he does love me', but afraid lest their love cause him any 'disgrace':

> and I canna bear for anyone to think I want to be anything but what I *am* to him. And so I want no one to know – I want to love him heartily and only him as I

always have. To be as useful as I possibly can to him and do as much as I possibly can for him.[82]

Four days later Arthur plucked up courage to tell 'Jamie', his first male friend, about his misalliance with Hannah:

after much hesitation, I told my old friend all the story, at least all we had time for – of her whose picture he saw the other day, and he gave me hearing and sympathetic counsel, though he could not fully understand the position ... And so I parted from my dear old Jamie, refreshed and brightened and more.[83]

One morning before she left the Hendersons, Hannah was photographed as she scrubbed the front steps: the only picture of her working. She had arranged for a street photographer to take two pictures of her that could be made into cards for Arthur. It was to be done quickly as she did not want the Hendersons to find out and was afraid of the remarks of passers-by.[84] She wore her scouring apron, her sleeeves were rolled up and the wrist-strap was visible. The Hendersons' house looked dingy: speckled by the smuts from the myriad of coal fires that burned all year round. As Hannah clenched the mat and broom her forearm muscles were flexed. Beyond her was the basement kitchen, Hannah's domain and the engine-room of the house.

On one of the last evenings she worked for the Hendersons, Hannah was sent to collect their visitor, Miss Beamish, from a party. This clergyman's daughter was curious about Hannah's 'gentleman' about whom she refused to speak. Miss Beamish probed Hannah for any scrap of information she could report back to her hosts, but Hannah held her ground and did not fall into the friendly traps that the lady laid for her as they walked home. Miss Beamish remarked:

'Well, Hannah, it does seem strange that you've known a man so long and been engaged and not married' and I said, 'Yes, ma'am, it's natural perhaps that other people should put the worst side to it, and think it strange but they don't *know* and I don't think I am forced to tell them, nor it wouldn't be right of me to tell a missis either without *his* leave, and there ought to be no reason either at my age.'

Hannah sidestepped most of the questions, but agreed to show the inquisitive lady 'a bit of his writing and his verses'. There was little chance that Miss Beamish would recognize his poetry. Hannah had derived pleasure from telling her even a little about Arthur: it was thrilling for Hannah to be able to talk of him. She confirmed that he was indeed a gentleman and that they had known each other for seventeen years, and implied that theirs was a celibate relationship: 'if anyone thought of it in a religious way or with commonsense they'd know such a thing couldn't of lasted *sinfully* so long or a quarter of the time'. Hannah was later racked with worry about what she had told Miss Beamish and if she had said too much, and what Massa would think of what she had said.[85]

As the time drew near for Hannah to leave, there was talk of going with Clara to Germany to meet her parents. Arthur was relieved when the idea was abandoned. Hannah was mystified by Clara's increased extravagance: she had four new dresses delivered to Gloucester Crescent by her own dress-maker, 'trimmed up so fine and she'd bought no end of things, new bonnets, and umbrella and parasol and things to take to Germany'.[86]

On the night of Hannah's last day at the Hendersons', Clara had insisted on sleeping with Hannah 'and seems to be very sorry I'm going away afore her. She leaves next week and is going to Germany to see her mother and friends'.[87] Next

morning Hannah said goodbye to Mrs Henderson, received
her wages and went to collect four guineas she had in the
kitchen drawer, and 'it was gone!' Hannah was sure it had
been taken by one of the servants, wondered if it was the lad
'cause he knew where my money was', but rejected him as a
suspect because she trusted him. She felt sick at the discovery
and too upset to do anything:

> I didn't feel very strong to say much or do much about
> it, so I bore it as quietly as I could. When Emily came
> home I told her of it and she turned everything over and
> Clara ran upstairs to tell the missis that I'd bin robbed.
> I shouldn't o' told her for I knew the missis'd blame me
> above all others for leaving it unlock'd so I meant to go
> away without saying ... and she *did* blame me and
> wanted me to have a detective in to search the boy's
> things. But I said, 'No ... leave it alone, ma'am, and
> don't you worry yourself – it'll come round some day.'[88]

It was a traumatic departure for Hannah. She cried in
shock at the theft of her hard-earned wages and the likelihood
that one of the people who kissed her goodbye had stolen her
money. A hansom cab was called to take her to Clerkenwell,
and Clara helped her up the area steps with her boxes and
bundles, and 'she above all the rest seemed to pity me for my
loss'. It was a cold, frosty night and Hannah reached the
Smiths at ten o'clock in low spirits.

The following evening she visited Arthur at his chambers
and had a shock. Rather than being sympathetic about the
theft, he was '*angry* ... and wouldn't be nice. So instead of
being comforted as I expected I felt more alone, unsettled and
unhappy.' Arthur left her to teach his class at the Working
Women's College and Hannah went to the eight o'clock
service at the Temple Church where she felt 'very *lonely* as if
there was nothing to live for, and as if it would be good for

me if it was *over*.[89] She visited Arthur the next day with trepidation, but was overjoyed when he apologized for being so hard the night before. Ten days later Emily came to tea at the Smiths' and told Hannah of her suspicions about Clara's honesty, suggesting that Hannah do some detective work by going to see Clara's previous mistress.[90]

Two nights later and Hannah was back at Fig Tree Court doing chores. While she mended his clothes, Arthur fell asleep. When she had finished he was still sleeping, and she took a photograph album out of a drawer, and was annoyed to see

a likeness of Massa took with that woman without a nose, what made me very angry as I heard her speak so freely to him when she went away. His hands were touching hers in the picture and she'd a rose in her hair. And it made me feel so angry, no one can tell, and so I was very disagreeable with Massa when he woke up but I wouldn't tell him what it was for ever so long.[91]

This is a rare case of Hannah expressing jealousy of Arthur's friendship with other working women. She told him the reason for her bad mood: 'when he knew he wasn't surprised at me, so I got a little better but I couldn't forget it'. One factor had been Arthur taking Harriet to be photographed by 'their' man Mr Fink. He apologized, reassured her and 'we got right again and cried together like children'.[92]

In March, Arthur considered renting a house in Richmond: maybe he thought that he and Hannah could live there as man and wife, where they were not known. He abandoned the plan.

In April, Emily went to have tea with Hannah: they talked about 'poor silly Clara being such a thief and how was the best way for me to stop her doing the same thing again'. Emily also brought a note from Miss Margaret who knew of a lady who needed a charwoman. Hannah and Arthur were pleased at the prospect of her finding a place and they arranged to meet at the South Kensington Museum the following evening after she had been to see a Miss Otway in Eaton Terrace, Belgravia. Hannah arrived at the appointed time but was kept waiting in the street for half an hour until Miss Otway returned. Hannah's first impression of her was of a lady walking a little dog on a string, followed by 'a funny looking little lad' who was her page-boy. She was eccentric in the interview, arranging for Hannah to return the following evening when the charwoman, Mrs Ingle, had been got rid of. They agreed on the wages, and while Miss Otway's manner and conversation were odd, Hannah reasoned that she looked like a lady and there was no cause for concern as she was a friend of Miss Margaret and Miss Beamish.

On 9 April, Arthur escorted Hannah to her new place. Once she was in the house Miss Otway told her to go down to the kitchen and locked the front door. Hannah's heart sank:

> it was such a miserable little kitchen ... and it didn't smell at all wholesome and there was no one down there, so I could only sit and wonder. There was a dull light of just a bit o' candle and bye and bye a charwoman came downstairs from doing the lady's bedroom. I got up and wished her a good evening and said could I go out for four-pence half-penny's worth of beer and she said 'No', she was sure Miss Otway wouldn't let me out at that time.[93]

Arthur waited for half an hour and then went home feeling apprehensive, not liking the look of the place. Hannah heard from the charwoman that Miss Otway had a high turnover of staff: she was reluctant to pay their wages and if anyone stayed longer than two weeks they were considered 'old servants'. Jane the housemaid appeared and said that the only way they would get their money would be by 'sticking up for it'. Jane showed Hannah her attic bedroom which was as grim as the kitchen: the room was dirty though the bed was clean. The following day Jane showed Hannah round the house, creeping past Miss Otway's bedroom for fear of waking the dog. Hannah had to ask for the key to the dining room before she could go in and clean. Miss Otway had taken all the keys to bed with her, even the key to the front door. Hannah rolled up her sleeves to do battle with the once smart town-house that was festooned with black cobwebs:

> it was in such a mess as I'd never seen, but I thought it was a capital chance for me to show I didn't mind doing dirty work, but that I liked it so long as it was doing some good and I was determined to make the best of the chance.[94]

Within three days Hannah found out how unbalanced Miss Otway was: her frugality in doling out bits of soap to clean a house that was squalid; her bedroom which was a complete mess as she had most of her meals in there and bathed there too; her insistence that the door handle should only be turned in a particular way. The strangeness of this new job was relieved by news from Emily that Clara was due to return from Germany. Hannah resolved to confront her. She explained what had happened to Miss Otway, who proved surprisingly understanding and allowed her some time off to go and find Clara. Hannah quickly tracked her down to 17 Hackney Road, in the East End, and there learned some uncomfortable truths. It was a 'little low house' where she met an old man and his young assistant, Clara's father and brother, who were supposed to be opening a bakery in Germany. Hannah sat and waited for Clara to return: it soon emerged that the German parlourmaid was a thief and a fantasist. She had not been abroad, and, confronted by Hannah's hurt and anger, broke down in tears, expressing her remorse for stealing the money. Hannah's impassioned words show her to be a kind woman:

> 'I don't want you cast down, only I want to be a true friend as I always was . . . and you always pretended to be so fond o' me, that I should never o' judged you . . . an' your deceit to me was worse nor the thieving, for you seemed so open and frank and almost as if you loved me and I said I *did* love you and I do now.'[95]

Hannah did not leave empty-handed, taking a brooch and earrings and 'two grand nightgowns and four shifts' in lieu of the money Clara had stolen.

Late one evening Miss Otway called Hannah up to her room and ordered her to search the building as she was sure there was a man in the house, making her 'go into the coalhole – the dusthole – the knifehole and any other hole under the stairs poking with a big stick as well as going right in there'.[96] Hannah knew there was no one there but had to humour her mistress.

A couple of days later Hannah was feeling very out of sorts: she had lost a stone and a half in recent months. Arthur 'was so anxious about me' and took her to King's College Hospital where 'lots o' poor folks go and sit on Wednesdays and Saturdays, but me having a letter of recommendation [from Arthur] I got up sooner nor the rest that haven't'. She did not dare ask for the time off, so she slipped out and hoped Miss Otway would not find out. It was an uncomfortable journey: Arthur was happy to walk with her but she felt too ashamed to be seen with him looking so

> shabby in my old milkwomen's bonnet and grey cloak and my ragged cotton frock and apron and my boots all wore down . . . and my bare hands looked rough and

black lined with dirty work ... I couldn't walk with Massa in the street cause o' been so poor looking.[97]

The doctor examined her and prescribed a tonic and Hannah hurried back where she collided in the hallway with Miss Otway, angry that she had gone out without her permission. Hannah could sense that her stay at Eaton Terrace would soon be at an end but she would not cut any corners: she cleaned the house from top to bottom on her hands and knees.

During the six weeks Hannah worked for her, Miss Otway's behaviour became increasingly erratic. She would delight in being vile to Hannah in front of her guests, yet at other times she would call her away from her work and play the piano for her and reminisce. One evening she sought her charwoman's opinion of an extravagant new bonnet: Hannah had learned to humour her:

I said, 'It's a very grand bonnet, ma'am, and looks nice,' and Miss Otway seemed so pleased. However I didn't think she looked nice in the bonnet, for she's elderly and grey headed with little hair and it was a fashionable headdress ... with flowers and feathers stuck high up, seeming to make her face look older.[98]

One day Miss Otway unlocked the door of a watercloset that had not been opened for years and ordered Hannah to clean it. The window was jammed shut and Hannah dared not open it for ventilation in case it disintegrated. There was a tiny hole in the corner of one of the panes and Miss Otway explained that

the Emperor sent spirits to hook the leaves off her plants through. They *fell* off as leaves do, but she often called me in to see the satanic fires going up, as she said *he* sent up and that he worked his sorceries in the rooms opposite and she would watch for hours – but it was nothing but lamps burning and as for lights I could never see them, but she said, 'Ah, they stop when they see you looking.'[99]

The following day Hannah had to pawn her watch to pay for food for their supper, the second time she had to do this. She was cross at having to ask for money and to pay the omnibus fare to the pawnbroker's. There was also the matter of the beer allowance which had rarely been paid. Hannah asked for the money Miss Otway owed her and for food for the forthcoming week:

> I told Miss Otway I should be much obliged to her if she would give me some money – that I was never so short afore and I thought that [it] was most disgraceful living with a lady and having to pawn my watch for one's own dinner. And I said I would ask Miss Henderson to lend me some money if Miss Otway would let me go to see her.

This bold tactic worked, but Hannah knew she could not stay much longer. On 7 May, Miss Otway wrote her a note of dismissal. Before Hannah had worked her notice she was in agony with a septic thumb and had to have it lanced at a chemist's shop. The man used a knife to 'give it such a cut as I shall never forget'.[100] Miss Otway developed a phobia about having to touch anything that might have come into contact with Hannah's thumb. In between painful visits to the chemist's to have the wound dressed, Hannah did her best to do her job but had to leave as the thumb was causing her such pain she could go on no longer: she wanted the six weeks' wages due to her. There was a dispute over how much: Miss Otway cheated her out of two weeks' pay, but Hannah was relieved to get three guineas, fearing she would get nothing at all. Miss Otway was aggrieved to have to pay and barely spoke when Hannah left the parlour. On her way back to Clerken-well, Hannah visited Arthur at the Temple where he was

> so pleased to see me I was just like one let out o' prison, but I daren't stop long – it was nearly eleven and Mrs Smith didn't know I was coming. So after a nice kiss or two and a little talk I started off again and had a [hansom] cab.[101]

The weekend of Hannah's thirty-ninth birthday Arthur took her to Greeenwich for the day, and on to Southend by boat to a hotel for a night, sleeping in separate rooms. It was the first time they had been away for a night together and was the beginning of a stage in their relationship when Hannah would be dressed up as a 'lady' and taken away for the weekend. This was a drama they had been acting out for years, in the privacy of Arthur's chambers. For him, the role was easy and he was only concerned in case she made a mistake; for Hannah, every time she walked out it was her debut.

On her birthday they went to church in Southend, walked through the fields and along the coast, she read poetry to him and they strolled in a heavily scented garden. In the hotel Hannah was nervous as she waited for Arthur to take her into the dining room. She was unused to having her head bare: for many years it was under a white cotton cap, and she struggled to brush and comb it into some kind of style. She coped in her first performance, however:

> I felt just a bit awkward . . . when my chair was put for me at the table and the waiter took the covers off and waited on us. But Massa said I behaved pretty well all through and it was soon bedtime and Massa was kind and took care o' my thumb all the while.[102]

Next morning they caught the early train to London:
Hannah had been awakened by the songs of the cuckoo and
blackbirds and thrushes, an idyllic start to the day. On arrival,
Arthur insisted on walking through the City arm-in-arm with
her and Hannah was thrilled when he kissed her 'heartily' and
invited her to Fig Tree Court the following day.

The birthday emboldened him in his plan to marry Hannah and install her as his housekeeper in his chambers where
they would live secretly as man and wife: 'And when will this
long tragedy be over and I be able to do justice to that divinely
beautiful soul and to myself?' He told Julie Bovet about his
plans and she tried to dissuade him.[103]

On 7 June Polly arrived from Ipswich, and on the eleventh
Hannah and her sisters travelled to Shifnal. The journey was
full of gaiety: this was the first time they had gone homewards
together. Hannah had meant to go before but had been afraid
of stirring up sadness:

> It generally has made me feel dull – going alone and
> having really no home to go to, nor anywhere as one can
> feel sure of being welcome for any time and then the
> remembrances o' one's home and mother and one's child-
> ish days all come up again and makes me so sad and to
> enjoy a cry to myself in the lanes or the churchyard more
> nor anything else. So as I never cared *much* about going
> but this time I've got company and we was all very jolly
> together.[104]

They did the usual round of visiting: brother Jim and his
second wife Lizzie at Wombridge, and aunts, uncles and
cousins in Shifnal. But by the end of the holiday the sisters
had quarrelled – Hannah thought they behaved 'too proudly'
– and she refused to say goodbye to Ellen and Polly before
they caught the train to London, which she instantly regretted,
and cried with frustration at how their happy holiday had

ended in discord. The silent presence of Arthur was never far
from Hannah's interactions with her sisters: they felt snubbed
by his earlier refusal to acknowledge them, and resentful that
she placed his happiness over theirs. Hannah was punished for
having a gentleman as a sweetheart, which they knew would
bring trouble if the secret was revealed.

Hannah stayed on and was visiting Aunt Sarah in Shifnal
when there was a loud knock and she was amazed to see
Arthur's face through a crack in the door. She just stopped
herself from calling him Massa:

> and he kissed my aunt and said, 'You know we've been
> sweethearts a good while and it's time things was settled –
> you used to tell Hannah to have nothing to do with me
> and I like you the better for it but I think you know
> pretty well now there's bin no harm in it and that I've
> always meant well.' And Aunt said, 'I thought not good
> of it at first, but I left it to Hannah's sense and I was
> never afraid of her going wrong' or something to that
> effect and Aunt looked as surprised as I felt and we didn't
> get over it till long after Massa was gone to the inn where
> he was to sleep. We sat talking it over and Aunt made a
> fresh cup of tea.[105]

Next day Hannah and Arthur walked to Wombridge where
he was to be introduced to Jim and his family. Oddly, Arthur
picked a quarrel with Hannah because she had not brought
the right bonnet to Shifnal. The way Hannah tells the story,
it was a trivial matter which upset her: she was relieved
when he 'forgave me and kissed me'. Luckily all was well
by the time they reached Jim's cottage where Lizzie provided
tea and 'they was very civil to one another . . . [Lizzie] was
respectful and spoke just as I could o' wished her so I was
glad.'[106] Two days later Hannah took Arthur on a nostalgic
walk to Tong where her mother's family, the Owens, had

come from, passing her old school on the way. The following day they walked to Ryton and saw the rectory where she had heard that her parents had died, returning for him to get the train back to London and then on to his parents in York. During this time Arthur had met several of Hannah's female cousins and aunts.

Hannah stayed on in Shifnal, working on a cousin's farm during July: haymaking, milking cows, fruit-picking, taking the women workers their tea. Her days were filled with brilliant sunshine, bread and cheese, homemade beer, moonlit nights, and plenty of interest from men in the fields. At the end of the month Hannah went to Newport to have photographs taken by Henry Howle in the High Street. She wore her own clothes as a Shropshire peasant and held a pikel, a pitch-fork used to gather up the hay. Mr Howle admired her arms which he thought 'big and fine'. Hannah was posed reading a letter from Arthur.[107] Arthur was pleased with Howle's work and sent Hannah back for more 'fresh likenesses' to be taken.[108]

On 8 August Arthur walked to St Paul's and bought a marriage licence from the office of the Doctor's Commons, enabling him and Hannah to be wed in the church of the parish that one or both of them had lived in for a minimum of fifteen days. Privacy was assured; it was the only option open to couples wishing to avoid the calling of the banns for three consecutive Sundays, which was how most couples were married. By 11 August Arthur was in York, their marriage licence in his breast pocket, waiting for the right moment to tell his parents about Hannah, and his plans to make her Mrs Munby.

On 14 August, Hannah walked some miles to Church Aston to see the wedding of a butcher's daughter. Suffering as she was with housemaid's knee, it is odd that she made this journey. Arthur's remark to her aunt that he thought it was time 'things was settled' was the reason for it. The wedding was quite a grand affair: 'three carriages with two grey [horses] in each'. The bride wore a mauve silk dress with a tulle veil. The ceremony was held up because the licence had been forgotten, and Hannah chatted to a local woman who had come to watch. While she waited in the church she read the burial and wedding services a few times. Perhaps thinking of her parents' unhappy marriage, she preferred the burial service:

> Somehow weddings always make me sad and I care very little to see the fine dresses or carriages tho' they do look gay. I suppose it's because o' that and knowing how empty it all is mostly seeing how unhappily they often turn out and I thought the burial service was much the best and to be coveted till I was forced to cry a bit and yet I was ashamed for the women to see me and I didn't keep it on.[109]

Two days later Arthur wrote Hannah a long letter about his plans for their future which he hoped 'if all's well' would materalize in September. He also told her of

> the trouble he felt over it too – he at home and not liking to tell his dear mother and father and still not to do it – so one may guess how I feel about it as well – more than I can say, or to make anybody quite understand how I wish it and yet *don't* wish it. Perhaps Massa will know and I wrote as much as I could about it.[110]

Arthur was so afraid of what his parents' reaction might be that he waited until the twenty-sixth, the last night of his stay, to broach the subject with 'the father'. Joseph Munby raged when he learned that Hannah was a servant: the bridegroom-to-be described it as a 'pathetic and terrible scene' and begged 'the father' not to tell 'the mother'.[111] Arthur wanted to get married, whereas Hannah was ambivalent.

On 9 September, Hannah started her round of goodbyes. Although she had enjoyed her time in Shropshire, she missed Arthur, but on the journey home she worried about what lay in store. Arthur met her at Paddington and took her to the Temple in a cab and 'kissed me kindly' and she 'did some little jobs for him' and went to her lodgings at the Smiths.[112]

On 12 September, Arthur employed Hannah to look after his chambers while he was on holiday in France. This was the beginning of her career as his caretaker, later housekeeper: it was an obvious solution to some of their difficulties, and Hannah leaped at the chance to go and work for him. On Friday the thirteenth she spent her first night at Fig Tree Court in her new role, packing his portmanteau ready for the next day. Hannah washed and rubbed Arthur's feet and 'they petted a bit and Massa knelt by me and prayed for both of us. I went to my bed in the back room.'[113] Hannah took his luggage to Charing Cross station and discreetly waved him off on his trip to Paris which might have been their honeymoon: instead, Hannah had to be content with Arthur's canary and tortoise for company. When she had seen him off she returned to the Temple and set about cleaning the place. She was nervous of meeting the chambers' housekeeper, Mrs Newton, who had replaced Mrs Mitchell, sacked for drunkenness, and was shy of the many male servants who thronged the courts and alleyways of the village within a city that was the Inner Temple. After a couple of nights in the back room, she slept in Arthur's bed, where she felt closer to him. She never minded him travelling without her, but since his riding accident she was often anxious.

Hannah had to learn about Arthur's tenants and any danger they posed in discovering the secret. Four other barristers were listed at 6 Fig Tree Court, sometimes they slept there, other times not: William Shedden Ralsten; Josiah Rees; David Featherbury and Owen S. Wilson.[114] Tarrant, an ex-soldier who was batman to a near neighbour, spent a lot of time in Hannah's kitchen and sometimes made a nuisance of himself. She worried that he might behave like Gower the footman and uncover who she really was in Mr Munby's life. Hannah was careful to handle him firmly and gently: she refused to appear prudish about him trying to kiss her and was not deceived by his mock dismay when she refused him.

When time permitted, Hannah visited her friends in Clerkenwell. She longed for Arthur's return on 29 September and spent two secret nights with him and then returned to lodge with the Smiths. Arthur returned braver about the situation, planning to tell the Reverend J. E. Vaux, a college friend who wrote for the *Church Times*, about Hannah, and planned to ask him to marry them.

Hannah's sister Ellen had left her place and they were sharing a room in Clerkenwell. Arthur allowed Hannah to store her boxes at his chambers: she was moving in slowly and sharing his life secretly. In the middle of October they discussed Hannah living at the Temple as his servant. On the sixteenth Arthur dined with Vaux but his shyness and fear of a bad reaction forced him to abandon sharing their secret with his friend.

On 21 October Arthur was called to York as his brother John was very ill and not expected to live. He died six days later of 'a congestion of the kidneys . . . and a congested heart'.[115]

During the autumn Arthur made the decision that while his family would not be told about his misalliance with Hannah, he would introduce her to his best friend, the Reverend Borland. On 14 November, after some coaching from Arthur, Hannah, feeling 'a little nervous', dressed in her best black frock, pinned up her hair and composed herself as best she could. While she waited she rehearsed what she planned to say. When Arthur introduced her to Borland he looked

white and worried. I got up and curtsied ... I rather
stammered and felt as if there was no use saying my
speech what I'd made up. Massa had told him all, but still
I felt I *must say something....* This is the first time I've
been shown to any of his friends and I never wished,
indeed hoped never to be. Massa and I have spent so
many hours together in this room *alone* and ours is like a
stolen love you know and when it's known it seems like
a *shame.* It seems as if the *charm has broken.*

Arthur left them talking together. Borland spoke to her
'kindly, but very seriously' and tried to persuade her to give
up the relationship. Borland, who knew Arthur's parents, tried
every argument he could muster to get Hannah to see that
her duty lay in ending the affair. An educated man with years
of sermonizing behind him could not dent her ardour, however:

he spoke his mind freely and so did I. I couldn't o' course
tell him *what* a peculiar love ours had bin, but I said it
was quite impossible not to go on loving one another, but
that I never wanted it known. I wanted to be a help not a
hindrance to him and I asked him lots of questions and
was quite free and open with him, not afraid at all ... we
talked an hour or two more and at last he stopped and
knocked for Massa, but he'd gone fast asleep and I'd to
call him.[116]

Hannah felt 'very sad' after her talk with the clergyman.
She did not 'like the meaning of what he said and I was
surprised and sad rather at Massa wanting *his* advice about
what to do with me'. As it was late and raining Arthur gave
her money for a cab to Clerkenwell. The following day she
tried to imagine what the men had said to each other.

During November Hannah was nearly caught washing
Arthur's feet when a lady and gentleman called unexpectedly.

She just managed to escape with the basin of water and hide in the back room while he put his stockings and shoes on. The unwelcome visitors stayed for ages and Arthur told them he was going out to hurry them on their way. Arthur objected to the indignity of Hannah having to hide more than she did, but her words of comfort probably made him feel worse:

> I told him that it didn't matter a bit to me, for many a time I've bin crouched in the cupboard and hid in the back room and no one dreamed of a soul being there.

Just before the couple had arrived, Arthur had shown Hannah their marriage licence and asked her what she felt about it. She told him she had '*nothing* to say about it' and hoped neither of them would ever regret it. She knew she was behaving 'so cool and said so little' but she was not acting for she 'really *meant* what I said'. In the period leading up to their wedding, Hannah was some days unmoved, and on other days unhappy about the prospect of being a secret Mrs Munby. It was not that she did not love Arthur – she certainly did – but she argued that their love was special and not like other people's:

> I said *very* little for the licence or being married either – indeed I've a certain dislike to either – they seem to have so little to do with our *love* and our union. They are things that every common sweethearts use when they love really or not and ours has bin for so long a *faithful* and *trustful* pure love, without any outward bond and I do seem to *hate* the word marriage in *that* sense. And yet I respect it as a *duty* which ought to be done on Massa's part, not as a *reward* to me, for I want *no* reward, but as a simple duty he owes himself, cause I canna be with him nor serve him as a servant, nor be a helpmeet for him as I ought cause of my name.[117]

Hannah left the Smiths and moved into Fig Tree Court as Mr Munby's maid of all work. Mrs Newton gossiped about their employer in such a way as to make his prospective bride smile. She told Hannah he was a 'good payer' and she liked him, but complained that he was 'very fidgetty and old-maidish'. Arthur would ask Hannah to be scrubbing outside in the court when he came home from the office. He looked forward to finding her cleaning the grating of the drains and washing the flags with her hands, and looking like 'a regular drudge'.

The first act of their new drama opened disastrously. They were unrehearsed and nervous and both got into a muddle about their lines:

> I'd forgotten about his coming and and it was nearly dark. 'Is that you, Hannah?' 'Yes, Massa, it is,' I said quite low – but it seemed he didn't hear me say it and then he said, 'What time did you come?' I felt confused and said, 'This afternoon,' still low and I crept in at the [kitchen] window. Then Massa came down to the kitchen and spoke again. I didn't say 'Sir' of course cause I'd no idea anyone was above listening. Then Massa went upstairs and rang the bell and I thought, 'Well that is showing off certainly' and I went upstairs with my temper up to its highest, and Massa begun to question me about not saying '*Sir*' to him as the lad was out on the stairs. I felt so *angry* cause I thought if Massa knew the boy was on the stairs he oughtn't to come down, not only for the humiliation [on] the first day, but because I didn't even know Massa kept a lad as a clerk. So I was really in a passion and said a great deal I didn't *mean*.[118]

A row erupted and Hannah shouted that if he 'tantalized her like that again she would leave him whether they were married or not'. She did not care about marriage, and was indignant that he had humiliated her in such a way. She did not sleep well and the next morning found a letter from Arthur telling her to take her things and return to Mrs Smith's: 'he felt it'd never do for me to be here in disguise. And so my trouble commenced again.'

Hannah did not regret what she had said: she had overheard him speaking 'crossly' and 'sharp' to Mrs Mitchell many times, and would not put up with Arthur speaking to her in that way. If she had tolerated this, she argued, she knew she would

> go out of my mind and a bad end would come to him as well as me, for I canna bear it, although I'm humble and wish to be only like a *servant*, but for him I've sacrificed so much and done so much for and loved so unselfishly and disinterestedly, that I will *not* be mocked or decried.[119]

Hannah sensed that Arthur was serious and wanted her to leave him but she was determined that if he sent her away now he would never see her again. She carried on with her chores and at three o'clock that day he returned to the Temple from Whitehall and took the keys to his chambers from her, then relented and gave them back. Hannah returned to the Smiths' and barely slept. The following day she wrote to Arthur and felt 'most wretched. I wished most sincerely that my time was nearly at an end by God's will, for my life seemed a burden instead of a joy as it ought to be.'[120]

Hannah persuaded Ellen to show her the letter that Arthur had written to her sister giving his account of their quarrel. He had told her that Hannah's conduct prevented him from using the marriage licence: but Ellen was being told only part of the story, and Hannah was ashamed to tell her sister that Arthur had expected her to call him 'Sir'. While Hannah was at the Smiths', he visited Ellen, and wished Hannah 'a kind good night'. Hannah felt discomforted by this alliance-building with her sister, and Ellen was probably bewildered to be the subject of Munby's attentions after so many years of indifference.

Hannah continued to work for Arthur. Four days after the row, he summoned Ellen to the Temple to discuss Hannah, who was sent out on errands. On her return she was unsettled to find them joking about her being jealous, and about being kissed by him in front of Ellen. Her sister had little faith in men and a jealous streak: she had a sweetheart but did not trust him, and Hannah agonized about Arthur's motives:

> If Massa only sent for her to tell her my faults and his not knowing what to do with me, I don't like that for it seems mean, but if it's to be friendly with her cause of me of course I *like* it, for I've always thought my sisters were prejudiced against Massa and would hardly be civil to him if he wished to see 'em – his never having spoken to them before they oughtn't to lay [sic] to me, cause I've always told 'em I'd never be anything nearer to him than I was till he *was* friendly with 'em. And yet they've both treated me slightly and unkind lately.[121]

Arthur gave Hannah orders for Monday, wished them both goodbye, and set off for two nights in the country. Hannah walked her sister part of the way back to Clerkenwell and returned to a restless night in the back room at Fig Tree Court. Early in the following week Hannah could tolerate Arthur's coldness no longer, and in an emotional speech on the evening of Tuesday, 3 December, she

> couldn't help telling him how he'd crushed my spirits altogether and that I couldn't bear for him to be cross with me. He *mustn't* if he car'd anything for me and I told him how he didn't seem to know *how* much I'd suffered and so he couldn't tell how *low* I felt. Massa

seemed almost surprised and yet I thought he knew everything at last and told me there was no one in the world he cared for so much as me. So I was a bit better and went to bed in the kitchen.[122]

Arthur relented a little. He had ordered Hannah to sleep in the kitchen rather than the back room in case 'folks talked'. A maid of all work would be expected to sleep in the kitchen, and if someone had known where she was sleeping they might have wondered why she had been given special treatment. Arthur was also punishing her for the emotional upheaval he was experiencing. After her tearful speech and their halting reconciliation, he came down to the kitchen bringing a rug for her to use as a curtain so that she would not feel the damp. Before a solicitous good night he told her to keep a good fire burning.

The rituals of their life were slowly re-introduced: she washed his feet, made his cigarettes and resumed all the duties and the appearance of a drudge. Hannah received an offer of a job via Miss Beamish, but after thinking it over she declined it as it was for an 'upper servant'. On 7 December Arthur became aware of Tarrant's interest in Hannah: he heard him tickling Hannah under the arms as she cleaned the stairs on her hands and knees. He heard her giggling and the two of them talking and later remonstrated with her that she should have shown

more dignity and not allowed Tarrant to touch me, but there was no one harmed and and I hate to seem prudish — besides I know better how to deal with a fellow like Tarrant better nor Massa can tell me. I don't *like* him . . . but it's only polite to be civil to a neighbour.[123]

Hannah was upset by Arthur's continued correspondence with Ellen. She felt he was keeping alive the misery of the

row, and driving a wedge between her and her sister. On 13
December Hannah walked over to Clerkenwell to attempt to
read the letter that he had just written to Ellen, but her sister

> was in two minds about letting me see it and it made me
> cross with her again, as usual cause she will *not* trust me
> nor behave sisterly and kind to me and when I told Massa
> this evening he was vexed with me again through it,
> for he seems determined that my sisters and me *shall*
> be friends. Of course I'm glad of it, but it's not so easy
> to be all in all when they've little by little forsook me
> through Massa, because he never asked to see them in all
> these years. So my happiness was checked again.[124]

Hannah seems to have worried about very little: when she
read the letter she was relieved that it was 'a very nice one and
I wanted my sister Mary [Polly] to see it'. She also wondered
why Ellen had been so reluctant to show it to her. Hannah
felt uneasy about the tensions in her relationship with Arthur
being refracted through her sister, and her emotions being
manipulated. Hannah could not understand why Munby set
such store by her 'not falling out with Ellen' and the anxiety
'made the *weight* come on my chest again and I was miserable
cause I *canna* understand what troubles Massa so'.

Arthur's mood improved noticeably after he saw her '*black*
doing the stairs. I cleaned the watercloset and the kitchen out
on my hands and knees.' The following evening he went
down to see if she was comfortable in her bed. Their old
unusual regimes were returning to Fig Tree Court. Seeing
Hannah black and watching her become black restored
Arthur's emotional stability and his tender ways returned. In
the mornings she woke him up and the first question he
would ask was if she was black, and he went to some trouble
to stage-manage her cleaning schedule.

On Saturday, 21 December, he ordered that she should be

'very black' cleaning the stairs when he came back after his half-day at the Ecclesiastical Commission. Hannah was still cleaning the kitchen hearth on her hands and knees on his return. Seeing him standing in the doorway, she smeared her arms with blacklead and rubbed them across her face, asking if she was not black enough. The effect was just what he had wanted and 'there was scarce a place clean enough for him to kiss me but he *did* and then went upstairs'. Hannah was wearing a red frock turned up to the mid-calf, striped apron and peasant's bonnet, and a 'blacker drudge you couldn't see in a day's march'.[125]

On Christmas Eve Arthur left London for York, as he did every year. They took his luggage to King's Cross station where he tenderly kissed Hannah goodbye. She walked to Clerkenwell, taking with her a goose for Christmas lunch. She feared that this might be the last Christmas she would have with Mrs Smith who was now very frail.

As Arthur travelled north he reviewed the events of the recent past: his father's fury at the heavily edited story of his sweetheart; Borland's horror; the stormy times with Hannah, and the sudden death of his brother John. The family would be in deep mourning; the menfolk were required to wear black armbands, but his mother, sister, his brother's widow, Margaret, and the nieces were swathed in black. Arthur's mother and sister had not been long out of the half-mourning of pinstripe black, purple and grey, and jet jewellery, worn after his brother Joe's death in 1867. Arthur found his 'dear mother, feeble in health and troubled' and 'the father' who was 'distressed at the loss of another son and anxious about his own affairs' concerned enough about money to sell some of their land. Arthur wondered how much longer his father would want to, or be able to, pay his rent on Fig Tree Court, and frightened himself when he thought about the prospect of being at the centre of a sensational misalliance story and the certainty of being 'divorced' by his family, friends, colleagues and society. While he was at home, he and his old nurse Hannah consoled each other about the death of John: she mourned the loss of the boy she had cared for as a child. She had no children of her own and she had been a surrogate mother to the Munby children. The time Arthur spent with Hannah Carter was a catalyst for memories of his childhood and adolescence to flood back.

Over the holiday his other Hannah slept at the Temple in his bed, and spent as much time as she could with the Smiths and Ellen. On New Year's Eve she went on her own to the circus in Holborn and to St Clement's Church in the Strand and curled up in bed and prayed 'for Massa and for me'.[126]

On the first day of 1873 Arthur's mind wandered down to London, to the kitchen, where he visualized Hannah preparing for his return:

> Hannah cleans and scrubs alone and waits for me, she the most noble and devoted of women who has loved and served me faithfully and purely for nearly nineteen years and is still in the world's eyes, only my hired maid of all work, and is treated as such by everyone but me – nay and by me also; for does she not wait on me and clean my boots and sleep on a servant's bed in the kitchen? Too late now to make a lady of *her* in spite of her sweet high-bred face and manners: but not too late to do her justice somehow.[127]

On 6 January Arthur was in London, calling to see Hannah before walking to work. His breakfast was ready, there was a roaring fire in the room she had decked with winter flowers: the canary sang. It was the warmest of welcomes: 'clasped in her master's arms', Hannah reassured him she was 'well and happy' and Arthur set off for the office a bridegroom-to-be.[128]

CHAPTER SIX

A Wedding in Clerkenwell

ON THE MORNING of Tuesday, 14 January 1873, Ellen Cullwick, her sister Polly and their cousin Elizabeth Morris walked
the short distance from the Smiths' house in Wingrove Place
to the church of St James, in Clerkenwell Close. It was a 'fair
grey day with sungleams'.[1] At the church they met Hannah
who had walked from the Temple. She had laid the kitchen
and parlour fires; cleaned Arthur's boots; served breakfast and
washed up before shyly showing herself to him, asking ' "Shall
I do?" ' To Arthur she was lovely and 'he kissed me ever so
long'. Plainly dressed,

> I went down to the kitchen where I slept and put on my
> Sunday clothes – red stuff gown [homemade] and grey
> cloak, and black straw bonnet wi' a white cap inside, and
> a white collar and cuffs.[2]

She wore neither gloves nor veil and carried no flowers,
and walked down Fleet Street, picking her way through streets
which teemed with people. Arthur followed so as not to arouse
suspicion. Ellen, Polly and Elizabeth, who was a lady's maid,
chatted to the nervous bride and groom as they waited for
John Henry Rose, the curate who was to marry them. Arthur
was on his own, with no friends or family present to celebrate
his wedding.

They stood before the altar which was bathed in red, blue,
green and yellow thrown by a 'sungleam' of low winter light
through a stained-glass window. The service began at nine:

weddings were required by law to take place in the morning.
When Hannah took her vows she called her husband by his
Christian name for the only time:

> Strange that his wife has never in her life called him by
> his Christian name, except once in the marriage service,
> on her wedding day when he compelled her reluctant lips
> to utter it.[3]

Arthur Munby told the curate that they were both of 'full
age'. He gave his profession as barrister, not clerk; her occupation was left blank. Hannah's address was 'of this parish',
Arthur's father's profession was 'esquire' and Charles Cullwick
was elevated to 'husbandman', more middle-class than saddler.[4]

When all was done, Arthur walked to Whitehall and
worked from noon to six o'clock at night; Hannah had a glass
of beer with her sisters and cousin at The Horseshoe public
house, close to the rear gates of the church. She walked back
alone to Fig Tree Court as the secret Mrs Munby, slipping
her wedding ring off before turning into the Temple. She
did not want Tarrant, Rees or Thornbury to see it. She put
on her servant's clothes 'an' come back to my work just as
if nothink had happened'.[5] Hannah was happy with her
wedding – the day had been in keeping with her shyness:

> dressing myself in the kitchen after my work and coming
> home to work again and getting thy dinner, but I'd liefer
> [prefer] a deal it was that way nor have such a many fine
> folks to see me and such a fuss an' all.[6]

Arthur made no mention of getting married in his diary
for that day: having devoted many thousands of words to his
Hannah, he recorded the weather, that he had received a letter
from his sister Carry and sent a letter to his mother, his
hours at work and 'to Clerkenwell by nine a.m.'. Years
later, however, he wrote a sonnet:

How well I recollect our Wedding Day!
She did her black work with a beating heart;
Then wash'd herself, and own'd a servant's part
Waiting on me, and then she went away
Down to the kitchen bedroom, where she lay
Among the pots, alone and quite apart;
There doff'd her servile dress, and with meek art
For once did make herself a little gay:
Her long dark cloak: a red stuff gown quite new;
Her black straw bonnet with white cap: Oh no,
No gloves, no flowers! 'Massa, shall I do?'
She cries; 'I have no looking glass, you know!
Now I am off! And mind you, all my life
I shall be servant still to you, as well as wife.'[7]

Once married, Hannah's life was unchanged: the routines she had established since becoming a live-in servant remained the same, those of a drudge. Vigilance was needed to ensure the other tenants did not discover their secret. When Hannah and Arthur and Josiah Rees, Owen Wilson, David Thornbury and William Ralston slept under the same roof, the newly-weds had to exercise caution in the evenings. Visiting each other's bedroom at the top and bottom of the house was fraught with danger. Arthur's tenants must have wondered about Munby's new servant: they recognized Hannah from somewhere – she was distinctive – and may have seen her sitting in the Temple Gardens, by the fountain or hovering outside Fig Tree Court. (Plate 16)

Shortly after their wedding day Arthur tried to put a stop to Hannah licking his boots. He felt it was wrong when she was his wife. He would only allow it on special occasions, such as their wedding anniversary, and at her insistence.

Arthur, who had always liked seeing Hannah 'in her dirt', noticed her appearance deteriorate in the winter and spring of 1873. The reason was the tenants' sexual advances:

Rees and Thornbury were the most troublesome, and then Tarrant. Arthur felt jealous at their familiarity, which she found tiresome, although her strength made it easy to repel them. Encounters when she was on all fours scrubbing the floors made her feel awkward, and disloyal to her master. To repel their advances, Hannah made herself as unattractive as she could by working hard to become almost black, and sweat like an animal: this strategy worked most of the time, but sometimes her earthiness was a magnet. There was always the possibility that she would go too far in this direction:

> Sometimes they met her in her dirt, carrying hampers or luggage and wearing an old crushed straw bonnet and striped lindsey scouring apron and her arms and face all begrimed with soot or blacking. And in such a case they disdained even to look at her. She quite understood their disdain. 'Aye, it's my black face . . . I lay if I keep myself pretty black, they winna want to kiss me.' And she acted on this discovery.[8]

Arthur had to treat them as tenants who behaved coarsely towards his housekeeper, and not play the part of an irate husband. This called for the greatest restraint and the best acting, qualities in which he and Hannah excelled.

They settled into domestic bliss. He went to the office, and she cleaned, singing at the top of her voice. She scrubbed the steps up to the chambers, collecting water from the cistern in the cellar. Fig Tree Court had narrowly survived the Great Fire of London in 1666. The court was rebuilt after another fire in 1678: the Temple authorities had strict rules governing the disposal of cinders in a communal dustbin every day. The buildings of the Inner Temple were a medley of styles and periods, grand and decrepit. Dickens described the atmosphere in *Pickwick Papers*:

low-roofed, mouldy rooms, where innumerable rolls of parchment, which have been perspiring in secret for the past century, send forth an agreeable odour, which is mingled by day with the scent of the dry rot, and by night with the various exhalations which arise from the damp cloaks, festering umbrellas and the coarsest tallow candles.[9]

The kitchen was dark and damp but Hannah was used to that. She made it homely by buying house-plants and adding other touches:

> with three big windows . . . but a low ceiling and so it's not light in the winter, but I fancy it must be pleasant in summer, cool and not *over* bright; as some are . . . There's a nice washing-up sink and plenty o' water, a dresser wi' shelves and cupboard and a nice little grate and mantelpiece, an oven too and now I've got a strip o' matting on the floor.[10]

When Arthur's evening meal had been prepared and served, she would change into her 'evening' frock and sew, make him cigarettes, wash his feet, read the Bible and other improving literature aloud, and play the part of a dutiful wife.

The first weekend they were married Arthur took his bride to Ockley in Surrey, by train from London Bridge station. Hannah the housekeeper performed a quick-change routine and dressed as the lady wife of Mr Munby. He had booked to stay the night but it poured with rain and there seemed no chance of going walking the following day so they dined at the White Hart in Dorking and returned to the Temple. He was proud of her, but nervous about her hands:

> She played her part very fairly by dint of nature and sweetness. But now that she was dressed in black silk, her shapely hands looked somewhat large and laborious and her dear complexion somewhat coarse, whereas her face

looks ladylike and her hands delicate when she is in her own servant's dress.[11]

During the first months of marriage Arthur tried to persuade Hannah to eat her meals with him when no one else was around, but to no avail. As a child she had hardly ever eaten with her parents, her table manners were basic and she was shy, insisting that it was not her place to eat with Massa.

She is so used to getting her meals anyhow and feeding on the broken victuals that I can hardly persuade her to eat and leisurely sit down by me, even now she acts on the pathetic assumption that only my leavings are for *her*![12]

Arthur had this struggle with her all their married life: she only relented when they went away, pretending she was a lady – stressful times. Hannah's self-consciousness about the clothes she wore on these occasions, in which she was physically awkward, together with the rigmarole of cutlery and etiquette, made it all alarming. On the other hand Hannah went to great lengths to be the perfect servant: she was never flummoxed when Arthur invited his tenants or neighbours to dine: she cooked the meals and waited on them with efficiency and 'meekness', very proud when Arthur reported that Captain Batten had told him '"What a nice person your servant seems to be!"' Arthur made an excuse to leave the room and slipped down to the kitchen to tell her what his guest had said and kissed her.[13]

One evening Arthur visited the Bovet family and Julie 'did her best to make me tell her all about Hannah; and failed'.[14] He had taken her into his confidence about his love for Hannah, and regretted leaving himself open to the risk of her telling mutual friends about his scandalous love affair. Arthur would dine out with friends, or at the Athenaeum, so that

Hannah could entertain Dick, Ellen and Cousin Elizabeth or servant friends in the kitchen at Fig Tree Court. He stayed out late so that she could spend time with them: he wanted her to build a social life, and insisted she visit the Smiths in Clerkenwell at least once a week. He came to understand that Hannah's equilibrium was sometimes rocked if she worked too hard and became isolated from her family and the Smiths.

On the evening of 17 February, Arthur met his closest friend, the Reverend Robert Borland, at the Craven Hotel where he told him that he had married Hannah. He must have been nervous of what the clergyman would say, and dreaded losing his friendship. Hannah went to the theatre that evening and sat in the gallery watching *A School for Scandal*, and thought it 'vulgar and wicked'.[15]

A barrister, Captain Batten, called in to see her one day when Arthur was out, and asked her to do some work. Hannah reassured Arthur that she was happy about the chores:

> I know he was fidgetting about *me* . . . he wants you to let me light his bedroom fire of a morning and clean his boots . . . 'Oh I shouldn't mind going into his bedroom when he was in bed, not a bit you know, I used often to have to do it for gentlemen when I was under-housemaid and quite a girl, so I might as well do it now I'm a married woman and I should like very well to clean his boots.'[16]

Arthur wished he could reduce her workload. Hannah had a manic zeal for dirty work which he had encouraged and over which he now had no control. He could see the toll it was taking on her: 'The longer we live together, the more I wish to take her away from her slaving and the more I regret that with all her intelligence she does not share such a wish.'[17] Hannah found it hard to accept that her place was in his bed and not in the damp, cold kitchen.

Arthur's diary records another obstacle in their lives: Hannah's reluctance and later refusal to go out disguised as a lady. It was only by coaxing, pleading or angry insistence that she accompanied him. She had excuses – her complexion was weatherbeaten and had to be veiled, or she had too much work to do. She wanted to be with him, but was ashamed of her rough hands; and did not want to be thought 'proud' and socially ambitious. She was happiest with Arthur when they were alone together at Fig Tree Court, or at Ockley where the landlady, Mrs Wickens, fell for the deception. After dinner they would talk 'for hours, she sitting between my knees, of the long fellowship of nineteen years'. Arthur had to wrestle with Hannah's self-esteem:

> a long evening with my Hannah; part of the time combating her strange fancies about herself, that she is 'not good enough' for one who is not worthy of *her*. Oh the divine humility of love! But it is my fault of other years, hard to be amended now, that this sweet soul has been brought so low in her own eyes. *That* wasn't what I meant by those strange trials.[18]

The following day Arthur went to Ockley to arrange their Easter visit: it was their belated honeymoon at The King's Arms, where he was sure Hannah would feel comfortable. Harriet, the 'rosy' chambermaid, greeted them when they arrived. Arthur was proud of Hannah when she came down and joined him for tea,

> her brown hair massed in rippling waves about her high-bred face . . . her tall lithe figure . . . why her smile, her whole face, is queenly now; stately in her courtesy to red-handed Harriet. And yet when we are alone, she wants to do things for me, instead of letting me do them for her.[19]

Hannah enjoyed her disguise, telling him how 'nice it is to be a lady'. Seeing herself in Harriet, remembering when she was a potgirl in Shifnal, made her feel comfortable. They walked for miles in the spring sunshine; visited ancient churches; took communion together for the first time as man and wife; picked primroses, and strolled in the starlit nights. When they left, they walked to Ockley station together: Hannah changed her clothes on the train and got off at London Bridge, taking the luggage home in a cab, while Arthur left the train at Charing Cross and walked to Whitehall.

Two weeks after their return from Ockley, wearing evening dress, Arthur was troubled by some familiar demons. When they were embracing and Hannah was in his arms,

> with her kitchen dress and servant's cap pressed close to me, how much more noble she seemed than those whom I was going to meet. 'How I wish I could show you there!' 'I'm sure *I* don't,' says she laughing, 'I should hate to be shown!'[20]

They left each other notes, and wrote to each other when he was away for the night. Worried about her becoming bored and gloomy, Arthur wondered how he could find a companion for her. To him, Ellen seemed an obvious choice: mindful of Hannah's anger when he discussed their problems with her sister, Arthur would have to tread carefully, however.

By early May Hannah was sleeping in the marital bed several nights a week: this was risky. One morning she was awakened by workmen who had come to repair the damp kitchen floor. Arthur feared that they might notice she had come from the top floor, not the kitchen where they would have expected her to be. He worried that one of his tenants would have seen her leave his room. At this time Josiah Rees put his arm around Hannah's waist and tried to kiss her: 'she pushed him away with wifely indignation and a strong right arm'.[21] Arthur and Hannah both enjoyed her telling him comic episodes of men showing their feelings for her, she could act out both parts. He loved her 'graceful archness' and was relieved when she said: '"I get happier every day, Massa."'[22] In the middle of May, Hannah and Arthur spent a weekend in Southend. The larks sang overhead as they strolled through the fields to church. The servants at The Ship Inn were taken in by Hannah's disguise: the waiter in the dining room called her 'ma'am'.[23]

While Hannah and Arthur had created a haven for them-selves at Fig Tree Court, the reality of their unconventional life could hit with brutal force. One weekend Hannah was ejected from the Temple Church. She had been a regular Sunday attender and she was tearful on her hasty return. Arthur writes:

> 'They know me as your servant but they let me in: but today I didn't know it was the ladies' seat and the man come and said to me, "You must go out." "Why?" I says. "You can't sit there, that's for the *ladies*." So they turned me out and put me to shame because I'm not a lady.' She knows, this loving one, that she *is* a lady, now legally of right, yet she never betrays her exaltation, nor wishes to claim her *right* ... and she doesn't want to sit among ladies, and she doesn't mind how many gentlefolks see her working 'in her dirt' out o' doors as she did yesterday and scorn her as a drudge. That she has always been used to; but to be publicly turned out of her seat in a crowded church because of her simple clothing, because she is not a lady, this is too much even for her meek spirit ... but what can I do to the man who did this thing?[24]

Arthur comforted her but was not surprised: he concurred it was unjust, un-Christian behaviour, but he knew the nuances of class. Marrying a man of his class, in 'normal' circumstances, would have conferred on Hannah the status of a lady, but this was not the case with them. On 26 May, Arthur gave Hannah a bracelet he had bought for her fortieth birthday: something to wear 'when she is a lady . . . a contrast to the leather strap she has worn for so long', but had to return it to the shop the following day as it was too delicate for 'the strong wrist of a tall English lass'.[25] In the evening he took her to the Bethnal Green Museum, which had opened in 1872, to see an exhibition of Rembrandt and Holbein. Later that week he told his college friend Henry James about his marriage to Hannah, while she spent the evening with her friends in Clerkenwell. Arthur told him a lot but omitted the details of her 'past drudgery and humiliation as a charwoman' in case it marred 'the pure idea of a rustic sweetheart'.[26] Henry listened intently for nearly two hours and Arthur was relieved when he said, ' "You have done right and you have given me enough to think of for a long time to come." ' They left in a cab for a party, talking about Hannah all the way; after supper Arthur slipped away and walked home in the rain. Hannah was worried about his friend's reaction to the news: fearing a negative reaction like Borland's, she preferred to keep the secret from his friends:

'But it seems to spoil all if it's told,' said my darling, 'they canna understand us two: they canna understand that I don't want to be took out o' my own place, nor to be shown to nobody.'[27]

At the end of the month Arthur took Hannah away to the Isle of Wight, the first time she had been at sea. They set off separately, she leaving the Temple in her working outfit, with her best clothes underneath. They met at Waterloo and after the train journey crossed the Solent: it was a bright, breezy day. They stayed at The Crab Inn at Shankhill which was a 'humbler sort of place'.

Arthur continued to note down details of the working women he came across: milkwomen, servants, anyone. Hannah often made mental notes of women she thought Massa might like to know. A summer tradition of theirs was to go to Isleworth and Brentford to look for the Shropshire pit women who had come to work in the market gardens when the demand for coal was reduced and they had been laid off. Over the years Hannah and Arthur got to know the stories of many of them and enjoyed looking for those who had become their friends.

Arthur went to the trouble of providing Hannah with presents to build a wardrobe for her role as a lady. On 19 July they met at Charing Cross station prior to the departure for a weekend in Ockley. Hannah was happy about staying at Mr and Mrs Wickens' inn and being waited on by Harriet, who even dropped her a curtsey. She enjoyed practising with her fan, a recent present from her besotted husband.[28]

In early August, Dick and Polly were due to spend some time at Fig Tree Court. Arthur was pleased as he planned to go to York and worried about leaving Hannah on her own. Dick was an 'innocent lad an' always helpin' folks and givin' away his wages'. Once he had sat on the stairs of his lodgings until midnight 'wi' that little lad on his knee as his mother was gone out and hadna coom back again'.[29]

On 5 August Arthur returned from the office and

> found my darling Hannah strangely hysterical and unwell so that I spent the evening in nursing her and putting her to bed. Among other burdens, this, of a possible illness is ever upon me.[30]

Hannah made a full recovery the following day and the cause of her malady is not explained. Polly's arrival took some of the pressure off Arthur, and he noted her closely and wondered how the differences between the sisters' childhoods and working lives had affected them. He wrote that Polly was 'very ladylike', and thanks to her aunt she had a better education than his wife. Polly would always be genteel in comparison to Hannah. The night before Polly left, Arthur played the piano and sang for them both.

Arthur worked on Saturday mornings and, in the middle of August, Hannah paid him a surprise visit. This was the first time she had called at his office: she was curious about his place of work and succumbed to a craving she had to see him. He was told a servant was waiting to see him, and he guessed it would be her:

> She was seated on the footmen's bench by the door where the humble folk wait; she was drest as a servant in her lilac cotton frock, clean coarse apron, her old straw bonnet, and her bare arms and hands visible beneath her grey cloak . . . she rose and made a curtsey to her husband. He, longing to kiss her, said a few hurried words as if it were a message and with another curtsey she withdrew saying 'Very well, Sir.'[31]

This brief encounter drained Arthur; he had to lie down in a darkened room when he returned home. He was 'ill with the indignation and excitement of the morning'. Meanwhile Hannah mended stockings, prepared food, went on errands and 'tended him . . . with all the love and skill and tenderness of a lifelong woman's love'. The following day they embarked on a new programme: to convince the tenants that everything was above board between them. Arthur worried they might think the relationship was sexual: 'for certain reasons we should prudently ask neighbour Rees to breakfast . . . to the carnal eye, the loving and vivacious wife sinks at once into a mere servant'.[32]

Arthur celebrated his forty-fifth birthday, and they prepared to go to France for a ten-day holiday. They went through the pantomime of him shouting goodbye to Hannah in case anyone should wonder about both of them going away on the same day. Later she met him at Charing Cross station where they caught the boat train to Folkestone: his heart swelled with pride when he saw her:

> a tall elegant lady in travelling dress. Blushing with excitement and pleasure, *my wife's* face had never seemed to me more lovely. 'How people did stare at me in the Strand!' she whispered as we walked together.[33]

They spent the night in Folkestone and Arthur delighted in taking Hannah to some of his favourite places: he watched her closely, noting her 'sweet good humour and gentleness' and intelligence. This was her first trip abroad and he enjoyed taking care of her, translating menus, and feeling proud of the trust she placed in him. He did not hide his admiration for the women porters who unloaded their luggage from the boat at Boulogne. He was glad that the team of five women assigned to the cart which carried their things had 'fewer old crones among them' and that 'the lusty young women, to whom the work is easy, were more [of them] than they used to be'.[34] They toured Lisieux and Caen, saw the Bayeux Tapestry, and returned via Rouen and Boulogne. Wherever they stayed they avoided eating in the dining room when English people were present. Arthur often described Hannah in the third person as if he was observing her from a nearby table:

> There is also an English servant of all work, staying . . . with her husband, and looking as ladylike as any other woman here. She however is neither self-indulgent, nor over delicate, though she is as gentle and tender as the best. She is always fearing to be a burden to him who loves her; she schemes to save him expense, and vainly pretends that she is not hungry or thirsty, but that *he* must certainly eat and drink.[35]

Arthur was relieved to reach England after suffering terribly on a rough crossing of the Channel. Hannah was barely affected, but 'could hear all going on and that my husband was very bad'. Because he was so ill they had separate berths, and early in the morning, before they reached Folkestone she:

> she run along the floor tottering a little and I found Massa still sick and hoarse wi' retching. I wiped his face and said I thought we were in harbour. He called me his child and said how ill he'd bin and told me to go and lie down again.[36]

They parted at Charing Cross station where Hannah took off the new holiday hat with its veil and 'plume of cock's feathers', and put on her battered black bonnet, covering her new skirt and jacket with an old plaid shawl which Arthur had carried in his knapsack on their tour, so that she wouldn't be noticed coming in to the Temple. She was glad to take off her gloves which she always found a nuisance. By the time he reached home, she was looking forward to cleaning the place in time for his return from York. France had been a great success: she was the perfect travelling companion, better than he had dared expect. Arthur had been impressed with her 'calm courage and self-possession . . . and such ladylike gentleness to all around her'. He had been relieved that there had been no signs of 'those strange moods of depression and "naughtiness" which affect her sometimes at home and which perplex and sadden me so. She will not give me the clue to them nor let me comfort her.' Hannah had acted the role of lady with ease and this encouraged Arthur to take her away again. He was uxorious on his return:

> In France, I saw for the first time how well my wife is capable of playing the part of a lady. Would that she could play it always, and yet also be the sweet and helpful

servant that she is! I have loved her for twenty years as a servant, and this year, now that I am her husband, I learn to love her as a lady too. One hardly knows which set of charms suits her best; but both together are supremely irresistible, and in both, she *is* mine for ever.[37]

Hannah threw herself into her work with zeal: she loved it, it was therapeutic; the busier she kept, the less time she had to brood. She dreaded the moments when she was on her own and the work was done. When Arthur kissed her goodbye, saying he hoped she would not be 'dull', she put on a brave face, but confided in a fragment of diary:

I said I shouldn't [be dull] and didn't mean to be, but I think it's not possible to be any other – quite alone in this very quiet place and not a soul to speak to confidentially, for I'm obliged to look at my words lest I should say anything to Mrs Newton or anyone to betray myself.[38]

On 3 September Hannah walked to the Strand, and had her photograph taken at the studio of Mr Dixon, wearing the French servant's clothes Arthur had bought her. She told the proprietor that she was a Temple servant, and he charged her the reduced rate of three shillings and sixpence for half a dozen copies. Dixon's 'boy' took her likeness and the session took longer than expected because a heavy shower of rain passed over the glasshouse studio, casting a gloom and requiring her to stand very still for longer than usual.[39] Hannah's lips were pursed and she seemed unfamiliar with her new outfit. The crucifix suggested that the wearer was devout: her left hand clutching at the apron showed no wedding ring.

Arthur went to the Lake District with his father: in Windermere he received a letter from Hannah. He was anxious that his father should not see the handwriting in case he recognized it from the many envelopes she had addressed to

Clifton Holme. After Windermere they spent two days in Keswick, where he said goodbye to his father and Arthur travelled on to Wigan. On 11 September he went looking for his pit-brow lass Ellen Grounds and was bowled over by the 'bigness of this bonny Ellen', who seemed 'to fill the lobby and the portrait shed with her presence'. Mr Little took two likenesses of her: one on her own and one with Arthur. She wore her wadded bonnet, striped skirt, breeches, iron clogs, buttoned coat, and she 'shouldered the spade in a workmanlike fashion'.[40] Ellen was the mother of a two-year-old son whose father had died of smallpox before they could marry. She brought the child with her and Arthur was impressed by this woman's femininity and gentleness despite looking rough and uncouth. He explained his role in the portrait: he was standing beside her to show how nearly she approached him in size. The picture is the only example of him and a working woman together. He paid Ellen a shilling for posing for him, and went to see another photographer in Wigan whom he knew well, Miss Louisa Millard, now Mrs Mawson, married and mother of a baby. The following day he visited pits in the area and sounded out the opinion of the pitbrow women on factory legislation, which had been much resisted. They were angry at the reduction in their working hours, could not afford the half-day's holiday on Saturdays imposed on them by law, and resented interference in their working lives. Other local people told him that the women did not get so drunk, and had more time to be with their families.

Hannah's mood was brightened by the presence of workmen in Fig Tree Court: one in particular, an Irish bricklayer called Robert, pursued her. He was attracted by her looks and earthiness. One day as she was on hands and knees, splashed with dirt, scouring the floor near her bedroom, he tapped her on the shoulder, saying: ' "I should like to come and have tea

with you o' Sunday." ' She said she was rarely in on Sundays.
Then he followed with: ' "Well, you're not engaged, are you?
Could I go out with you?" ' Hannah brusquely told him that
she did not want any company. She was disappointed at
having to speak to him in this way: she enjoyed having the
men around – they stopped her feeling lonely, but she did not
like the confusion that her open personality caused:

> I like to be free wi' all the workmen and civil o' course,
> but somehow I hate them to pretend making love to me
> – it annoys me and then I can look so straight and tho'
> I look a drudge and am ten times blacker than they are I
> feel as if they've no right to speak to me on that subject.[41]

Munby's thoughts turned to Hannah and he felt homesick.
He re-read a letter 'filled with love and tenderness unutterable'
he had received that morning and 'my absence from her, my
daily thoughts of her, were brought to a crisis by that letter.
I could do nothing else than go straight to London to see
and cherish that unexampled wife.' He sent her a telegram:
'Coming tonight, Friday from ten to one, to see black work
tomorrow – sleep downstairs, French dress.' Hannah understood immediately: that he wanted to sleep with her downstairs in her bedroom; that Hannah was to be wearing the
new dress she had been photographed in at Dixon's when he
arrived, and that he wanted to see her dirty the day after.
Arthur arrived and she told her diary how he was 'looking so
well and jolly and he clasped his drudge and kissed her for
ever so long and she was as pleased to see him tho' she said
not much'. He told her all his news and then went into detail
about how he wanted to watch her work the following day,
what she should do and how she had to be 'thoroughly
black'.[42]

Hannah had followed his instructions and was wearing
her new French frock, cap and apron, and a red shawl: 'How

bright and cosy the kitchen seemed with such a servant sitting by me there.'[43] That night he spent below stairs with Hannah was 'the first time in my life, in a servant's bedroom in a kitchen – a cellar'. And for the first time he woke up to the facts of Hannah's life. As he lay there on her straw mattress, oppressed by the low, dark room, he noticed that her patchwork quilt was made up of old cotton frocks, and she had two boxes of possessions in the corner. There was an old chair and a wash-stand, but no basin or ewer or looking-glass: she washed at the sink in the kitchen. He ate the breakfast she prepared for him in her humble kitchen and he told her that she was his 'own wife and that we can never be parted now for ever'.[44] Before he had finished she threw herself on the floor between his knees and put her head on his breast and 'her bare working arms around him'. But there was little time for 'petting' and she kissed him and lifted him up in her arms 'to show her old strength'.

Arthur spent the next day directing her dirty work. One can imagine him as a watchful boy, quiet and intent, observing the servants at work at Clifton Holme:

> I got up and put my dirty things on. Lighted the fire and swept up. Washed me at the sink, where I always do – in the tin bowl and Massa was pleased to see me do it. I've no looking glass down here and as I told Massa as I'd not seen my face for days – only yesterday I looked to see how black I looked after being out on the errands, and there was a streak o' black across my nose and my whole face more or less dirty . . . Massa saw me clean his boots and this morning I fetched the bath downstairs for him to use and brought a basin down. But Massa had to wash at the sink and he said that's one part of a servant's life he wouldn't like and seeing the dirty clothes hanging about, but he supposed that this was nothing to me . . . [after breakfast] I read a chapter of the Bible and we knelt down

in the kitchen and had prayers . . . And I lighted the fire
upstairs for Massa to sit and see me scrub. I put my
bonnet and apron on and took my pail and things and
Massa told me to kiss him afore I blacked my face – so I
did and then I rubbed my black hand across my face and
arms . . . and when I'd to go down for a fresh [pail] o'
water Massa said he hoped to see me blacker still when I
come back, so downstairs I blacked both my hands and
wiped them all over my face and that pleased Massa and
he said it was blacker even than any o' the pit wenches.[45]

Although Arthur left later that day, Hannah was overjoyed
to think that he had dashed back to London, a lengthy train
journey, for a night and day of bliss. She treasured it as proof
of his love: 'to come from impulse two hundred miles just to
see me . . . all for *love*'. When they were kissing each other
goodbye 'so heartily', they were nearly undone: Josiah Rees
walked into the kitchen and found them together. Luckily it
was a dark room and it seemed as if he had not seen, although
Arthur was embarrassed at even being in the kitchen. Thinking on the work she had done for him she asked:

Should I have felt *such* pleasure for a common working
man? I *might* if I had found a working man as could love
me purely and be as Massa is (I mean in everything but
his learning) and honour him as much but that's the
difficulty I doubt – finding such a one. And so when I
was young and *did* meet wi' Massa (whose face I'd seen in
the fire) I made my mind up that it was best and safest to
be a slave to a *gentleman*, nor wife and equal of a vulgar
man. Still wi' the wish and determination to be independent by working in service and without the slightest hope
of being raised in rank either in place, or by being married
– and so at last after all these twenty years by God's help
and Massa's true heart and fervent love to me (more than

ever I could dare hope for from anyone but him and I always trusted Massa) I am as I am – a servant still and a very low one in the eyes o' the world. I can work at ease. I can go out and come in when I please and I can look as degraded as ever I like without caring how much I'm despised in the Temple or in Fetter Lane or in the streets. And wi' all that I have the inward comfort of knowing that I am loved and honoured and admired and that I am united heart and soul as well as married at church to the truest, best, and handsomest man in my eyes that ever was born. No man I ever see, or ever saw, is so lovely. And Massa is pleased wi' me and after all this time there can be no doubt of our bein' made for each other.[46]

The following day there was a letter from Arthur and a parcel of photographs from Mr Little in Wigan of a very fine pit wench: 'Massa knew her and had her likeness took in three ways and in one *he* is standing by her. *Am I jealous?* No.' Hannah remembered Arthur lying in bed with her and describing her knees as 'feeling like a nutmeg grater'.[47]

Hannah's rebuffal of Robert the bricklayer was a challenge to one of his mates, a carpenter, who tried to woo Hannah by complimenting her on the size of her biceps. He told her: '"I never saw a woman with such a muscle in all my life,"' and the following day he asked her to go with him to the theatre and

pretended or seemed to want me to be a sweetheart of his and tried two or three times to kiss me but he'd no chance wi' me for I'd only to put up my arm and I told him besides that I'd no *right* to kiss anyone but the right one neither should I. Still I wasn't put out wi' him but talked civilly and freely as usual.[48]

David Thornbury also tried his luck with her: he would send her out on errands and then inveigle her into his

chambers, asking her to stay with him while he wrote letters
'as he rather liked to see me about'.[49]

In the autumn Arthur invited the Reverend Borland to tea.
It was the first time Hannah had seen him since they had
been married. She was nervous, but acquitted herself well.
Dressed demurely, she agreed to serve tea seated at the table
like a lady. Borland greeted her as such, but Arthur saw that
the greeting was less formal than if she had been a real lady.
Arthur sensed a snub when Borland invited Arthur to stay,
not looking at Hannah and thereby not extending the invitation to her. The tea lasted two hours, during which Hannah
said as little as possible.[50] She was no more pleased with
Borland than the last time, but was respectful. The first time
he had made her

> feel vexed and dispirited rather than pleased, for all
> because he was so gentle and kind in his manner to me –
> for I told him then it was quite impossible for *him* or
> anyone else to understand our love.[51]

She resented that their privacy could be invaded at any
time by the tenants or casual callers; having to be vigilant was
exhausting, and the isolation sometimes lowered her mood,
causing her to be 'bad' or 'naughty'. The term 'dull' was used
by Hannah and Arthur to mean sad and depressed:

> I often think they must feel that I am dull here, not
> knowing as well as I do *what* I am besides just a servant
> and what pleasant evenings Massa and me spend here
> together, especially when I am really good, but that isn't
> always I'm glad or sorry to say – or both. Sorry because it
> vexes Massa so much at the time, but glad cause it makes
> me more humble and sorry afterwards and anxious to be
> right again.[52]

On 22 November Arthur returned from his half-day at the office to find his wife in tears, writing to her sister Ellen in Putney that their old friend Mrs Smith was dying. She was over eighty and had been Hannah's 'only friend and protectress in London for years'. For the Cullwick sisters, and Dick too, the Smiths' house was a safe haven. Arthur had been miffed at Mrs Smith's refusal to meet him, and he tetchily recorded that 'she cannot read and she refused to see me on the ground that she has never had anything to do with gentlefolks, and couldn't begin now'. Being so old and once a 'servant who worked afield', she evoked his interest and he wanted to interview her, and he would have canvassed her help during the stormy times before his marriage to Hannah, but she would have none of it.[53]

On Monday Hannah took Mrs Smith beef tea. Arthur went with her and met the old lady for the only time, and they all prayed together:

> 'This is Mr Munby, my husband. Will you shake hands with him?' said this dear soul tearfully: and then we knelt down and I prayed aloud . . . I took the dying woman's hand – a large strange hand . . .[54]

Arthur had hoped to take Hannah away to Hayling Island but bad weather prevented the trip, and she immersed herself in scrubbing, her enthusiasm leaving her with back pain. He panicked: the gloomy mood at home lowered his mood and brought fears about Hannah's long-term health to the surface:

> The fear that she might be ill has always been to me a living and present horror: but only since my marriage have I realized that this sweet but terrible burden, I being utterly *alone* with one who is dearest and being unable to consult friends or have ready female aid if she should suffer.[55]

On 4 December the news came that Mrs Smith had died. Arthur hailed a cab and went straight to Clerkenwell. His reaction to the scene is class-ridden: his annoyance that the grieving household did not treat Hannah (and by association, himself) with more deference and respect rankled:

> My Hannah was in tears and the graceful tenderness of her grief contrasted strongly with the homely vulgar ways of the good woman [Emma] of the house who yet called her 'Hannah' and treated her as one of themselves. She went upstairs when I left and had tea with a simple Welsh milkmaid who lodges with her husband in the house.[56]

Arthur worried about how Hannah would cope with the loss of the affection she had enjoyed in Clerkenwell for the past twenty years. He knew enough of her fragile emotions to be fearful of the next months. Hannah's loss had heightened her attachment to Massa.

He comforted her as best he could, but he worried about Christmas when he went to York, and wrote to Ellen and Polly asking them to stay with Hannah at Fig Tree Court. He was relieved that they could both get leave from their mistresses at short notice. Polly was to arrive at Shoreditch station at four o'clock on the morning of Christmas Eve. Hannah tied a long piece of string around her wrist and dangled it out of the bedroom window for Polly to tug when she arrived. On the train journey home Arthur was concerned for their futures:

> And then the porter took up the luggage and went away and then that servant [Hannah] came into her Master's arms, and his cab was kept waiting for a while. I have been troubled about leaving my Hannah this Christmas, and have had to feel more than ever her lowliness and loneliness for now that the old dame of Clerkenwell is dead, she has not a house in London to go to, except a

few kitchens where she herself once lived and one or two
poor dwellings of her old fellow servants.[57]

Arthur seems a little detached as he writes that Hannah
had no 'home' to go to: after all, she was married to him and
Fig Tree Court *was* her home. By the time he returned, Ellen
and Polly had left. When he appeared at Fig Tree Court in
the moonlight on New Year's Eve morning, a scene of
domestic bliss greeted him: there was a roaring fire, tea was
ready, the rooms were decked with holly, and Hannah was
lying in her kitchen bedroom waiting for his return. She told
him how Thornbury had visited her in the kitchen, a little
tipsy and speaking to her in a 'very free way', asking if she
had any mistletoe as he would like to kiss her underneath it.
She offered to shake his hand instead. She told Arthur the
story, wondering if he would be 'vexed' by it, but he seemed
pleased as 'it showed how Mr Thornbury never suspected I
was anything but a servant and I thought so too'.[58] They
spent New Year's Eve together, she wearing her wedding gown
and a black silk apron. As the midnight bells rang they prayed
together for the year ahead.[59]

A new anxiety started to appear in Arthur's diary: his
frustration at sometimes failing to persuade Hannah to dress
up as a lady and go away with him at the weekends. During
1874 they grew to love Ockley, where she felt comfortable
about her disguise with the homely Wickenses and their
servants. It was difficult to coax her to be a lady anywhere
else.

The year opened with Hannah insisting that Arthur watch
her scrub the yard of his chambers in the drizzling rain.
Arthur remarked at the men who 'could look down into this
yard, and behold my Hannah'.[60] In the middle of January
she warned him that her hands were so bad that she could
not be a lady until the winter was over. But Sunday, 25

January was a bright, frosty day and Arthur succeeded in getting her to go for a walk in the woods in Weybridge, but an old injury to her foot flared up and on 26 January she had an operation at Charing Cross Hospital. She insisted on going there as a working woman, not a lady. Arthur arranged for her sister Ellen and Emma Smith to take her, and he explained their marriage to the surgeon. Arthur was present during the operation and marvelled at her determination to be brave:

> one house surgeon pumped ether spray on her foot and the other prepared to operate . . . Hannah laid her head on her sister's breast . . . I held her hand and kept my face to hers. She never screamed nor started only her noble beautiful face kept working with pain and her dear lips moved against mine in half convulsions . . . kisses all the time. In five minutes or so it was over and for a while she lay on the sofa looking faint.[61]

Arthur found the experience shocking and wondered how he would have felt if 'she were about to have a child'. This is a rare, oblique reference to their sexual life. Once Hannah's foot was bandaged, the women went home in a cab and he followed separately. He left them looking after the patient, and went to teach his Latin class as usual. Mrs Newton and her daughter Hetty were hired to look after Hannah. Hannah told him: '"Oh how glad I am it was not *your* foot, and yet I should like it too for then I should nurse you!"' On 10 February the Newtons had gone. Anyone peeping through the kitchen windows would have seen Arthur sitting: 'on her knees in the twilight'.[62]

At the end of February, they went for the weekend to the Royal Hotel, Southend. Hannah's foot had healed sufficiently for moonlit walks along the clifftops: she complained about all that was needed to transform her into a lady: 'I found my

darling Cinderella busy transforming herself into a princess
. . . but oh what a bother it is to be a lady. It's a good job it
doesn't come often!'[63]

Having the Newtons around to help gave Arthur the idea
of hiring the Skeatses to move into Fig Tree Court and relieve
Hannah of some of the heavier work. Mr Skeats, who had
been a porter, and his wife, a servant, arrived in Fig Tree
Court on 20 March. Hannah was unused to delegating the
heavy work. At Easter the Munbys went to Ockley for five
days: Hannah was pleased to see 'stout and cheerful Mrs
Wickens', but afterwards was equally pleased to resume the
role of Cinderella amongst the cinders.[64] A week later Hannah
made an 'odd proposal', that she go and help her old mistress,
Miss Knight, get ready for the summer season. The prop-
osition sounds as if Hannah was making a bid for her
independence of the past. Maybe she felt the need for fresh
air after a long winter in London.

Hannah explained her relationship with Mr Munby to the
Skeatses before they moved in. Mrs Skeats quizzed Hannah
about their life together. Hannah's workload was the same as
before, as Mrs Skeats preferred to do the lighter jobs. Needled
by the woman's insinuations, Hannah was forced to consider
matters which she would have preferred not to discuss: the
experiment was not a success. Even the Skeatses' daughter
Rachel felt she could encroach on Hannah's privacy and
comment on her marriage:

'It must be awkward for you, you haven't got your rights'
– meaning as a gentleman and wife. But I said, 'Why, it
was my own wish to be like this and it's most convenient.'
I *couldn't* be a lady here, nor anything like one. I'd leifer
live here and work as I like and behave as I'm used to,
than live anywhere else and be set up and stared at . . .
'Besides, I'm forced to be a sort of a lady, when Mr

Munby and me go out together.' You see, Massa, they canna understand it – *no one* can. They're all for finery and being thought much of.[65]

On the first weekend in May Arthur went to see the Reverend Borland at Harford Rectory near Southampton: they talked about Hannah, Arthur extolling her praises, desperate that his friend should grow to like her. It worked: Borland gave Arthur a posy of flowers to give to her and this helped cement the trio's relationship. The visit was important to Arthur: he enjoyed the chance to talk about the woman he loved, and Borland was his only friend who knew the full story. Smoking his pipe, Arthur told him of

> the other traits of her beautiful double life of wife and servant, lady and laundress, for he is the only man to whom I can talk on the subject and his nature is broad enough and gentle enough to do her justice.[66]

In May, Arthur invited Polly to stay with them at The King's Arms. There would be no risk of her sister betraying them: Polly was genteel in her ways, and the Cullwicks' origins would not be guessed by the Wickenses. Arthur thoroughly approved of Hannah's youngest sister as a 'good girl, gentle and comely ... a Sunday school teacher and devoted to the Low Church ... and tells with pride of "the many ladies who come to our shop and high ladies too". Innocent Polly.'[67]

Hannah celebrated her forty-first birthday while Arthur was away visiting his parents. Her letters told of Josiah Rees asking her to do more jobs for him, being stared at in the street on account of her dirt and strength, heaving heavy ladders she had borrowed to decorate their rooms, and the joy of working to make *their home* more homelike: 'the blacker I get with work, the more ardent I feel towards you'.[68] She was overjoyed with the fisherwoman's bonnet he had bought her on a day-trip to Filey, and she remarked on the drama of their life: 'How nice it is to be your servant too [as well as wife]. It's like a *play* only better nor all the plays that was ever wrote.'

Hannah was well read in popular fiction, and had seen many melodramas and tragedies on the London stage. Thornbury had asked Hannah why she did not get a better place where she did not have to get so dirty:

> Because I like it, Sir, I've always been used to rough work and enjoyed it and I hardly reckon *this* as service for I've got a *home* here in the kitchen and no missis over me, and Mr Munby's a good master and he lets me do all the work as I like.[69]

Thornbury never gave up his pursuit of Hannah, even when she was 'in her dirt'. He told her: '"By Jove you are wonderful . . . I declare you're as fine a woman as ever I saw in my life!"' Then he grabbed one of her arms 'to inspect and admire it'. Arthur noted that Hannah submitted to Thornbury grabbing her 'strong stout arms' like a 'slave might submit to be handled by her purchaser'. Then Thornbury pounced and said, '"Give me a kiss!"' Hannah told Arthur that she had shaken him off 'quite quietly and stood farther off and said, "No, Sir, I never kiss *anybody*." She continued sweeping and he said, "Perhaps you are right but shake hands before I go,"' which she did. Hannah told her husband that she was not afraid to be alone with him or any other man, and that '"No man is strong enough to do me any harm."' Three days later Hannah and Arthur were in the parlour in the evening when Josiah Rees nearly caught them together. She had to dart into another room where she fell asleep listening to Rees telling her husband what a great servant she was. Arthur knew what the repercussions would be if the truth was made public. They would have to leave Fig Tree Court.

Arthur was shocked when the messengers at his office sniffily told him that a servant was waiting to see him: he could not bear their condescending looks or the danger that his self-control might give way. The day after he had spent the night with a friend in Surbiton, Hannah walked to Whitehall with a note she had written. Arthur recalls:

> I went down to the hall and found my blessed wife there, sitting on the servant's bench . . . she wore her big straw bonnet and an old green plaid shawl and short cotton frock and clean apron – the leather strap round her wrist, and in order not to appear young or bonny as she is, she had purposely soiled her face and hands, and took the note.[70]

During 1874 Hannah's company was sought out by her old mistress, Miss Margaret Henderson, who had dismissed her because of her relationship with Munby. She was staggered to hear that the 'gentleman' had married her servant. Over the summer Miss Henderson would invite herself to tea at Fig Tree Court, and insist that Hannah visit her at home. Hannah did not like being intruded upon, nor did she enjoy returning to her old place as anything other than a servant. Arthur hoped that the tea parties would give Hannah practice at being a lady, and she went along with it.

The last weekend in June, Hannah and Arthur were in Ockley, but the pressures of the week, Miss Henderson's tête-à-têtes, and working too hard in the hot weather, meant that Hannah took a while to calm down. When she met Arthur at Waterloo, she was dressed as a real lady in 'black silk, delicate muslins and veil, ornaments and gloves' but sounded far from ladylike, telling him she was 'in a muck sweat wi' hard work'. She told him, ' "I do *hate* these fine clothes! and these gloves too!" '[71] By the time they arrived and had a word with Stephen Piggott, the station-master, before walking off to The King's Arms, Hannah was reconciled to her new lot. Arthur wrote about her irascibility and feared for the future:

> I think somewhat sadly of her unwillingness to become a lady yesterday and apprehend that since she cannot be a lady always, she may have to be always a servant, and so lose something of her versatility and delicacy of manner.[72]

One weekend in mid-July he was with a friend in Croydon, planning to return to the Temple on Sunday night. He changed his mind at the last moment and decided to return to London the following day, 'trusting that Hannah with her calm good sense and her courage would go quietly to bed'. But she panicked that he had been in an accident: memories of his riding accident were rekindled, and when he called on the way to the office he found Hannah in a state. She had sat up worrying about him, 'having no one to comfort her but the silly old dame downstairs [Mrs Skeats], who said to her, "Well, if anything has happened to Mr Munby, shall you go into service again?"' Hannah was so desperate that she asked Thornbury if he thought anything had happened to her master. Arthur stayed with her, and when she stopped crying, he went to work.[73]

Two weeks later Hannah again refused to go to Guildford for the weekend: Arthur went straight to Whitehall on Monday morning and was not surprised to hear that 'his servant' was waiting to see him. She had been kept an hour before they disturbed him. One wonders if the messengers and clerks ever guessed there was more to them than master and servant:

> She stood up. There was no one by, so she did not curtsey, but smiled freely: and shutting the door I clasped and kissed her: 'Don't shut the door, Massa!' she said with

a wise instinct. 'I'm only come to bring your letters and carry your bag home.' 'Darling,' says he and kisses her again! and then he parts from her as a Master lest anyone should see.[74]

In early August Arthur bought Hannah more lady's clothes for their two-week holiday in Ockley. Always frugal, and careless about her appearance, she despaired at the amount he had spent. She was annoyed at having to wear gloves as 'they make my hands as foolish as a stuffed tabby'.[75] Arthur was concerned to see Hannah talking on her own to the Rector of St Margaret's, the Reverend DuSautoy and his wife, but panicked unnecessarily. Another trial lay ahead when they were invited to tea at the rectory, and at the last hurdle, when taking their leave, she 'made a dreadful mistake', saying 'Goodbye, Sir' and 'Goodbye, Ma'am' to Mrs DuSautoy, something a real lady would never have said. Hannah told him: ' "I'd leifer be shaking mats than calling on Mrs Du-Sautoy. But if you think I ought to call on gentlefolks, I must try and bear it as well as I can." ' Arthur felt despondent about his plans for her to practise at being a lady, so she would be able to live openly as his wife.

On 1 September came a welcome distraction: a visit to the only photographer in Dorking, William Usherwood. Hannah wore her best black silk frock and 'Gainsborough' hat that Arthur had bought her, and her white muslin. She was aware that these images were part of his plan of making her a lady, a project with which she grew more uncomfortable with every outing. Her hand was posed to flaunt her wedding ring. Remembering the tensions around tea at the vicarage, the drama of Pygmalion comes to mind.

At noon on Friday, 11 September, the Munbys met discreetly at Somerset House, and went on to Gilling's studio in the Strand. Hannah posed in her working dress as if on an errand, with her plaid and peasant's shawl. She was bundled up as if against the cold, the leather strap on her right hand peeped out. Arthur liked the pictures:

> very picturesque and charming she looked . . . and though the pictures are a contrast and complement to those at Dorking her manner and aspect were almost as ladylike in these servile clothes as then, only she said 'Sir'.[76]

The Working Women's College opened at 5 Fitzroy Street, off Tottenham Court Road, on 16 October. Arthur persuaded Hannah to attend and she enjoyed it, although judging by the stares of the lady patrons of the college, she looked too much a working woman for their tastes.

A few days later Arthur's emotions were churned up by a visit to the Lushingtons at Wheeler's Farm in Pyrford: they had refurbished the place he called 'Eden', scene of his dalliance with Sarah Carter. Whenever he went there it made him feel guilty: on another visit he would learn that Sarah was now a governess in America.

Hannah and Arthur spent a weekend in October at Southend, she playing the lady in an exemplary manner, and one of the waiters at the Middleton Hotel was clearly smitten by Mrs Munby. On 8 November Hannah cooked breakfast and waited on Arthur and two of his Pearson cousins. While she prepared for their visit, she flew around the place, laughing and talking, rushing to kiss him, and was 'youthful, graceful and radiant'.[77] There must have been a frisson in the parlour as she set down the dishes and stood behind Octavius and Henry as they talked, removing their plates and making coffee and toast at the fireside. Hannah was not perturbed and with her sense of fun enjoyed Arthur's nerves. She was proud and Arthur was glad when it was over: the two men did not notice anything untoward about their cousin's relations with his virtuous servant.

There was one visit to Ockley before Christmas: it was foggy and frosty outside and snug in the parlour. On their return, Hannah told Arthur that that was the last time she would be a lady until the spring: her hands would again be too rough to disguise in the cold weather. On 23 December came the usual leave-taking: Arthur left for York for his last Christmas with his father. They prayed together and 'kissed many a time at the door and so with divided heart I left my darling, not alone, but with only the old folks [the Skeatses] of the kitchen to keep her company'.[78] The day was foggy, there was a hard frost, and the Thames was covered with floating ice. As Arthur went off he was pained to remember Hannah's parting words: '"You are going home to see your mother, that is a pleasure I never had once in my life. Oh how I should have enjoyed it!" And her dear eyes glistened at the thought.'

Hannah spent Christmas Day with her sister Ellen, a nursemaid in Putney. The children in the nursery told their mother that Hannah looked just like Queen Elizabeth. Arthur agreed in part: she was like the Queen in 'features, if not in expression'. Otherwise she kept her promise to him and made herself busy, making up hampers of food and parcels of his cast-off clothing for her brothers Jim and Dick, visiting her friends in Kilburn, reminiscing with the Skeatses over the kitchen fire about her years in service and politely accepting a Christmas box of two shillings, rather than kisses under the mistletoe, from Mr Thornbury. Arthur hurried back to London, leaving York with the River Ouse frozen over.[79]

At dusk on New Year's Day 1875, Arthur hurried home to Hannah from Whitehall. His footsteps crunched on the frost. As he turned into Fig Tree Court, he saw her hanging over the balustrade talking 'freely' to the lamplighter, and stood in the shadows listening to their conversation. She assured the man she liked hard work: '"I'd liefer go down on my knees and scour a floor, nor write a letter." ' The man asked her: ' "Don't you wish to get married?" ' Hannah replied: ' "Not I – I've seen too much of that, with father and poor mother." ' As soon as they saw Arthur they stopped talking.[80]

After dinner Hannah read to Arthur from Fanny Lewald's *Italian Sketchbook*, part of a plan to persuade her to accompany him to Italy and Switzerland that summer. Earlier that day under the blotter at the office, he started to write *Hannah*, an account which he kept for two years, alongside his diary. *Hannah* opens with a poem:

> Love, only love, was her reward:
> Her hands were still with labour marr'd,
> And still she swept the kitchen yard, My Hannah,
> But oh, she swept it merrily!
> For not a hireling now was she;
> She worked for love, she worked for me – My Hannah.

The rhythms of Hannah and Arthur's life remained undisturbed during the second year of their marriage. His tenants and other Temple men continued to be attracted to her and she put them in their place. Arthur's relations with her relatives had improved steadily and on 14 January Ellen and cousin Elizabeth were invited for a tea party, a celebration of their wedding. He was pleased with Hannah's greeting when he entered the kitchen: 'And when her "master" came in to join them, she did not call him Sir nor wait in silence, but ran boldly up to him and kissed him before them all and called him a "dear old darling".'[81]

She had transformed herself from drudge to lady, wore her best black silk dress and a camellia in her 'lustrous hair'. Arthur gave Ellen and Elizabeth identical brooches 'as memorials' of their wedding day, and sat and had tea with them until half past six, leaving them to dine at his club.

Arthur spent as much time as he could with Hannah,

rushing home after work to spend a couple of hours with her before going out, sometimes barely enjoying the social round of his other life. On 10 March they were taken aback at the arrival of his clergyman brother Fred from Turvey in Northamptonshire, to stay the night. Arthur panicked: Hannah said that Fred would never be able to guess that she was his sister-in-law:

> 'I can sleep in the kitchen quite well, Massa, and I shall wait on your brother of course. I shall *enjoy* it; and he'll never notice me! I'll make myself look so as he'd never think for a moment that you could care for *me*!'

The brothers went to see Henry Irving's *Hamlet* at the Lyceum. When they returned, Arthur crept down to the kitchen and saw Hannah fast asleep on the 'rude sofa bed'. Next morning she cleaned Fred's boots and took hot water to his room: he walked Arthur to his office and returned to the Temple to find her on the stairs and 'so black . . . looking a poor hardworking drudge with my dirty cap and frock and coarse apron and arms and face blacked o' purpose. But that was how I *wished* to look before *him*.'[82] Hannah carried Fred's box and carpet bag to the cab, he tipped her a shilling and rode off without saying goodbye.

At Easter they travelled to Ockley: Arthur was concerned that Hannah's appearance had deteriorated over the winter. He urged her to wear her veil and her gloves at all times and sit with her back to the light: but the Wickenses and their servant Harriet treated her like a lady, as in the past. On Easter Saturday, mindful of the gaffe Hannah had made on their last visit, Arthur went to see the Rector, the Reverend DuSautoy, and 'told him vaguely about Hannah'. He explained in confidence that his wife was not a lady born, but did not 'venture to confess that she is a servant'.[83] His confidant 'seemed surprised and said emphatically, "I should never have known it."'

There was a gaiety about Hannah: she loved to tease Arthur that she was going to tell their secret. She joked that she would tell Mrs Newton at the Temple the truth:

> 'Some day I shall say to her, "Mrs Newton, do you know my master's very fond o' me? I almost think he'll *marry* me!" "Marry *you?*, never fear!" "Oh, but", I'll say, "the other day I really thought he was going to *kiss* me! and he speaks quite *loving* to me when no one's there; he only speaks roughly to me when anyone's by."[84]

Arthur smiled nervously, hoping that no one ever discovered the thrill it gave him to kiss her when she was dirty. He especially liked to kiss her when he was in full evening dress. He did not mind Hannah making him dirty as it would not show; he even treasured the possibility: 'If any black did come off her it was from her lips.'[85] Arthur had to learn not to show his feelings when he saw men being familiar with her. An elderly man, Jemmy, a messenger who also took down the shutters of a nearby wig-maker, would often tell her, '"I could kiss them lips for ever."' Once Thornbury asked her to clean out his chambers, that had not been touched for years, and paid her in old *Law Journals* rather than cash. She did the job and sold the periodicals to another of her admirers, Josiah Rees.[86]

In the middle of May Arthur arranged for Hannah to spend five days in Shropshire with brother Dick. As soon as she left he missed her – 'The Light of the house was gone' – but he was about to leave for a visit to his parents. Hannah and Dick were met off the train by their brother Jim and his wife Lizzie: Dick took their things to Jim's cottage at Wombridge and Hannah went to help Lizzie sell fried fish at Oakengates market. Jim still had his wheelwright's shop in

Oakengates: and they had a market stall every Saturday to earn extra money.

Arthur was pleased with Hannah's 'ruddy, blooming and rustic' appearance and her broad Shropshire dialect 'which long years of service in alien kitchens have disturbed'. He studied the regional accents he came across and recorded the words of his subjects in dialect. Hannah reported to him her conversations with Lizzie's neighbours, local colliers and other country folk.[87]

On 2 June Thornbury caught Hannah leaving Fig Tree Court apple-cheeked, clean, and wearing her grey stiff frock with the frill round her neck, on her way to her weekly French class at the Working Women's college. He called her as she was leaving and looked up from his papers, saying:

> 'Why how nice you look – you look prettier than ever I saw you!' 'It's only my frock, Sir,' said Hannah calmly. 'If you was to see me in my dirt as you generally do you wouldn't think so!' 'Well, dress *does* make a difference!' 'Not with me, Sir . . . if I'm as black as a sweep, as you *have* seen me, or if I'm drest up like this, I'm just the same country wench.' 'I don't take you as a country wench," said he, "you're a very sensible woman and I respect you highly. 'Here,' he added, rising and approaching her and offering her a couple of shillings, 'take this – I do wish you'd give me a kiss.' He seized her hand, but she wrenched it from him and drawing back, said respectfully, 'No, Sir, I've told you before, I never kiss anybody: I respect you when you behave to me like yourself, but I'm not afraid of you, nor of any man, and I don't want your money, Sir; them little things I do for you, you're very welcome to 'em.'[88]

Arthur left England on 14 August for Italy and Switzerland with his young cousin Henry Pearson. He would have preferred to go with Hannah: 'poor fellow, a sorry substitute for Hannah and in spite of his good nature, a strange comrade on such a pilgrimage'.[89] This holiday would prove a disaster: Henry died of sunstroke at the Hotel de la Poste, Bellinzona on 16 September. He was taken ill on 19 August and Arthur did his best to make his cousin comfortable: he hired nurses to care for him; wrote to his aunt and uncle about their son's condition; contacted the Consul at Turin, and booked rooms for relatives to come and stay in the hotel. Then he carried on with his holiday: on the fatal day, he was in Turin, enchanted by a chambermaid who reminded him of Hannah: 'she brought me my bath and stayed to talk for a while'.[90]

Arthur had hired Ellen to help Hannah with cleaning, wallpapering and whitewashing their rooms, and to keep her company while he was away for five weeks. Hannah liked to martyr herself by insisting on doing all the hard jobs and then complain that Ellen was weak and could not do the work. Ellen had problems with her 'young man' and her big sister was a good listener. Hannah remarked that her sister was over-religious, grumbled too much and was jealous. The summer of 1875 heralded Ellen's increasing presence at Fig Tree Court and Hannah's resentment of Ellen's influence with Arthur.

On Saturday, 3 October, Arthur travelled north to see his family and visit Molly Nettleton in Flamborough. On the first day he walked to a service in York Minster: in the afternoon he visited his first Hannah, who was now living at Dame Middleton's Hospital, an almshouse in Sheldergate. His father's influence ensured her a comfortable place after years of loyal service to their family. Meanwhile, Hannah Munby enrolled in the English Literature class, her second at the Working Women's College. She was in high spirits and sounds a little manic: sometimes she wondered aloud if she was 'too happy'.

All plans were abandoned on 2 December when Arthur

heard that his father was unwell. Later that day he went to York and walked from the station in bright moonlight. His mother was in the morning room with his sister and brothers and he saw 'my dear father in bed, calm and tranquil: and read by his desire Psalm thirty-four'. The following day Arthur's father assured his family that he was ready to die: and at nine o'clock that evening Arthur assumed the role of paterfamilias and took his father's place to read a sermon to the servants.[91] Mother was 'feeble and in pain, sat on the sofa in the morning room with her head on my shoulder'. Arthur read his father more psalms and helped him change his will and 'looked on his calm and manly face ... while he prayed aloud and earnestly said that he knew in whom he believed'. Arthur kissed him goodbye and caught a train to London, arriving at three o'clock in the morning. He walked from King's Cross to the Temple through quiet streets deep in snow. Hannah was waiting up for him, a fire blazing in the grate. After a few hours' sleep he went to work, but could not concentrate: 'spent sad and anxious day, haunted by the dear memory of my father's saintlike face and solemn in prayer and my mother's love and feebleness'.

The following afternoon Arthur received a telegram telling him that his father 'was much worse and that I had better return'.[92] Hannah helped him pack and prepared a hamper of food for his journey. He arrived in York at 11 p.m. to find that a doctor was staying the night. The next few days saw Joseph Munby rally and sink. In the early hours of 21 December he died of congestion of the lungs. Mother had sat in 'silent agony by the bed, in my arms; and then we carried her away'. Afterwards Arthur walked with Dr Ball to York in the starlight. For the next two days he was preparing the funeral.

Sixty-eight carriages joined the family as they left Clifton Holme for the burial at Osbaldswick, two miles out of York.

Many mourners followed on foot: the blinds of every house were down and all the shops were closed along the route. On Christmas Day Mrs Munby, with many tears, had put on her widow's cap, and Arthur took his place as the head of the family and read the sermon to the entire household. On the twenty-eighth he left for London and started to write a memorial to his father. On New Year's Eve Hannah had a bad cold, and Arthur had 'no spirits to go' to the midnight service at St Clement Danes. When midnight struck he said a prayer for Hannah by her bedside. His last diary entry for 1875 reads:

> So ends a year in which I have had the infinite delight of seeing Italy; but in which I have suffered the greatest loss and keenest sorrow that I have ever known yet. Beloved father![93]

Arthur's tribute to his father consumed his emotions through the winter and spring of 1876, and for a year he wore a black armband. The more material he gathered, the greater the eulogy: a chance to honour a father whom he disappointed and outraged the time he discussed his love for Hannah. Arthur may have felt crushed by the memory of a man who was held in such high regard.[94]

Abiding by the Victorian conventions of mourning, Arthur's social life shrank for the first half of the year. He visited Borland and went to the country, but the social whirl of the past – two parties in an evening, concerts, 'at homes' and the theatre – was inappropriate. References to Hannah in Arthur's diary are glimpses rather than full appearances: her sayings and doings remained blank until 21 June.

Arthur did not benefit from his father's death: the £32,500 (nowadays worth about £1½ million) left by Mr Munby went to his widow: the children would not inherit until their mother died. On the first day of the New Year, 1876, Hannah is merely 'my faithful servant [who] ... has lived here alone, cleaning and caring for the house, occupying the kitchen and sleeping in the back room'.[95] Arthur's gloomy mood meant that the third anniversary of their wedding was not mentioned: the weather seemed to sum up his feelings: 'day was cold, raw and dreary'.[96]

On 15 April, Arthur went to see his mother and Hannah went to Shropshire for a working holiday: Ellen was hired to take her place. Arthur found Ellen to be 'an excellent servant', and he enjoyed her childhood reminiscences of her elder sister. On 20 May Arthur joined Hannah on a visit to Shropshire and was introduced to more members of her family: she met him at Newport and showed him round the town where she had been a nursemaid in the late 1840s. This trip marks a lifting of gloom in his diary: their walk through the 'pleasant and quiet little redbrick town' was the first moment of colour in a monochromatic few months. They rambled through 'charming woods and lanes beyond and by these in a glowing evening across fields to where cousin Gosling had a nine-acre farm'. There was a cordial reception from Thomas and 'sprightly Ellen', and they were given 'tea in state in a little parlour'. He and Hannah slept in a little room which 'overlooked the buttercup meadows'.[97] For the next couple of days Arthur explored the coal banks and talked to the local pit wenches: it was a joy for him to see a gang of them leaving Oakengates at the start of their annual trek to London in search of work in the market gardens of Isleworth and Brentford where he and Hannah would visit them. Arthur soaked up the atmosphere: the hysteria at the railway station, the kissing, the crying, the waving of hands and handkerchiefs, the crowds of lads seeing the lasses off.

On 21 June Arthur again picked up the account of *Hannah* he was writing. His retreat from life over the last six months had been accompanied by Hannah's withdrawal from the dressing-up dramas of the recent past. There is despair in his first entry for 1876:

> All this year, my Hannah has been receding from the possibilities of ladyhood, and becoming more and more what she used to be – a servant, and nothing else. She will not be persuaded to go with me into the country, even to Ockley where they have always supposed her to be a lady and where the Rector and his wife called on her and evidently thought her one: she will not appear with me anywhere as an equal; she can hardly be made to go to her French class at the Working Women's College ... 'What's the good of a drudge like me learning French wi' such hands as these?'
>
> All the dresses and bonnets and ornaments which I bought for her at first and which she wore in France and elsewhere are worn out or put away and she will not wear them any more. She wears nothing now but common kitchen clothes and even on Sundays never wears gloves ... when I ask her to go out with me, her excuse is always 'I've no clothes to go in wi' such as you; and besides folks 'ud know me for a servant by my hands and I canna behave – I like to be respectful and wait on 'em and not to have to talk nor pretend to be an equal.'[98]

She had had time to polish her arguments for leading the life *she* wanted to lead. Having a break from the charades may have given her the psychological space to see this part of their lives as hopeless and dishonest. Arthur was deeply disappointed when she told him that she was 'too old to change' and begged: ' "Let me alone and nobody shall never know what I am to you." '

He returned unexpectedly to the Temple, hoping to see her at dirty work and she told him: ' "Don't kiss me, Massa – I shall black you!" But I clasped her to me and kissed her just as she was beholding her sweet looks through the dirt; and knowing that all this was the sacrament of love and humility.' Hannah told Arthur that she had decided 'to live entirely in the kitchen' and had moved her things out of the room in the basement that had been her bedroom. This would now be Ellen's room. Hannah would answer his bells and wait on him upstairs, but withdrew from those secret marital spaces.

On 21 June Arthur had returned to London from Oxford and gone straight to Whitehall: at noon a messenger came to his room and announced that 'your servant has come to fetch your luggage'. As she stood in the doorway, Arthur noted her appearance:

> She was drest as the humblest of servants. She wore her old-fashioned black straw bonnet, with a snow white cap inside it which contrasted sharply with her face, for to say truth, her bonny face, though ladylike in feature and expression, was afire with labour and the heat of the day, and was bathed with sweat. Her old grey cloak, thrown back from her shoulder, showed underneath it her short sleeved lilac cotton frock, cut short at the ankles, and her large brown holland apron, and showed too her bare muscular arms and working hands, all ruddy and clean.

She dropped him a 'rustic curtsey'. Arthur told her gruffly that she had ' "better sit down and wait a moment" '. She had also brought him his letters, including one to her 'darling Massa' from 'your faithful drudge'. While she sat bolt upright on the stool near the door he wrote her a note 'not like my spoken words'. He told her, ' "Give this note to Mrs Cullwick . . . and tell her I shall be at home this afternoon." ' He held the door open for her because her hands were filled with his luggage, and as she left the room

> with a tone and manner more like a lady's she passed the door with another curtsey, smiling towards him with her

lips, but keeping her eyes cast down that she might not betray herself by looking at her master.

On the last day of June, Ellen was formally engaged by Arthur as a servant at Fig Tree Court. The Skeatses had proved troublesome: Arthur liked having Ellen there as a buffer. On 3 July Hannah and Arthur went to Isleworth Fair and met up with six working women they knew. When he sent her to Drury Lane to hear *Fidelis* she came home when she found how expensive it was, saying she would not allow him to spend so much money on her.[99] There are times in *Hannah* when he reminisces about how they used to be, observing:

> I saw Hannah go out of the house and across the court, just as she was; not dirty this time but clean and bright for she had just been preparing my breakfast. She wore a short cotton frock of dark lilac such as I love, without sleeves; a large white apron, coarse but clean; and a large snowy cap, of a French maid of all work. But she carried across the court a tub of cinders, and emptied it into the movable dust bin which the men bring round every morning . . . but I had forgotten that she had to do it and drest thus out of doors on a bright morning, I wondered if others admired her as much as I did. 'Oh yes, Massa! several gentlemen saw me and they *did* stare at me and my cinders!' It was Cinderella they stared at, not her cinders . . . this tall comely 'slavey' in a foreign cap and an English paysanne's dress moving erect and lithe in the open air, modest but unabashed.[100]

The following evening, with Ellen out of the way – her presence at Fig Tree Court inhibited their lovelife – he was allowed a favourite ritual. Earlier that day he recorded his anger – jealousy was the subtext – at hearing of Thornbury's treatment of Hannah. Thornbury grew more mercurial, sometimes ardent, often cruel when Hannah spurned his advances, giving her the dirtiest of jobs by way of punishment. What Thornbury never found out was Hannah's indifference to his pettiness and cruelty. Arthur was upset to hear from her that when she waited on Thornbury he had flung scores of dusty old letters over the floor and commanded her to pick them all up. Hannah was not concerned, but Arthur was jealous of the attention his tenant was able to command from his wife. After she had waited on Arthur at supper (she had eaten the remains of his dinner for her own supper), she returned:

> she came up again unbidden and invited me to go down and see her in the kitchen, that she might wash my feet there. I went, and she, kneeling before the fire, washed her master's feet for the thousandth time.[101]

Hannah withdrew into a world of scrubbing and more scrubbing. When Arthur returned from the office he had been taken aback at her unusually black and dishevelled appearance. He had found her on her knees scouring the public stairs: 'clad in a sacking apron, and looking black as a sweep; and her hair sprinkled with whitewash'. Arthur wondered at the wisdom of having Ellen in the house:

> Hannah insists on being allowed to clean my boots always for boot cleaning being the lowest work of all was ever a *sign* of her being *mine*: and especially since the days when she cleaned more than one thousand pairs of boots a year in service and was known as a first-rate shoe-black – but chiefly Ellen's function is to keep her sister company when I am away and help her when I have company. Hannah is glad of this but a little jealous for she is apt to look on Ellen as a poor creature who has little strength and is good for nothing but dressing fine o' Sundays and doing 'little finickin' work' such as dusting and serving.[102]

Hannah and Ellen had a fuller social life than most servants. When Hannah was satisfied that all the chores had been completed, they would go for walks, take a trip to the Botanical Gardens at Kew, visit old friends, and invite brother Dick and their cousins to tea parties in the kitchen.

In early August there was a new note of resentment. Arthur had been to see the Reverend Borland and called Hannah up to the parlour to tell her his news. She listened and asked: ' "Please thank Mr Borland for remembering me and give my duty to him, but what will he care for my duty?" '[103] A few days later, Arthur received an old looking-glass and summoned Hannah, who was taller than the delivery men, to move some paintings to make room for it. They enjoyed playing the parts of the meek servant at the command of her 'brutal master'. When the two workmen had gone he was delighted when 'the drudge, black as she was, flung her arms about her master and kissed him ... "But you nearly betrayed yourself, Massa, once or twice you all but called me *Dear!*" ' After she had cleared away she came upstairs and sat by him in her old chair and read aloud to him as in the past.[104]

On 19 August Arthur and Hannah left the Temple for a two-week touring holiday in Shropshire. Judging by the number of their visits to old churches and the remarks he made about their recent restoration work, this must have been a working holiday for the Ecclesiastical Commissioners. The day before they left Thornbury had told Hannah, ' "You are a beauty," ' as she waited on him at breakfast. She had bought a new pair of gloves 'to please her master'.[105] Arthur reported that Hannah had started the day cleaning boots and blacking the grates, carrying coal and water in her rough servant's dress, and now, twelve hours later, she had 'sailed into the ladies' coffee room' at the Raven Hotel in Shrewsbury where they were staying. He marvelled at the way she was dressed and adorned as a lady, self possest and elegant and comely as if she were to the manner born; and she knew how to behave with such condescending grace to the obsequious chambermaid who showed her to her room.[106]

The following day 'she was with her master all day and pulled against wearing gloves and said it was harder work being a lady nor being a servant'. They explored Church Stretton and its environs for four days, where Arthur made a note of all the pretty servants he saw and other 'comely wenches' they chanced upon on their walks and rides. A week into their holiday they were in Ludlow, staying at The Feathers Hotel; then at New Radnor, where Hannah stayed at The Eagle Inn on her own while Arthur visited Aberystwyth for a couple of days. He was relieved to find her happy on his return, and to hear that she had been treated as a lady. On their last night in New Radnor she told him she was looking forward to not having to pretend to be a lady and on the way back from Monmouth to London she changed to being a servant, happy to put her gloves away.[107]

At the beginning of October Arthur spent a week with his grieving mother in Scarborough. Before he left Hannah had scrubbed Fig Tree Court from top to bottom, and been ' "under the beds, flat on my belly!" ' and

Hannah says that my new grates make her hands blacker than ever; since she has to clean the cakes of soot off the glazed tiles every morning. 'But I'd liefer have my hands black nor clean ... and I'd liefer go to bed tired wi' scrubbin', nor wi' climbing great hills or staircases of hotels. I *will* be your servant to my life's end and I hope you'll never take me out again as a lady. It makes me miserable, I feel so useless and idle!'[108]

Faced with her refusal to go away dressed as a lady, Arthur went away on his own. In the weeks leading up to Christmas he visited Gillingham four times, Brighton, his brother in Northamptonshire, Ockley, Ripley and Southend. Meanwhile, Hannah immersed herself in her work, singing at the top of her voice as she manically cleaned Fig Tree Court, taking on more work from the tenants. Rees was to be married in December and Arthur would take back his rooms: perhaps the extra space would give them privacy in which to restore their married life. Thornbury continued to pay attention to Hannah: Arthur overheard an incident:

> Yesterday, came my tenant Thornbury, and Hannah left her dirty work to open the door to him. As he entered, 'Hello, how are you?' he said to her: and condescended to add 'Shake hands!' She, glad to see her 'other master', obeyed and then cried, 'Oh dear, Sir, my hand is black, an' it's soiled yourn!' Whereupon, she told me, 'I wetted the corner o' my apron wi' my lips, and wiped his hand, an' he let me do it!'[109]

Thornbury's compliments became more extravagant and his tips more generous. Some routines, such as Hannah reading aloud to Arthur after supper, were re-introduced: '"What can be more pleasant than our meetings in the evening, and our reading, Massa?"' One day Arthur went down to the kitchen and watched her clean:

> She crept out of the kitchen window into the area and standing there washed and scrubbed the frames and sashes of the three windows. Then she climbed into the yard above, and swilled it with pailfuls of clean water, and swept the wet flags end to end vigorously with her besom: then she did the same to the area, stooping also and unstopping the drains and gullies, and searching and cleaning them with her hands. She wore her old peasant's bonnet and coarse striped apron, her frock tucked up, and a red kerchief over her shoulders, and a pair of my strong

boots. Her face and arms were black with sludge. After
working thus nearly an hour, she came in, washed herself
in her tin bowl at the sink, and went up, rosy and clean,
to tea with Ellen.[110]

She drew Arthur's attention to a huge lump of coal she
had found in the cellar which she 'carried upstairs poised on
her right hand from the cellar to the first floor. It all but filled
the scuttle and weighed twelve pounds, for I bade her weigh
it. No collier wench could have carried it in the same way.'[111]
Sometimes Arthur spotted Hannah hurrying about the Temple, doing errands, putting out cinders and cleaning, and saw
what an incongruous figure she must have cut to people who
were unfamiliar with her rustic look: that battered straw
bonnet she had for years; his cast-off shooting boots; her
layers of plaid shawl and comforters to keep out the cold. She
asked him with great glee: ' "Don't I look rough, Massa?" ' On
4 December, Arthur writes, she 'showed me a paper describing
her preference for hard work over being a lady'.[112]

Hannah's kitchen was busy in the days before Arthur's
Christmas in York. She decked the parlour with evergreens,
cleaned and cooked, and packed his portmanteau. When he
left on 23 December, instead of a goodbye kiss, she insisted
that he wait a moment and made a sign which cheered him
for his journey:

> When my Hannah saw that she was not to carry my
> luggage nor fetch my cab, she found another vent for her
> wishes: she, my darling, unbidden, fetched her blacking
> brushes, and went down on her hands and knees at my
> feet, and cleaned my boots; first wiping the mud from off
> them with the coarse apron she had on. Who else would
> do this?[113]

On his return, she was delighted with his gift: a pair of
clogs, and pattens (shoe platforms) to wear when she cleaned

the courtyard. They reminded her of when she was a pot-girl at The Red Lion. He was impressed how she 'looked gigantic'. On New Year's Eve, she gave him 'a satin cushion stuffed with her own hair'. In the winter twilight he sat on her knees, feeling safe in the arms of his 'gentle giantess'.[114] Ellen was away and that night they went separately to the service at St Mary-le-Strand. He watched her, in her grey cloak and black straw bonnet, sharing her hymn book with some poor children. At midnight they knelt by her bedside and prayed: her first words of the New Year were 'God bless you, Massa!'

One of Hannah's favourite malapropisms was 'Truth is stranger than friction', which she overheard one day when at the market. It is relevant to the events of 1877. Arthur was relieved to take over Josiah Rees's rooms on the ground floor in the New Year, so that they could have 'more privacy and quiet'. He planned to rent the rooms during business hours, and then use them as a retreat after the rigours of the day. Hannah insisted on taking on more work, asking to be hired as the laundress to whoever rented the rooms. Taking on more work and denigrating her sister's abilities were factors in her later illness. Ellen, who was a 'good and devout soul . . . and willing' must have despaired to know her sister's low opinion of her. Hannah often told Ellen she was 'a poor creature': '"She's no good at real dirty work, she canna kneel down and scrub the floors for hours together – no! nor will she swill wi' pail and besom neither!"' Hannah would compare Ellen to her obsessive self:

> Besides you know I clean grates wi' my bare hands; I blacken my hand inside and rub it as brisk as can be up and down the bars till my hand is as bright and stiff as the bars almost.[115]

On 15 January Thornbury brought his new bride to chambers and gruffly ordered Hannah to 'Show this lady in somewhere'. Hannah took her into Arthur's parlour where Mrs Thornbury stared at her 'but spoke no word, not even "thank you".'[116] Arthur started his diary reminiscing about Hannah's childhood and years in service, and imagined how he might appear:

> To look at him, indeed one would not think he honoured her much. Before the world he treats her like a mere servant such as she has been and wishes to be; and she for her part is his maid of all work and daily exhibits before everyone the lowly servile dress, the rough ways, the kitchen dialect, which she prefers to the finery and daintiness and delicate speech that nevertheless she can assume and adorn at pleasure ... she flatly refuses to be a lady ... Since her marriage she knows what it is to be a lady; to be respected and admired and waited on and called 'Ma'am' and driven about in carriages. *But she has no heart for such things.*'[117]

One evening Arthur went home to dress for a soirée in Chelsea and found Hannah cleaning out Rees's rooms in an ecstasy of pleasure. Hannah's cleaning was an act of penance:

> She luxuriates in the dirt and dust ... she lay down on the floor and placing her cheek on the dusty boards, thrust her head under the bedstead and drawers to see the under surfaces by the light of a candle beside her ... and thrusting her arm under the furniture she drew it back again and held up her arm and hand, covered with a fur of black dust ... The dirt was softened with the water and brush and lay like a thick film of black slime over the boards ... and this slime, being driven to and fro by her fierce scrubbing, flew up in great splashes over her face and arms, till she was pied and spotted and striped all over with liquid grime.

Massa had sat silent, watching this picturesque Rembrandt creature at her work and thinking over it: now that she had reached the utmost of toil and blackness, he said to her, 'And do you really like this work dear?' She stopped, the fair black quadruped – for so she seemed – and spread her wet hands on the floor before her, and rested her weight upon them as if they were feet: her face, blacker than ever and bathed in sweat was illuminated by the candle from below: but her eyes were shining with pleasure, and her rosy lips all smiles, as she had turned her face up from the floor, and answered him in these words: 'Yes, Massa, I *do* like it!'[118]

Arthur went upstairs to change. He rang the bell for her to help him. She told him she was too dirty but he insisted she stayed: '"for I cannot do without you"'. She looked on while Arthur dressed for an evening with ladies and gentlemen: 'he arranged himself in fine linen and broad cloth, the unmeaning varnish of civilization'. She stood, black, dirty and soaked from head to toe, wearing 'so many signs of self-sacrifice, of lifelong love'. To Arthur she was 'noble and most womanly in her outward degradation'. He told her he would see 'no one so sweet as you' at the party, and asked her to wash her face a bit so that he could kiss her before leaving.

At the end of January Arthur awaited his brother Fred's arrival from Turvey Rectory. Hannah was excited at the prospect of the visit, combining as it did extra work, play-acting and the joy of knowing something that Fred did not. It went well. Hannah was triumphant to have coaxed Fred to take his boots off so she could clean them. She was pleased to report that he had been haughty with her at first, but then her winning ways had caused him to praise her as a 'most attentive and devoted servant', before tipping her two shillings and sixpence when he left. Hannah chuckled at her own performance: ' "Well, Mr Frederick is gone, and I managed it all so well! I was as demure as an old hen; and I kept it up to the last and behaved to him like a thorough drudge." '[119]

Hannah determined to whitewash Rees's rooms on her own. Ellen was not allowed to help as she was a 'weakling'. In the midst of the muddle of decorating, Thornbury ordered her to scrub his floor while he wrote letters. When Hannah had finished, Thornbury thanked her and told her to shut the door and said to her, ' "I'll show you such fine things." ' Hannah told Arthur that she 'wondered whatever he meant'. Thornbury opened a box and inside were 'all his jewels and rings and suchlike – gold and diamonds all sparkling', and gave her some pieces to look at:

> 'He spoke so free it made me free wi' him; and the rings fitted me so I put one o' the diamond ones on my rough black fingers; and I held out my hand with 'em on and said, "Look, Sir, see how well your grand rings look on such a hand as mine." And then he took 'em off, and he laughed when he saw the contrast of the rings and my hand.' That was just like Hannah: to lose no opportunity of humbling herself and of appearing as the very opposite of a lady.[120]

Hannah's report to Arthur also mentioned that Thornbury had given her a two-shilling tip, saying, ' "Here, get yourself something to drink." ' Arthur was annoyed: 'this insult was the last straw of endurance'. Hannah made it worse by saying, ' "Oh Massa, that's nothing; whenever he given me a shilling he always says that." ' She thanked Thornbury and told him that she was 'a teetotaller now'. He asked her why she did not drink and she explained that she had enjoyed her beer, but ' "I give it up, and I feel ever so much better for it." '

In the middle of February Hannah appeared one evening 'full of spirits . . . drest from head to foot in Rees's Volunteer uniform' and looking like a handsome man of twenty-five. Hannah had found this uniform left behind and helped herself to it, intending to wear it as a winter coat.[121]

During the spring of 1877 Arthur, in the face of Hannah's intransigence, went away alone for weekends in Gillingham, Cheltenham, Rochester, Southend and Folkestone. He could talk to the Reverend Borland about her and often stayed with him overnight. With his encouragement, Hannah enrolled in the physiology classes at the Working Women's College. In writing *Hannah* Arthur was clarifying his thoughts: he compared and contrasted her with every woman he met.[122]

He was fascinated by the relationship between Hannah and Ellen. Despite Hannah's carping about her sister being 'feeble', they lived together in the kitchen in a companionable way. He noted that they never kissed and that no 'endearments of speech or act pass between them'. Sometimes Arthur had to intervene when Hannah was being intolerant of Ellen, and used 'the plain language of her class if Ellen is stupid or indolent, and calls her sister a fool, without mincing matters'.[123] It was not terse all the time, however: they would go to temperance teas and concerts at St Paul's and elsewhere together.

On 4 April Hannah visited Arthur at his office. He had returned that day from a short holiday in Cheltenham. Ostensibly she was there to deliver his messages and collect his luggage, but it was really to act out the master–slave routine and to hand him a note from herself. As soon as the boy had gone and the door was closed:

She was willing to smile and to be kissed and petted as she sat there in her short lilac frock and large brown holland apron and her rosy face a glowing within the white cap inside her black straw bonnet. 'Someone'll be comin', Massa!' at length she said . . . and she took up his hat box and his hand portmanteau in the other, as easy as a porter, and with a smile and an arch curtsey, said, 'Ouvrez la porte' and disappeared down the stairs into the hall.[124]

When they were together in the parlour later that evening Hannah told him how people stared at her old-fashioned bonnet and cap and the way she carried his heavy bags through the streets. He was more interested in her reception at his place of work:

> The head porter recognized her straight away and she waited as instructed and while she waited in the footman's seat some lads pointed and stared at her . . . but the boy soon come back and beckoned to me and I got up and followed him without even thinking that such beckoning was a kind of insult.

Even after twenty years of being in service Hannah had blushed at their stares. She was proud of being a servant, especially *his* servant, but had felt humiliated by the young minions. They were exerting their power over someone below them in the pecking order. Arthur reported her defence of the career she had chosen:

> 'Why do I choose such a low station and like it? Because I think the lowest station is the most useful and what others *wouldn't* choose and you know I wouldn't be in a high or upper station for the world. I should hate it. But I like to be respected in my own.'

Arthur was delighted when Hannah agreed to go to Ockley for a weekend at Whitsun. Earlier in the spring, she had dressed up for him, without being asked, and they had spent a joyous evening together. Satisfied that no one else was in, she put on her best white muslin dress, covered her hair with her best French cap and wore some of her jewellery, even her wedding ring, Arthur remarked with surprise.[125] On 19 May, after 'much scrubbing of her hands and brushing of her hair before she donned her finery', Hannah set off for London Bridge station on her own, meeting him in the pre-arranged carriage. After such a long gap they were tested when they found themselves travelling with the Rector of Ockley, the Reverend DuSautoy. Hannah coped well: they were relieved to be in their old rooms at The King's Arms, given a cordial welcome from the Wickenses and their servant Harriet. Lewis Morris, a poet whom Arthur knew, was at Ockley church when Arthur and Hannah went to take communion. This was the first time Arthur had met someone he knew when he was with Hannah, and he may have worried that word of Munby's 'lady friend' might have been passed on to others. Hannah and Arthur enjoyed walks together, 'she with childlike joy gathering ladysmocks and cowslips and exclaiming at the beauty of the woods'. On their return to the Temple they were relaxed: Hannah was invigorated by her short holiday, keen to get back to scrubbing and blacking. Wanting to build on the success of the weekend, Arthur hoped to go to Southend for her forty-fourth birthday, but Hannah refused: '"No, Massa, it's too soon, besides I want to clean the place."' At the end of May Fred came to stay: Hannah enjoyed these visits more than Arthur: her mood was 'joyous and half-amused'. She cleaned their boots, waited at table and served the food she had lovingly prepared.

By June Hannah was happy to go out with Arthur dressed as a lady for the day or evening. She also arranged to meet him at Piccadilly Circus and take his luggage back to the Temple after his weekend with Fred and his family, rather than endure the embarrassment of going to his office. One summer's evening, wearing her best cloak and Sunday bonnet and white cotton gloves, she met Arthur at Cannon Street station and they caught a train to Bexley Heath, then an omnibus to tea in Welling with Eliza, a servant friend of Ellen's.[126]

On 11 August Hannah went to Shropshire for an eight-week working holiday, staying with Jim and Lizzie at Wombridge, and with cousins in Shifnal. Arthur had bought her an old-fashioned black straw bonnet and paid her twelve-shilling rail fare and outstanding wages. While she was away Ellen looked after him until the end of September, when he sent her to the All Saints Convalescent Home in St Leonard's-on-Sea, for reasons unknown.

In Shropshire Hannah lived the life of a peasant, helping on the fried fish stall at Oakengates market and 'leasing' or gleaning when the harvest was being gathered in. Arthur left for a month's holiday in Switzerland, returning on 16 September. They wrote to each other and looked forward to the return to Fig Tree Court. While Ellen was convalescing, Arthur hired Miss Cooper, the head porter's daughter, to keep house for him. He had been on his own for a fortnight when he sent for Hannah to come home early. On 4 October, after a single knock at the door, she walked in, a rustic vision. She wore her Sunday-best clothes and was weighed down with country produce: eggs, cakes, fowls and hams, and 'roots of flowers' for her little scrap of garden in the Court. She wanted to roll her sleeves up and get to work. At breakfast Arthur rejoiced to see her so 'bright and bonny' with 'rosy cheeks and lightly sunburnt face, contrasting with her large snowy French cap, as her round apricot arms did with her clean lilac frock'. She was in high spirits at the prospect of the work that lay ahead: clearly Ellen and Miss Cooper had been slacking:

'My word, Massa, what a state things is in! It's a mighty good job as I've come home to clean for nobody can do for you as well as I can!' And all day long she was cleaning, and waiting on gentlemen.[127]

On 6 October, Arthur left the Temple for a twelve-day break in Yorkshire: he was with his mother for a few days at Scarborough and then spent some days visiting his flither-lass friends in Filey and Flamborough. As Hannah said goodbye before she carried his luggage to a cab, she promised she would be happy:

'Don't you fret – you know I like to be alone, especially when I'm cleaning – and I shall have a good week now all by myself, to clean all them dirty rooms and floor and stairs, and yard and passages as well. I shall enjoy it. And *wasn't* it a good job I came home?'[128]

Arthur had learned that it was not wise to leave her on her own for long to brood. On 16 October she wrote: 'I am often tired, and I am as black as a sweep nearly every day; but I like it and I never was happier nor I've bin since you left me all alone in the dirt!' And she spoke of the contrast between her large hands and the small white ones of a 'lady' who sat by her in the theatre gallery. 'Mine were red and swollen wi' scrubbin'.'[129]

Arthur arrived back on 19 October: the place was sparkling. Hannah proudly showed him her hands which could not be scrubbed clean: everything had been dusted, polished, scrubbed. She had been scouring the stairs until ten o'clock the previous evening, and his three new tenants had stared at her: she was the blackest they had ever seen. Arthur went to work, then came home for a brief time with Hannah, and then went out to dine, not returning until midnight. The following day was a Saturday and Arthur asked Hannah to go away for the weekend but she said that her hands were too bad, and besides, she had plenty of work to do. So, after a morning at the office, he left for a walk on his own in the countryside, and spent the night at The Talbot Inn at Ripley. His friend Vernon Lushington came to see him on the Sunday, and they walked over to the house at Pyrford which Lushington and his wife had rented until recently, trying to persuade Arthur to take it.

He caught the train to London the following morning and went straight to the office, returning to the Temple at four o'clock for two and a half hours until he went out to dine in Fleet Street with two friends. Hannah is not mentioned in his diary on Monday, or on Tuesday, when he went to work, then dined and read at his club, not returning home until eleven o'clock. As he stayed out late at his club a terse entry in the diary is appropriate. On Wednesday he went to Richmond after work and walked along the river bank: 'a fair and soothing scene'. By seven o'clock he was back at the Temple: no mention of Hannah. On Thursday, a day of steady rain, he left work and went shopping, then home to dinner at six o'clock:

> Hannah in bed: went to 85 Harley Street at 8 p.m., to Dr Julius Pollock . . . who came back with me and saw her, and stayed till 11 p.m., most courteous and patient and kind. He advised me to send her into the country at once.[130]

Hannah must have stayed in bed the following day. On Friday, Arthur went to the office, dined and read at his club at six o'clock and returned home in trepidation at half-past ten. Saturday would be Hannah's last day at Fig Tree Court. She got up and did her usual work in the parlour; she:

> lighted the fire, cleaned the grate, laid the breakfast table, prepared my breakfast: and as usual too, read to me the Psalm for the day; which (as usual too) was singularly

appropriate. At twelve o'clock she started for Shropshire. I went by train to Woking arriving there 3.20. Walked by the mossy old barn, along White Rose Lane.[131]

Since Dr Pollock had advised Arthur that Hannah be sent to the country, Arthur asked him what was the cause of the trouble, and if she might return to Fig Tree Court. It sounds as if she had a breakdown triggered by over-work. There had been an awful scene, the memory of which would frighten Arthur for years. It made such a profound impression on him that he always feared a repetition if she returned to the Temple. On 30 October, three days after her exile to Shropshire, she wrote to Arthur. It was presumably an angry, heartbroken letter: we cannot know for sure as no letters survive from that time. Letters sent a few years later are still bitter and impassioned and she would cry at the rejection she felt at being sent away from her home by her husband. During the first months of her banishment she pleaded to be allowed to return, assuring him she had recovered and that her 'illness' was gone. Whenever Arthur consulted Pollock again about Hannah's return he was advised she should stay where she was.

On 1 November Arthur told the Reverend Borland about Hannah: it was a relief to discuss events which he barely understood and had difficulty describing. Arthur did not feel strong enough to reply to Hannah's letter until 5 November: thereafter there was a flurry of letters backwards and forwards, from the Temple to Jim's cottage in Oakengates.

On 22 November Munby entertained Borland at Fig Tree Court and Arthur told him that Hannah had 'become a costermonger and likes it. And I too honour her for this.'[132] Ellen served their breakfast the following morning and she brought memories, 'in a large white cap and apron and buff cotton frock; she handy and willing, and looking just nice enough to make me miss Hannah the more.' Calm returned to Arthur's diary: he is relieved to receive a letter from Hannah the following day sounding happy with her lot: 'I wear my peasant's bonnet all day long in the cottage . . . and about the village road and my black straw bonnet I wear at the stall.'[133]

Ellen's return on 17 October after a three-week convalescence which had been arranged and paid for by Arthur may have been a trigger. Hannah resented Arthur involving Ellen in their disagreements, and felt they conspired against her. Perhaps Hannah had accepted Ellen living with them as a servant, but minded a great deal deep down. Years later there are references to Hannah's conclusion that her sister had been the cause of her ejection from the Temple by coming between her and her husband.

In the weeks up to Christmas Arthur reverted to his bachelor life, paid social calls, dined out a lot, went away for the weekends and thought hard about whether he should rent Sarah Carter's old home at Pyrford. He may have considered having Hannah to live there either as a wife or as his housekeeper, or he could have considered it too special to the memory of that disappointed girl. On 10 December, Jim's wife Lizzie came to London for the first time and stayed with Ellen in the kitchen bedroom at Fig Tree Court. Arthur made her welcome and took her and Ellen to the South Kensington Museum. After four days Lizzie left with armfuls of parcels and hampers: Hannah's possessions, her working frocks, caps and aprons, her clogs and pattens. Hannah had been told she would be in Shropshire until the doctor was sure it was safe for her to return to London.

Arthur went to Clifton Holme for Christmas and Ellen travelled to see her sister Polly in Ipswich. Fig Tree Court was shut up, the tortoise was in hibernation, and the canary taken to one of Arthur's barrister friends nearby. His mother was unwell and spent Christmas Day in bed: the day after Boxing

Day he walked to Osbaldswick to lay a wreath in memory of his father, before walking home in the crisp snow. While he was away Arthur made no mention of Hannah in his diary, other than the code he used for letters sent and received. The painful memories of late October prevented him from writing about his darling Hannah and their mad love.

CHAPTER SEVEN

Hannah's Story 1877–1909

A YEAR AFTER HANNAH's banishment from Fig Tree Court,
Arthur wrote of her abrupt return to Shropshire:

> Was there once, my heart a woman
> Whom I loved when I was young;
> Whom so ardently I worshipped,
> And so tenderly I sung:
> Whom I thought all pure and stainless,
> Meek and gentle, sweet and mild,
> One of God's selected children –
> Nay his own peculiar child:
> Whom her lowly birth debarr'd not
> From such higher nobler grace:
> One who owned a lady's nature,
> As she had a lady's face:
> One whom labour could not sully,
> No, nor drudgery degrade:
> Who was still in soul a princess,
> Though she seemed a servant maid? . . .
> What, was that glad beginning,
> And the ending such as this?
> Loathsome words and shameless spewings,
> From the lips I used to kiss?
> Do not tell that hideous story –
> Do not rouse that piercing pain!
> Love would chase himself to madness
> If he dwelt on it again. . . .

Therefore, thus I tell my sorrow,
Only then, my heart, to thee
I have injured, I have lost her,
And she was not made for me.
Love himself cannot restore her;
Never more shall treacherous time,
Give me back that stainless woman
Whom I worshipped in my prime.[1]

'Loathsome words and shameless spewings' show Arthur still wounded by the storm. At the time the verses were written, Hannah was living in limbo with Jim and Lizzie and their two sons in Wombridge, wondering if she would be allowed to return to her husband and her home in the Temple. Arthur may have hidden behind Dr Pollock's professional advice to keep her in the country for the good of her health, and to avoid a repetition of the row which had shaken him so badly. For the first few months of her exile Hannah made the best of it, resuming the peasant's life she had been living just before her breakdown, waiting for a letter from Arthur telling her she could come home.

But the letter did not come. By the summer of 1880, decisions had been made: Dr Pollock could not be satisfied that it was prudent for her to leave the countryside, and Hannah was told that she could not return to Fig Tree Court. On 3 August, Arthur received a letter from Hannah, the first we know of since the 'hideous story' of late October 1877. It was written in Somerford, in Staffordshire, ten miles from Shifnal and Wombridge. Hannah had gone to live with her cousin Charlotte Cullwick, a needlewoman, in her secluded cottage: Arthur gave her a monthly allowance which she paid into her post office savings account, opened in 1880 in the name of Hannah Cullwick, not Mrs Munby. As well as sewing, Charlotte sold vegetables she grew and was glad of

Hannah's rent and help with sewing jobs, her enthusiastic stick-gathering and the work she did around the cottage. Three years after her breakdown, Hannah tells us about her feelings at this time, and how she was adjusting to the decision that she might *not* return to the Temple.

My Darling Massa

If you have never read *David Copperfield* I wish you would – you know how I told you how the clerk downstairs had said I was like one of the characters in it, but I can only find David's aunt – and she is odd to anyone else – anything like me. The book altogether is so homely and life-like. I *should* like you to read it. Poor Traddles is such a simple and grand young man – a barrister in the Inner Temple and he hid his wife in the chambers all day and so it's something like and yet so different to you and me for they're equals and they enjoy themselves heartily among the few friends they have and at last he comes to be a judge and well off with a family of nice children . . . Oh by the way I was dreaming about poor Ellen [her sister] last night . . . she was ill, very ill and I was carrying her about and nursing her but she was tetchy and impolite to me as usual and I was obliged to leave her in disgust and give her up as beyond my endurance and whenever I dream of her it's something the same, something she says cuts me to the very heart till I'm writhing with pain past describing and yet I do pity her and am *sorry* for her. I'm sure her life must be a sad one – a sweetheart marrying another and then a friend dying and no society in London or anywhere else hardly . . . The reason why I haven't written to you sooner is because you gave me 'till next month' to write and because you didn't send a card just to say 'Flowers doing well – thanks' . . . I like to feel sure my sending is not too troublesome. And again I rather thought you shirk'd answering my last letter by saying I

asked you not to write sooner. And I couldn't understand
how you could take so patiently my three months silence.
You vex'd me so I think I should have pulled the telegraph
wires down to know the reason. But it's best, my darling,
to feel no compulsion in this if we are to dwell apart
always as you say to forget is the only way to be comfortable. Your loving letters set my soul on fire and I cannot
rest and yet I would not hurt a hair of your head nor have
you think me unkind to you. I know what I know and
what I do not know I will not seek to learn. You know
the hours you've spent in writing to me – you know the
hours I've spent in writing and working for you – but all
I might wish to say could never make you understand me
nor the nature of my love for you. I am very well in
health and in my mind wonderfully happy. God bless
you, my *sweet* Moussiri, but do pray that I may forget you
as I do heartily forgive you.[2]

She signed the letter simply 'Hannah'. Arthur had a bad
summer: Hannah Carter had died in May, his mother in July,
and the situation with Hannah had to be worked out. He had
buckled under the strain: 'my unutterable private sorrows
came to a head, and gave me work enough to keep my wits
together under it'. The house he took over from the Lushingtons from May 1878, a reminder of Sarah Carter, was a
sanctuary. He was well off following the death of his mother.
Clifton Holme was sold at auction in 1880 and along with the
considerable estate his father had left, the proceeds were
divided between Arthur and his three brothers and sister.

From Somerford, Hannah moved to Wolverhampton, to
lodge with her brother Jim's daughter, Emily, a former servant
who was married to George Gibbs, a groom. She paid them
part of her weekly allowance from Arthur, and cleaned, sewed
and knitted for them. One of Hannah's letters to Arthur from
Wolverhampton shows an intimacy: she advises him to 'take a

pint of common good ale a day to keep the bowels open and then I feel sure the piles would leave you'. Hannah reminisces about her time at Ryton Rectory (prompted by reading an obituary of the Reverend Eyton) but her emotions are mixed and there is a detachment in her mood. She describes a recent dream in which she and Arthur were out riding on horseback: her horse was as big as his, she points out. When she dropped a few pennies she dismounted to pick them up and 'you went off and I couldn't find you again'. Her feelings are both positive and negative:

> Indeed, my own darling, I have felt my love for you as much as ever this last six weeks although I have as it were given you up and have no desire to see you. I consider we have been married ever since the first month we met – certainly going to church didn't cement us any stronger than we were before – except to the world's eyes ... kindest love, dearest, and I am your own Hannah.[3]

By 1882 Emily and George's first child, Ada, was a toddler, and the need for space prompted Hannah to move. From Wolverhampton, she went to lodge with George Gibbs's widowed father, Charles, in Bearley, a picturesque village five miles outside Stratford-upon-Avon. Charles Gibbs was fifty-two, an agricultural labourer, a rough-and-ready fellow who had been born in the village. In the 1881 census his youngest daughters, Ellen, aged fourteen, and Mary Ann, aged eight, are living with him. Ellen is described as his housekeeper. Next door was his mother, another Hannah, aged seventy-seven, a gamekeeper's widow, and two unmarried sons, John, forty-six, and Edward, forty-one, also farm labourers. Hannah went to live with a tightly knit family to whom she was related by marriage, meeting them for the first time in the summer of 1882. They gave her a warm welcome, as she wrote to Arthur:

My darling Massa

    . . . they are all kind folks giving a very hearty welcome as well as being very respectful to me . . . As I expected there is not much room for me to sleep in this cottage . . . the house is three old cottages opened into one and I have to go through in and out to reach the stairs leading to my room. I have to stoop to get in and out of the doors. . . . One thing, dear, I feel *happy* and that's what I haven't done in many a day. I go to bed and get up again with a lighter heart nor I have had in a good while. You didn't say anything to make me *permanently* happy, my moussiri, but I enjoyed your visit – you was very nice and as sweet-natured as ever for kissing and I enjoyed working for you and waiting on you so perhaps you'll wonder what made me *alone* happier. It's this, darling – I see that you love me as much as ever your nature will let you and I also see that you enjoy being alone as a bachelor and having no inclination like other men for a wife – it's decidedly better that you shouldn't be bothered by the ones about you and so my mind is more settled and it would be weak and foolish of me to fret for what we have as if it were done on purpose, tho' *I* was quite [sic] as to the consequences of such a long engagement, but I must say I used to wonder how ever it would end and I used to feel every year that the rod was the longer for my own back – so it has proved, tho' I didn't expect this sort of suffering – to be *alone* in the world that's of all things the worst thing a *woman* can have to endure I am sure, still, dear, I do not complain, and indeed you will not let me – so I will not seem to. Time passes wonderfully quick with me, so quick that I hardly reckon it, therefore don't you be anxious about me, nor trouble for me. I only want civility – from them about me – and a little work as I like, and then I am happy . . . I send you my love and best wishes, darling, hoping nothing I've said will vex you, for I am sure I

don't want to do that. I wish you all good and may God
bless you as well as myself.[4]

Bearley had 215 inhabitants. Hannah lived here from 1882
to 1887, during which time the Reverend Robert Kempthorne,
then the Reverend John Dover, were the vicars of the tiny
church of St Mary-the-Virgin (there are only fourteen pews)
which she attended. A reading room and library had opened
in 1878 and 'was well supplied with useful and entertaining
literature. Refreshments on temperance principles may also be
obtained.'[5] Hannah had not planned to live with the Gibbses
so long: she had thought to stay for a couple of months. She
hoped that one day she would be able to take a place as
housekeeper to a gentleman, as old ladies were so 'fidgetty'.
Hannah went 'leasing' or gleaning when the harvest was in,
gathered sticks, picked mushrooms and berries, went sightseeing to places associated with Shakespeare, and wrote long
letters to her husband, counting off the days until his next
visit. In June, Hannah signed a letter to him: 'kind love
and kisses for you, my darling. I am ever your true slave and
wife'.[6]

Hannah's letters from Bearley show her subtly informing
Arthur about her point of view. Amidst village gossip, or an
account of a book she was reading, or of local working
women, she would correct him where she felt he had mistaken
her motives. In the weeks leading up to his visit in the
summer of 1882, she wrote that she had never been jealous of
the ladies he knew:

> I am glad you find so many interesting ladies and from
> Shropshire too. You like company and I have not bin
> used to fresh faces and I don't enjoy company only *some*
> children's. I *never* felt jealous of you and ladies for all
> I knowed as you liked to be among 'em and it wasn't
> because I couldn't see my own defects either nor yet know

the value of ladies' abilities but I knew *you* and I loved *true* [even] if I didn't understand and I am thankful after all, I am not disappointed in much.[7]

Word soon got round a tiny village: folk wondered about the relationship between the newcomer, Mrs Munby, and Charles Gibbs. When the new vicar, the Reverend Dover, called at the cottage he made Hannah feel uncomfortable: 'I thought Mr Dover looked a bit dubious o' me staying here.'[8] Hannah sensed that people did not believe she was properly married. She had a poor opinion of the Reverend Dover who 'gabbled his prayers ever so fast and there's most of the old folks here as can neither read nor write a letter so how are they to be impressed if the prayers and psalms are not said distinctly in his sermon?'

Arthur was able to judge for himself when he spent a week with Hannah in August, staying with William Beesley, the blacksmith and shopkeeper in the village. The Gibbses' cottage would be empty much of the day when the family worked to gather in the harvest: she wanted to cook his meals, wash his feet and engage in their favourite rituals: 'we can enjoy it better nor going to towns or abroad because there's *no* gentlefolks, nor no one to be afraid of meeting and I shall dress in your way as much as I can'.[9]

The visit was a success, and Hannah looked ahead to where she would spend the winter. She wanted a 'little cottage of my own where you could come sometimes, but it wouldn't do for me to be in it *alone*'.[10] Until she felt strong enough to do that, she would continue to store her possessions and lodge with various relations. Hannah decided to stay at Bearley 'until she found it too cold'. She was jittery about returning to Emily and George's: her niece could be 'uncivil', and had refused to let Hannah have a fire in her room. If she and Emily fell out, then she would return to Bearley, find a cottage or a place to work and 'do for someone. I rather fear that tho' lest I should have to forget you more nor I do, but I am not afraid o' liking anyone else much less o' loving them.'

Hannah proved indispensable to the Gibbs household. She paid to lodge with them, she took Charles's brother Edward to hospital in Birmingham where she was able to get him better attention. The Gibbses were illiterate and Hannah read aloud to them, and wrote their letters and read out the replies. Hannah accepted that Ellen was Munby's housekeeper at Fig Tree Court. Although she did not write to her sister, she frequently sent her love in the pages of her letters to Arthur, sometimes adding advice about her housekeeping duties.

Relations with Emily and George were cordial enough for Hannah to spend the autumn and winter of 1882 and the first half of 1883 with them. During the summer her help around the house had been useful when Emily gave birth to another girl. In their letters, Hannah and Arthur discussed the special nature of their love, savouring its rigmaroles and enjoying the memories of some of its more outlandish features:

> As you say, my dearest . . . no one else would *ever* understand *our* love – if they knew I had been up the chimney and rubbed the bars of the grate wi' my hands and blacked my face all over wi' blacklead and let you wipe your boots on my face and let you walk over me in the street when I've been kneeling at the missis's front door and all that and they would say, 'Pray, what has that to do wi' love' – doesn't it show Hannah to be a poor fool and he is an oddity. So, darling, it must be. I only wish the end could have been better, but thank God I am happy and well.[11]

Sometimes Arthur dreaded Hannah's letters: he could not be sure that there would be no reference to the pain of their love. Every letter she sent him mentioned the past and he felt

defensive about how things had turned out. In July she wrote
him a letter from Wolverhampton, with confidence:

> I never feel any older but somehow the experiences of the
> last six or eight years has learnt me a great deal, so as I
> feel that whatever may happen I should never fret again,
> nor be astonished at any thing. I have always known the
> peculiar circumstances you was in concerning me and I
> was always willing to love and serve you, under a cloud as
> it were. Indeed it was and is painful to be with you before
> anyone so used as we had got to being alone together and
> coming so long as I did to your rooms on the sly like,
> afraid o' the sound o' my own footsteps almost in the
> Temple I think has made me so nervous and shrink from
> seeing anyone strange or anyone belonging to you. It's a
> pitiable feeling to get into and I think since I've been
> going away from you so long and my desire to see you is
> less. . . . I dislike the thought o' seeing you because I know
> it can never be but for a short time and you must be gone
> again. I wonder that you should allow yourself to have
> tears of love for me – it's hardly prudent I think but of
> course I'm not sorry to hear you say so – and it's all that
> I have to warm up the old love and old times – memories
> of you. I am what you may call happy and gay even. . . .
> God bless you, my dearest, and with my best love I am
> yours faithfully and affectionately.[12]

By September Hannah was at Bearley, 'a-nutting and
blackberrying' and picking up wood for the fire. She got on
well with young Annie, and decided to stay with the Gibbses
'as long as ever I can'.[13] Her mood was buoyant: Arthur's two
visits in 1883, which had caused Charles Gibbs to mutter that
surely his home 'was not fine enough for *him*', had lifted her
spirit. She addressed him as 'precious Massa' and was 'lovesick
all the day as you went away'.[14] Hannah hoped the winter

would not be too harsh as Emily's new home in Clarence Street was smaller, with little space for her. In November there was trouble with Charles Gibbs: his daughter Annie was sleeping in the next cottage with Granny Gibbs and Hannah had to reject Charles's advances, sleeping with furniture wedged against her bedroom door. She was happy there but for his unwelcome interest, was confident she could deal with him, however, and made no attempt to find new lodgings:

> My darling Massa . . . I seem to be settled down here and I feel quite content and find it quite as pleasant in the winter as in the summer. It's so snug having the fire and cooking all to myself. Annie still sleeps in the next house and I have got over all compunction – or *nice* feelings about *Gibbs*. I hope he never has the least thought now. I look at him firmly but kindly when I have occasion to look at him and we do sometimes a sitting over the fire when I'm reading to him.[15]

At the same time the Reverend Dover called and questioned Hannah about her relationship with Charles Gibbs. Regarding her as a social inferior, he felt he could pry into her life: 'He asked me what relation I was to Gibbs and how long I was going to stop, and said, "Of course Gibbs likes you to be here."' Hannah refused to answer his prying questions and simply replied, ' "Well, perhaps cause I make myself as useful as I can," ' and wished him good day. Hannah reduced the amount of beer she was drinking: she only had a pint of porter when Charles Gibbs went to collect it from The Golden Cross on Saturday nights. She was astonished by how much better she felt: 'I am not like the same person, but twas always the same.' Hannah spent Christmas with the Gibbses but felt 'screwed down to Bearley somehow' for the immediate future. Charles feared he was going to lose his job in the New Year and Hannah decided to stay until he found work: her rent would help them survive the winter.[16] Their lives became more difficult when he was given notice to leave by the owner of the cottage, the landlord of The Golden Cross: Hannah fretted that she was the reason, but Mr Hawkes changed his mind and their lodging was safe.

From 1884 Hannah and Arthur sent each other postcards in French, to encourage her to practise her elementary French, and as a way of communicating that the postman would not be able to understand. Gossip about Hannah living at Charles Gibbs's cottage had intensified, and she arranged that Annie stop sleeping in Granny's cottage and come and sleep with her in Charles's cottage. This was uncomfortable as the young girl was a restless sleeper, but Hannah 'felt more satisfied having her with me, but only for what people may *think*'. The Reverend Dover had been to see her again:

> I opened the door and he said, 'Oh are you still here.' 'Yes, Sir, will you come in?' He did but would not sit down and kept me standing. He said, 'I thought you were not going to live here.' I looked at him and said, 'I shall stay here till March most likely.' 'Oh yes,' he said and looked as if he would have liked to say more but he never said why he called nor anything hardly and never offered to shake hands when he said 'Good morning'. I said 'Good morning' too for I began to feel indignant with him I can tell you and if he *does* come again like that I shall tell him not to be afeared to speak to me of confession if that's what he wishes. Once he was preaching about temptation and I *thought* he looked pointedly at me when he said we should avoid temptation in everything.[17]

Apart from the affront that she, a married woman, would be 'carrying on' with Gibbs, Hannah's pride was hurt: 'the idea of his suspecting me with a loutish man like Gibbs is preposterous'.[18] The Reverend Dover called to see Granny but 'did not look in' on Hannah. Sometimes Hannah's semi-nomadic existence made her miserable, and she felt alienated by not having her possessions around her. She had arrived in Bearley 'with just what I stood up in and carried in a bundle and they've been enough for me' and wished she did not have 'half so many things to lug about with me'.[19] But there was Arthur's visit to look forward to: she told him she would be wearing her cotton bonnet and would carry his luggage to 'the meadow as before'. Arthur planned to meet the Reverend Dover and explain their unusual arrangements, although she was unsure whether to reveal themselves to a man she disliked:

> I think him too stupid for you to acquaint him with ourselves but for all that I should like you to go with me to the Communion one of the days. Your verse to me is very nice. It's impossible for me to write all I *think* like you do, my darling, but oh I do hope all will be right in the end as I don't ever doubt.[20]

The middle of April came, and Arthur had just left Bearley. She told him proudly that she had not shed a tear, or

> even felt sorry to part with you. I don't love you less than aforetime – it's because I am older and have had experience enough to learn me the folly of fretting at anything as may come or go but I shall never give up feeling a pleasure in doing for you whatever I can and whenever I can.[21]

Arthur was relieved and dared to hope that the worst was over. But he was anxious about her drinking, and she tried to allay his concerns: drink had probably lubricated her 'loathsome words and shameful spewings' of 1877: 'It quite overpowers me sometimes to think as you should be afraid o' me drinking a pint o' porter! You seem to have lost confidence in me, dear, over that and you needna for I only have little.'[22]

Hannah made a mention of her menopause: she was fifty-one years old, and she felt she was looking and feeling her age:

> my hair is quite grey and do you know my eyes are beginning to get dim. I cannot see things close half so well as I used to. I suppose I am very well indeed for my time of life and am getting over all that wonderfully well to what some do, but I *do* feel tired generally.[23]

In the autumn Hannah had likenesses taken by Mr Charles William Smartt, in Rother Street, Stratford-upon-Avon, the first photographs of her in seven years.[24] On the day of the 'Stratford Mop', 13 October, when servants gathered in the market place hoping to be hired for the year, she was photographed in her hood bonnet and working clothes, as if offering herself for work. It was a characteristic pose, biceps on show and no concession to 'flummery', Hannah's word for fashion. The leather wrist-strap and wedding ring had gone. Arthur annotated the reverse: 'Hannah after thirty years of rough hard work in service'. When she arrived at the studio she had been nervous, but found Smartt 'civil' and was flattered when he called her 'ma'am'. When he asked for her husband's name she would not tell him: ' "Ah that's what I mustn't tell you – he's a literary man from London and if you make a good likeness o' me in my peasant's bonnet I am sure he'll be pleased and it'll be for your good." '[25] Hannah was also photographed in her finery, her biceps hidden, nothing other than a lady.

Hannah's last letter to Arthur in 1884 shows indecisiveness about her plans and weariness about the village gossip:

> I feel strange and upset at the thought o' leaving Bearley ... but I feel sure it'll be cold here this winter and a

change will do me good perhaps ... Mrs Hughes [a neighbour] said one day there's them about as think and even say as you and me aren't *married* and she says we must be or you'd never seem so fond o' me nor speak o' me as your Hannah and so on ... As I always told you I *expect* folks to think the worst o' us instead o' the best and I care very little *what* they think.[26]

Hannah spent Christmas in Wolverhampton, staying until the middle of April 1885. Her third year in Bearley was overshadowed by the effects of the menopause on her physically and emotionally. Mood swings dominated her letters to Arthur: the same letters could be filled with joy and contentment, but also bitterness and self-pity, and she brooded on her expulsion from the Temple. She hoped her change of life was over in 1884 but it is clear from her letters, and his attempts to placate her, that she was far from well:

I'm very poor at writing letters to you considering how much you send me. I feel quite angry wi' myself over it – and my mind's never at ease and this doesn't satisfy me no more nor my last did. I keep well only them terrible flushes will come over me and they tell me I shall have 'em worse yet.[27]

While Hannah was in Wolverhampton she had gone to a lecture on John Ruskin, and knowing that he was an acquaintance of Arthur's, she worked herself up into a critical mood:

and there's certainly been one thing sadly lacking in you and that's you encouraging my own backwardness to talk to you – you've never let me come close to you like, nor made me open enough wi' you like I see the other women as are nothing to you can be. I *have* got used to even *that* way o' yours and am so used to it as I have so little to say to anyone else and am only really happy wi' you and I

don't suppose *any* woman alive would be happy along o'
you as a wife as I am; when you're always reading and are
so quiet and only like going about and smoking as you do
and yet you *knew* I was happy when I really believed as
your weakness was not an excuse for me being only a
servant and not an equal – I'll say no more about that,
dear, for you'll be sure to mistake my meaning. Perhaps
all has turned out for the best both for your purpose and
mine. I *know* you have always loved me and *you* know
that I have loved you from the delight I always had in
working for you and not for myself.[28]

Hannah began to blame Ellen for being thrown out.
Arthur visited at the end of April, the first of two trips to
Bearley that year, and though they had a happy time, the first
letter she sent on his return was angry about the past:

how I do wish now that no one [Ellen] ever had come
amongst us to break our peace. However, dear, we can
only be thankful things are no worse and I am sure there's
no one more ready to forget and forgive than I am if I see
the least encouragement to do so. And you must know
that my love and devotion was and is so entirely to you as
it was no wonder I should be drove mad as it were, when
I could find you could write them words. But I am sure I
don't wish to recall them and I was glad to know you had
burnt 'em but that hasn't hindered the thoughts o' 'em
gnawing at my heart all these years and making me enjoy
no life and only wishing for death. You canna stand me
telling you as much and I think you are wrong for that.
You *ought* to be able to stand that much . . . you may
depend on it, darling Massa, that I am quite as willing to
live on and *be happy* too in the *thoughts o' you* when I
canna see you . . . I canna help loving and respecting and
admiring my own moussiri now as much as ever and even
more perhaps in a different way and it's a good thing

when love is settled down to contentment and deep
respect ... I am glad for I've so often thought you had
sacrificed the greatest pleasure o' life as some folks think
for me knowing all the while I wasn't good enough for
you.[29]

Eventually, Hannah goaded Arthur to answer some of her
questions. Drinking seems to have been the catalyst for her
breakdown, about which she was still in denial. She was sorry
for her behaviour and embarrassed about it. Hannah reminded
him that 'I love *truth* and I should like to know where and
when it was I had that DT [delirium tremens] twice as you
once wrote I had, for it's a tremendous untruth whoever told
you.'[30]

All through 1886 Granny Gibbs was a malevolent presence:
an irascible old lady, for the last ten months of her life she
made Hannah's life miserable. Charles Gibbs and his two
brothers, like all farm labourers, were suffering from the falling
price of wheat. Charles's wages had been reduced to eleven
shillings a week and the farmer threatened he would have to
'take another shilling off next pay if the wheat's no higher'.[31]
Hannah wanted to leave but felt obliged to stay to try to help
make ends meet. The Gibbs family needed the money that
Arthur sent her.

In early February her friendship with Granny was tested
when the old woman doubted that she and Arthur were
married, and accused her of being a 'kept woman':

I haven't been in a very happy mood lately and I dislike
telling you the nasty little tales I have to hear and bear
with coming from Granny Gibbs who is so old and ought
to know life and things better than me and this being her
home and that when she says hard things of me it
naturally makes me uncomfortable – being only a lodger

among 'em. She has been very spiteful or spleenish again me.[32]

Charles Gibbs had other worries: his thirteen-year-old daughter Annie was spending too much time with a lad in the village, and later in the year she would have a child which died shortly after birth. Learning of Annie's pregnancy, her father sent her to live with his mother. With Granny's encouragement, Annie also turned against Hannah. On 10 February:

> Last Saturday morning brought it *all* out. Annie mouthed and shouted at me so. I couldn't bear it. I'd scoured the table outside and because I took a cloth to wipe it and dry she begun her impudence and shouted as her granny could hear her. I shut the door and slapped her mouth with my hand. She kept on mouthing and saying things I couldn't bear and I hit her again and when I turned away she struck me across the bridge o' my nose with her father's book, hurting me so and making the blood spurt. She was frightened at that I reckon and made off into her grandmother's and I followed her to hear what tale she told and I showed Granny my nose and begun to tell her what made Annie impudent – for nothing – she wouldn't look but . . . kept saying why didn't I *goo* away and I said, 'Granny, how *dare* you speak to me so' and she got up and stared me full in the face and said, 'You bin only *a kept woman*. Mr Munby's got a wife and family in London and you've bin in bed with Charles many a time.'[33]

There was only one solution and that was for Hannah to live in her own cottage. She had the means to buy one: she wanted to spend her life savings on a house with its own little garden. She guessed that the old woman was near the end – 'so tottering and grey looking' – forgave her behaviour, and was as civil as such intransigence would allow. She counted the days until the first of Arthur's visits that year, and asked him to explain their marriage to Granny, which he dreaded doing. He stayed with the Beesleys again and the trip was a great success: his diary does not record a meeting with Granny, but he did visit the Reverend Dover to explain their circumstances, whereupon the clergyman insisted that 'he had never heard a breath of scandal against her since she came into the village'.[34] Hannah bombarded him with tales of her encounters with Granny: after all the years, Arthur could still be amazed and a little frightened by her:

> Hannah held forth about Granny Gibbs. When she speaks to her equals – and is excited, her Welsh blood – wild barbarian blood – comes out strangely. She thrusts her head, flings her great bare arms wildly about, wiped the foam from her lips with the back of her hand; a rude bardic figure, she is, a handsome Meg Merrilees, with flashing eyes and widely planted feet.[35]

Even in the face of continued name-calling by Granny and Annie, Hannah stayed. Although she was not easily frightened, she had a bad time with her landlord in July:

> Gibbs turned on me ... and I see how it is he got so wherrited [worried] having all the [grand] children ... and he being at home ... and it's too much for his temper. And I suppose he thought I was at the bottom of it and so he let me have his spleen and ... someone told him about you looking over the farmhouse and me going to the bank and to the house in Snitterfield Road. He said I had been axing for lodgings. I told him such a thing was never mentioned but he was *furious* with me. I kept upstairs from then [Monday] till Sunday morning and never saw him but I knew he'd be in all day and dinner was to be got, so I came down at the usual time. We looked each other full in the face and I bowed my head

and said 'Good Morning' and he said it too and then he talked as before. But I am afraid of that man and of his daughter Annie as well – not of their fists but of their tongues and so I've been in a terrible frame of mind ever since not knowing where to go for the best, nor having a soul to speak to for if one says a word to anyone I always feel an intruder and in the way.[36]

Hannah was sure the old lady was going to die: she had heard the deathwatch beetle 'in the corner' where she sat and dreamed of 'a shower of cherry blossom falling near me – that seems a sign of death'. On 3 August Granny took to her bed, unable to walk. Ten days later she had another stroke and was paralysed down one side of her body: Hannah nursed the old woman until she died on 3 October. Hannah's stomach turned at the smell of Granny's bedroom: she had to clean the place when the Reverend Dover called:

I put her room straight and scoured the floor and stairs next morning before Mr Dover came and I took her sheets and clothes off and have washed and changed them three times since as well as washing her feet and legs. She was in a most offensive state and is such a gross person and her not being a woman as I like either and that you may know and really it was almost more nor my stomach could bear altogether with doing all.[37]

In August Hannah wrote to Arthur telling of her plans to visit London soon: although she was sad at not being allowed to visit him at the Temple, she reassured him pointedly that she would spend time with friends, and go to an exhibition. She promised him she would 'not think of the hardship of not seeing inside my old place. I canna help loving it and London for your sake, dearest, and I always shall look on it as my home. I can be happy anywhere through experience and time.'[38]

Granny's rapid decline prevented Hannah going to London: instead, she nursed her until her death. Arthur was visiting when Granny died. Hannah felt she had to help Esther and Eliza, the dead woman's two older daughters, to 'wash and shroud her and lay her in her coffin: it was a sickening job ah do believe her hadna washed herself for years'.[39] Arthur attended the funeral (the first in Bearley for nine years) on 7 October, noting that no blinds were pulled down in the village and no spectators stood on the route to the church, signs of Granny's unpopularity:

> The neat elm coffin with black ornaments was laid out on the ancient carved bedstead upstairs; and in it lay the Granny, dressed in seemly white garb and in her own frilled cap: and looking far cleaner (thanks to Hannah) and more amiable than she did when alive. Flowers in wreaths and posies and long drooping fantasies were laid around the head and across and about the body, arranged in good taste and both gathered and arranged by these poor folks, her children, grandchildren, who stood around her, silent and tearful.[40]

Although Hannah's life was better without the poisonous presence of Granny, her rent was more vital as Charles was on short wages and he had to pay for the funeral. Hannah would remain at the Gibbses' until May 1887. She was now on better terms with the Reverend Dover: the improved relations had been brokered by his wife who liked Hannah and asked her to teas at the vicarage. Hannah made shirts for Arthur, knitted stockings, and wrote letters to help Charles's daughter, Jane, find a place as a parlourmaid. On 23 December she wrote wistfully to Arthur saying how much she would like 'to have thee with me another Christmas and perhaps in one's own cottage which would be better and I am looking forward to a pleasant time now'.[41]

Hannah's move back to Shropshire was hastened by the illness and death of her favourite brother Dick. His chaotic bachelor life meant he spent his last months living with Jim and Lizzie at Wombridge. Hearing of his gasping for breath, fainting, and suffering from swollen legs, the three sisters rushed to see him before he died. Worrying about Dick brought back memories of their childhood: father hitting them and 'ill using their mother', her ears being boxed, and her father's coldness when she left home.[42]

On 19 April she received a note from Dick addressed to 'My dear sister and mother to me' which made it clear he was much worse. He could not breathe properly and had to sleep sitting in a chair: 'Lizzie is very kind, she tries to bolster me up but it's of no avail . . . I do not think I shall last much longer.'[43] A note two weeks later shows that his last wish was for Hannah and Ellen to patch up their differences. Their relationship had taken a turn for the worse after Ellen's marriage to a legal clerk called William Cooke in 1882. Hannah was bitter that Ellen, who still worked for Arthur, was able to live with her husband at Fig Tree Court while she was banned from there. Dick told Hannah: 'my dear, I am ill. I do not know what to do for breath and fainting attacks. My legs and feet are swelled – they are so thick . . . I should be so pleased to see you and Ellen friends before I go home [die].'[44] Hannah and Ellen called a truce, but ill-feelings resurfaced as soon as their brother died. On 24 May 'Poor Richard breathed his last . . . he hadn't three minutes' sleep the night before . . . nor had half an hour for this seven or eight weeks.'[45] Dick's death made it easier to escape from Bearley: the time Hannah spent at Wombridge got the Gibbses used to the idea that she would not be around for ever.

For the next twelve months Hannah's life was nomadic. She was with Jim and Lizzie until September, and then stayed secretly at the Temple for three weeks while Arthur was abroad on holiday. She decided to go to her old home without telling him and give it a nostalgic spring-clean. She knew that her sister and her husband were on holiday, and made friends with Arthur's other servant Harriet, telling her she was Ellen's sister and hinted at a special relationship with Mr Munby. She was happier than she had been for ten years, to be in 'this long-loved place . . . it seems now as if I'd never bin away at all while I've bin working away all these three weeks wi' such a joy as no one in the world could imagine but myself and it's you who's made me love it so much'.[46]

When Arthur returned he was shocked when she walked into the parlour:

> I rang but no one came until I rang again, and then a tall figure in a plain servant's dress entered the room in answer to the bell. It was Hannah: why had she come and when without notice and without leave to this place, so full of loving but also of terrible memories. She was pale and silent, tremulous with suppressed excitement. 'You made me speak and I meant to be dumb and never say nothing, only wait on you . . . I felt I *must* see my old home again; so I came by the excursion train and when I seed what a lot there was to do and how folks serve you, I felt I must stop and set things to right.'[47]

Arthur was dumbfounded, but when he saw how calm she was, he was relieved. He dreaded being reproached for sending her away. Neither Hannah nor Arthur mentions her seeing Thornbury and Ralston, who were still renting rooms. He was relieved when he heard that she had got on with Harriet: Hannah had treated her to a river boat trip and they had been to church together each Sunday. She proudly showed her 'grannered' hands: 'I kissed them, rough as they were and especially that which has the ring on it and we spent the evening alone together.' The morning after his return he rang the bell for prayers, and Hannah and Harriet knelt down together: then he sent Harriet out for the day and 'when she disappeared I took Hannah in my arms and kissed her and said: "My darling, two female servants kneeling one on each side of me at prayers and one of them is my *wife*!" She answered: "Yes, Massa!" with passionate fondness and "Oh isn't it nice!" '

At Easter it was decided that Arthur would rent a four-roomed cottage for Hannah in Trench, Hadley, that Jim had heard about. The owner was Mrs Chilton, 'a buxom post-mistress', and the rent was two shillings and ten pence halfpenny a week. There was a small garden behind and it had a 'pleasant view ... over fields to distant trees and farms'.[48] At 6 Trench Road Hannah shared a privy in the garden with her neighbours the Rickerses, and grew vegetables, kept hens and chickens, and a pig in a sty in the garden. She gathered her possessions from where they had been stored and looked forward to their first privacy.

Hannah was happy to be making a nest: she liked Mrs Rickers and her daughter Lizzie whe were 'so willing and simple'. Jim had sown spinach, potatoes, peas and beans before she moved in so she would have food for the winter. She bought furniture from auctions in Wellington and Shifnal that summer. The folk of Trench were curious about them: 'Mrs Rickers said to me the first day I come – Mrs Chilton was proud as you and Mr Munby are coming to live under her. Why they say as he's a *squire*.' Hannah told her neighbour he was a '*gentleman* and his father afore him and *I* am like you a working woman and the difference makes us a *match*.'[49] She gathered twigs and berries for the winter, and copied out Arthur's poems, some of which he published in 1891 in *Vestigia Retrorsum*.

During her first summer in Hadley, Hannah wrote to Arthur she 'was never so happy in all her life as I am in this little house'. Saturday nights she worked on Jim and Lizzie's stall at Oakengates market. Depending on their health and the weather, Arthur would come to spend at least three months of the year with her. On his rambles around Hadley, he made friends with some of the local pit-brow women: one, Becky Price, became a good friend to both of them. Thirty years of note-taking had not dulled his appetite for dirty wenches, he was still keen to collect. He was enchanted by Becky: 'A sweet bonny girl of thirty with a healthy rosy face and rugged hardworking hands. Works at Ketley Bank Pit, earns seven shillings a fortnight.'[50] She was a widow with four children and lived with her parents in Wombridge. Jim and Lizzie were friends and paid her to do their washing and housework.

Hannah had missed the camaraderie of her family. She, Jim and Lizzie relied on one another, but she could not be close to Ellen. The poems she copied out for Arthur put her into a reflective mood about their long love:

> I have done my best for *thee* and everybody I've had to do with but there is no mistake that thou is first and all to me and always has been and you ought to know it too for having given me so much of thy self. I think God must favour us and give us peace in the end and you can see even my sisters hath forsaken me cause they know I am thine, but I never did mean to forsake them and they drove me to it.[51]

One evening Hannah disturbed a chopper-wielding burglar in Jim and Lizzie's cottage looking for the takings from the stall. She was afraid of being robbed when she was out at her brother's, leasing at harvest time, or gathering horse shit off the roads to manure her garden. So she made a dummy of herself in a chair near the window that was visible from the road – 'I put a silk handkerchief on the head and a newspaper and light at its elbow' – and had fooled some neighbours who banged at the door wondering why they could not wake Hannah up.[32]

In autumn 1888, everyone in the country was looking for Jack the Ripper: Arthur, a newcomer to Hadley, was accosted by a gang of local men who thought he might be the serial killer. Hannah's account shows how fortunate he was to get away unharmed:

> This is how Lizzie [a neighbour] heard the tale. Joey Phillips and Mosey Lawrence . . . saw lots o' men and lads rawdling a man with a satchel on his back – but it been dusk they didn't see it was *you* and besides Joey's eyes are bad – just had 'em took out and only one put in again and they've give him a glass eye but he won't wear it, and Mrs Phillips says there's nobody about here carry's a satchel but Mr Munby and rushed off to tell Lizzie. Mrs Rickers heard of it at Trench and a woman said, 'Why I'm told as a lot o' chaps set about a gentleman last week and took him for Jack the Ripper . . . and Soppy as led the gang and Tommy Jones . . . is frightened now and disguised himself thinking the bobby'll be after him every minute.[53]

Christmas 1888 was their first together: Hannah explained to Arthur her insistence on being his slave. Her troubled childhood, combined with the deep impression that Byron's *Sardanapalus* had made on her, suggested to Arthur that she had been looking for him, as he had for her. By coincidence they had found each other in Oxford Street. Arthur knew the plot of *Sardanapalus* but he did not know that for thirty-four years he had been playing Sardanapalus to her Myrrha:

> So that was the genesis of her love; as instantaneous and as lasting, as mine has been for her. Before she went up to bed tonight, she called my attention to her hands. 'You

haven't noticed my hands yet; this time, Massa, you see how rough they are!' . . . I took them and felt them and kissed those laborious palms. 'I honour your hardworking hands; but I never wish them to be again as hard as they were when I used to cut the horn off for you and your Missis said you wasn't fit to wait at breakfast with such hands. *Now* you're to work as much as you like, and when you like and no more.'[54]

When Arthur left the cottage Hannah would roll up the rugs and put them away with the best crockery, cutlery and scented soap, which were for his use only. He described the kitchen, used as a parlour on his visits:

In front of the fireplace the Japanese hearth rug I bought for her which she will only use when I am here. In the middle of her room is her ancient oval table of black oak with solid framework of the same, and is covered with a clean and handsome white tablecloth which was spun by Hannah's grandmother . . . The table is a century old or more – one half of it stands in the window between the net curtains and bears two rows of plants, geraniums and hyacinths and posies of primroses and Lent lilies and has room for some of my books and papers. The other half stands opposite against the inner wall and close to the plain deal door that opens on the front of the bedroom stairs and had upon it Hannah's musical box, and a few books, her Bible and a volume of Mr Pepys . . . next to the window in the other side opposite is the housedoor with steps outside and leading straight down into the lane. . . . The fourth wall . . . at right angles to this door is covered, like the inner wall with pictures of Hannah's choosing, *Graphic* and *Illustrated* pictures sent to her by me, old framed prints which she has picked up at village sales and photographs of herself and me.[55]

Hannah's happiness was secured because her neighbours knew that she was Mr Munby's legal wife. She helped Mary Rickers the postwoman to deliver telegrams, wrote letters for neighbours and copied out his epitaphs of faithful servants. She wrote 'characters' for a couple of local girls seeking work: she was instrumental in helping Becky Price's daughter, Polly, get a place in Blackpool.

On retiring from the Ecclesiastical Commission in 1889, Arthur was able to spend longer with Hannah. He busied himself on writing projects with which she helped, dedicating his collection of faithful servant epitaphs to her in 1891. He spent more time at his country retreat, Pyrford, which was a source of jealousy to Hannah who resented the servants who worked for him there. It took Arthur years to summon up the courage to tell Hannah that he spent much time there, and longer to admit that he had rented the farmhouse and had a housekeeper, maid and gardener. He had started renting in 1878, but even in 1890 he only dared tell Hannah that he was lodging there from time to time: 'My darling, I feel a bit vex'd as you've got, or getting what you call lodgings. Remember Miss Carter. Not as I'm anyways jealous tho.'[56] After her surprise visits to Fig Tree Court, Arthur must have been afraid that she would turn up at Pyrford unannounced and find out the truth of his living arrangements.

In 1891 Hannah loaned Jim £100 of her life savings to buy their old family home in Shifnal which was up for sale. Scrubbing and whitewashing the place ready for Mrs Stubbs, the tenant, brought back mixed memories. Jim was a man of means, renting out two other cottages which he owned. Lizzie was 'so tottering on her feet', suffering from dropsy and rheumatism, that Hannah had to fetch her buckets of water from the pump in the yard and take away gallons of water that was 'sludgy from the workmen's feet and the old dirt'.[57] The Cullwicks became firm friends with Mrs

Stubbs and her eighteen-year-old daughter who opened a
shop selling bread, butter, eggs and poultry in the downstairs
part of the house that Hannah had not seen in forty years.
The Stubbses were 'bettermost' folks who had fallen on
hard times: Arthur was taken to meet them in the summer
and was impressed with the widow: 'she is a very fine handsome woman; as fine as Hannah herself and about the same
age'.[58]

Hannah decided to move to the cottage next door. Mrs
Chilton was still her landlady, and the rent was three shillings
a week. She moved because the wash-house in the garden was
nearer to the back door, and she could make a better parlour
for Arthur in the front of the house. Arthur suggested they
live abroad, which she rejected: but some days she would
daydream about living on an island:

> Our love is made to live for ever . . . all is suspicion here
> by them as don't know us and though I am above caring
> for that it makes things unpleasant – you and me to ha'
> been perfect should have retired to an island where there
> was no one else but birds, beasts and fishes . . . where
> there was no ladies to court you and no common folks to
> wonder at me.[59]

There is no explicit sexual intimacy in their writings, but
a handful of erotic moments. One hot August day in the
cottage, she insisted on bathing him, and he records it as if it
was a ritual:

> 'You mun let me soap you all over, Massa; it's good to get
> the sweat off you; I always soap myself.' And as I stood in
> the bath, she did this for me with vigour . . . rubbing me
> down afterwards with equal skill. She stood there tall as
> myself nearly; drest humbly in blue cotton frock . . . her
> loving face and bare strong arms glowing red with the
> work; an obvious servant and yet an obvious wife; for

none but a wife might do such a thing and few wives would have the strength and devotion enough to do it. 'This is a slave's work, my dear,' said he, 'but you don't like it the less for that.' [Later that day] ... I did for her what she had done for me in the morning. To me it is nothing carnal or voluptuous but a thing of infinite sacredness.[60]

As they lay in the four-poster bed above their heads was an arrangement of valentines he had sent around Hannah's embroidery of 'her favourite letters M O D M' (my own dear Massa), and the 'sacred monogram' she had stitched forty years earlier: 'IHS'. She translated: ' "What a many things them letters IHS stand for! It stands for I, Hannah, Slave; and I, Hannah, Servant; and I Have Suffered ..." '[61]

For ten years at Hadley, from 1893 to 1903, Hannah battled with depression and drinking. Her 'dullness' and 'gloom' at Arthur's departures ran through her letters after a visit by him: these feelings were worse in the darkest months of the winter, and especially when lubricated with ale and porter. Arthur must have opened her letters with a heavy heart. Even though much of the time she was happy with her life, she had not put her exile out of her mind. In nearly every letter there was a mention of her pain and loss, decribing herself as a dog, all chained up and alone, with descriptions of her undying love and devotion. Hannah would sign her letters: 'your affectionate wife and servant', 'thy own slave and loving wife' and 'affectionate and faithful wife'.

Just before Christmas 1892 she had her purse stolen by local children but managed to catch the thief. Her nephew George, Jim and Lizzie's son, had been with 'bad wenches' and Hannah paid the doctor's bill; and there is a feeling that she is enjoying her misery. She was surprised at her own sanity:

You have not been unkind to me, dearest, but it's what I canna forget in past days as I think of that is so unsatisfactory. A woman has just been took to the asylum – her mind is gone all through bygone days – her husband's dead – but it's over him her's mad – there's nothing has such an effect as been hurt over love and I wonder often as I've kept so well as I have – but I'll never acknowledge that I've done wrong to anyone but myself and I have suffered enough for it without been reminded. I trust that I shall never be so wretched again and that in time my case will be bettered by *some* companion, but I shall always be your own slave and wife.[62]

Hannah was upset and confused at the beginning of the New Year: her thoughts were disordered. She picked up her pen on 13 January, the day before the twentieth anniversary of their wedding day: she may have had too much to drink before telling him that she has decided to give up ale and drink stout instead. She told him:

If you'd known or considered a bit I was overworked and hadn't got over my disappointment of you altogether or believe the reason and Ellen upset me . . . with telling me as I was to go. Then I told that wretched man Pollock everything again myself, and you didn't act wisely or rightly – so I've had that to work on my mind ever since – but I am going to grow callous if I can and care for nothing nor nobody – just me unto the end (as that canna be long now as I'm sixty) doin' as best I can and *lookin'* for the end wi' joy. . . . And I feel sure I could ha' shown myself as a true servant and yet have elevated myself in all ways if you hadna took my will away and made me resign myself to all your fads and making me a laughing stock to my fellow servants by blacking my face in the park and all that – not as it hurt *me* but it was unnecessary all that endurance – then after all them years of trial you couldna stick true to me, for all you knowed I'd no other friend . . .

Now *dearest* Massa, mind you this isn't a sermon for you nor a reproach. I always knowed what you was doin' on me – and that *I* was making a rod for my own back but I've never felt unkind towards you nor have I spoken cross to you really. When I have it's been the outlet of passion as I couldna keep in at them times . . . My darling, you know very little about me when you say I don't feel any sorrow or shame – not only that it's the *pain* I feel is enough to make one pitiable as well as loathing oneself. But I know that as long as I don't acknowledge it to be a fault I *canna* overcome there's no hope, for I *know* what has caused it and if I can only carry out my resolve I shall keep straight. Circumstances has so much to do wi' it tho' and them I canna curtail. I told you plainly enough as if I go quite without [ale] the neuralgia comes on in two months or so. . . . But this is what I am going to do – have *no ale* but a bottle of stout regular twice a week – that's half a pint at a time . . . that'll about keep the nerves steady I think . . .[63]

In the summer, while Arthur was away, Hannah went on a day-trip to London and met her sister Polly, to see the pomp of a royal wedding. She could not resist taking Polly to Fig Tree Court and introducing themselves to Arthur's house-keeper as Ellen's sisters. Arthur would have worried in case Hannah let their secret slip while drinking tea in the old kitchen with Mrs Denny. This visit helped her, she told him; she had

sat in the old armchair and rested . . . but I couldn't help having a faint sickening feel at bottom over it all and had lost all interest in everything belonging to it since I knew it was all nothing to me now and I must be there only by permission of the housekeeper and soon to say goodbye to it all again perhaps for ever. So I was thankful to be alone and *glad* you wasn't there. How different to times when I have been afore and felt nearly mad and prayed out loud that I could see you in the room if 'twas only your ghost. Thank God he has weaned me off that madness over *you* and I can go up and down again without a pang. No, not without a *pain* but I mean I can bear it without showing it or shedding a tear.[64]

Arthur's affectionate poem 'Susan', published in 1893, was about Hannah. He persuaded her to go with him to Church Stretton in the spring: they had not been there in twenty years. It was a successful outing: her disguise as a lady worked so well that he considered renting her a cottage there. But the next ten years would be erratic because of her moods and drinking, and 1893 was the start of the process of moving her away from Hadley: in 1903 she went to live in Shifnal. The core of the problem at Hadley was that some of her neighbours were jealous of her imagined wealth: she would lend small sums of money, at no interest, to people in Trench Road, and whilst most debts were repaid, some, like the Morrises, were tardy about paying her back and bullied her to lend them more. When Hannah refused they started a witch-hunt against her and they were instrumental in driving her out of Hadley.[65]

But as long as Hannah kept busy, and sober, her spirits remained on an even keel and she was able to ride out the rough times. While she could get out and forage for food and fuel, and clean her cottage, and read the Jane Austen, George Eliot and Charles Dickens novels Arthur sent her, she was content. (She loved Hardy's *Tess of the D'Urbervilles*: he had chosen it because Hannah reminded him of Tess.) When she was not gripped by depression, their strange love rituals were practised with enthusiasm, more on her part than his. Hannah, at sixty years old, was still as playful as a puppy: 'she went up to him and pretended to be a dog, she threw herself on the quilt and laughingly said, "Now I'm your big dog, as covers you all over; like I've heard o' them St Bernard dogs in the snow!" and she licked his face.' There was even a return to boot-licking, an activity that had almost been banned since their marriage: when it happens we can imagine Arthur indulging her to keep the peace:

> She often licks his boots as she cleans them; I have seen her do this openly at the cottage door. 'Ah just lick some o' the dirt off afore ah put the blackin' on,' quoth she. She has strange uses for her tongue, as well as for her hands.[66]

Revival of aspects of their past lives excited and subdued Arthur. After the rocky winter of 1895, he felt he had to allow Hannah such things from the past, and he offered an insight into why this practice had been a part of their lives:

> And as her own duties were the humblest and lowest of all they did not satisfy her where he was concerned. It was not enough for her to clean his boots: *she must also lick them*: for boot cleaning was her trade, she had to do it for everyone: so she must do something lower still for *him*. It was not enough for her to be as dirty as the other maids of all work; she must be dirtier and coarser than any of them, because she was *his*.

He arrived at Hadley in the middle of January 1895, but left in a hurry after an awful row: for the next four months a stream of angry letters reached Arthur who was suffering from bad eyesight and painful sciatica. On 22 January Hannah wrote:

> May God deliver me out of this fearful feeling and comfort *thee*. I know thou hast not wilfully harmed me. I

must lay the blame all on myself . . . God help me! I will be as happy as ever I can but I doubt you coming and going upsets me terribly and yet what can I do? I canna get quiet over it, nor self possessed. I trouble too much but I canna help it.[67]

Three days later her mood was calmer but she was snowed in and Mr Ceaser, the doctor whom Arthur had instructed to take care of her, found it hard reaching her cottage. She put on a brave face, but she was still not well: 'Make yourself easy o' me – it's so nice to think you love me and yet it makes things harder for me to bear.'[68] On 2 February Arthur sent her a questionnaire to elicit some more detail of her life. After his opening enquiries about keeping warm, and her rheumaticky arm, and if she felt calmer, he asked the question which troubled him most: 'Have you kept your promise over sending to The Bush and all that?' She replied: 'Yes I have not sent since, but I have had some ale and ginger beer . . . I have left off now.'[69] Three letters sent in February become acrimonious and self-pitying. Her rage boils over:

> Your letter is kind and loving but *oh* you don't seem to know how many years I have loved and *feared you* – both together so that while I long to see you – even to trembling with delight I am and at the same time have been dreading as something'd be wrong either in my dress or in myself for you to find fault with and it had always been as ever since I knowed thee and what with service so many years as the fear as I came to you lest anyone should see me and tell . . . all that has helped to make me fearful and nervous. But I know the greatest cause of all is me never caring to eat well.[70]

Hannah felt annoyed at his manipulation, and guilty at her own weakness. Her emotions and reasoning were in a tailspin:

I *believe* one great reason for my going wrong is been too much of a slave to you – indeed I'm sure it is – and however much *I* love to be a slave or servant to you that's no reason why you should urge me on to it. Love should make a perfect freedom on both sides and thou knowest how I have been always bothered by you over my bonnet or my cap or my hands. When I first knowed you I was going to do my work heartily but keep my hands as nice as I could. Then you was always saying they wasn't coarse enough – same over my dress – never letting me dress a bit smart, so that I've got thoroughly disheartened – having *no* joy in life and so you coming and going only irritates and excites me. Mind you I do not blame you – after all it must be my own weakness, but, my darling, let us help one another in forebearance and pity. I will *not* be bound over to any more promises nor will I write any more about my dress or work – only if I like. I'll do the best I can. I'm too old now to be troubled with trifles.[71]

He was right to fear that she was still sending out for refreshment from The Bush. He must have winced to learn that the wooden butt outside the cottage, on which she usually depended for her water, was still frozen solid, a metaphor for her feelings for him:

but ever since you went off I have been like spellbound and I scarce know how to write to you or even dare to see you again and yet that seems more than I dare think of for that'd take away what little charm there is in my life . . . I hope the water'll melt in the tub and with the change I look for a change in our future – only don't write much to me and whatever you do don't mention *that* and please God I shall live yet to master the evil.[72]

Arthur half-heartedly asked her to go abroad with him, but to no avail. In April a clearer picture of the scenes which had driven him away in January emerge: Hannah had been drinking beer and rum with a friend before he arrived, and seeing him she became hysterical with excitement, as she explained:

> I lost heart altogether – this comin' and goin' has always been an upset to me and *you* canna understand *my* feelings over it and I haven't the candour and boldness to tell you, so that I have felt that I couldn't live. I never was one for eating enough . . . and the beer . . . seems to do one as much or more good and up to a few hours o' your coming that day I had tasted no drink at all for a good while – then Martha Williams came and that excited me more so I had some rum for her and me and so I was got over excited. I know it isn't the first time but I do know the sole reason of it is as I don't eat enough but then I'm alone and haven't the spirit to go out and perhaps if I send to the shops I can get nothing tender. However, I hate making excuses for myself and I'll say no more about it and I hope I shall hear no more from you about it. I *am* better and I have had some tiny dinners lately, but I am very nervous.[73]

Arthur coped as best he could: he kept in touch with Hannah's sisters, paid Dr Ceaser to supply her with any medicine she needed, and waited patiently for her to tell him when he could see her again. His declining sight and mobility made these periods when she was 'dull' more difficult: the secrecy meant that he posted the letters himself at the nearest pillar-box which was not very close. He could not ask his servants to post the hundreds of letters he wrote to Mrs Hannah Munby of Hadley. The temperature of their correspondence was raised when he was sometimes not able to reply quickly. Hannah often interpreted this as a cause of gloom.

There is a photograph of Hannah taken in 1895 in Wellington, Shropshire, at the studio of Mr J. W. Bowler. Arthur first
mooted the idea at the end of April when she seemed to be
over the worst of her madness and sadness. On 23 May, she
put on her wrist-strap, which she had not worn for some
time, and trudged to the studio in her working clothes. Mr
Bowler caught her looking resigned, her wedding ring displayed at the end of her still-powerful arms. If the time Arthur
spent at Hadley is a barometer of her mental stability, then
1895 was one of the worst years of the 1890s: he spent only
seventy-three days there; 1897 was worse, he was only there
for sixty-five days. Happier times were in 1898 when they lived
together for 121 days and 1902 when they had 161 days of
togetherness.[74]

Arthur's visits to Hannah in 1897 were curtailed by her
annual and ale-fuelled breakdown, but also by an operation
on his right eye: he had glaucoma. On Good Friday 1897,
Hannah admitted she had a drink problem, but was in despair
and unable to give it up completely. Perhaps she was taking
ale as medicine, but it only made her worse: 'I know my fault
is drinking instead of eating – I never *could* eat much but
could always drink. Why is it my sisters are so different? Can
I help it?'[75]

At the end of April, Arthur was relieved that whilst she
had not stopped drinking, she was helping her brother and
his wife on the stall on Saturday nights, had spring-cleaned
the cottage, was collecting fuel for her fire and helping Becky
Price with Jim and Lizzie's washing, so she was well enough
to receive him. He travelled to Hadley on 10 May for a three-
week stay. Reassured that she was better, he returned to
London for an operation to relieve his glaucoma. On 9 June
his oculist, Mr Juler, was to perform an iridectomy on his
right eye. He could have been blinded by the operation which,
though brief, was risky:

The operation means cutting out a segment of the upper half of the iris. Cocaine, poured into the eye, numbs it *protem*: and the operation, which lasts only a minute, gives no pain other than the sense of being twice struck lightly with a *blunt* instrument. In bed all day, both eyes bandaged.[76]

Arthur was at the 'clinique' for two weeks. Hannah's next letter to him was barely sympathetic. He was due to visit her in August but she put him off coming. She was 'indulging in 'the nasty stuff', as Polly described it. She had suffered her worst relapse and her sister's letter of 2 September shows Hannah to have been suicidally depressed:

> My dear dear Hannah
>   . . . God alone can deliver you from Satan's devices and flesh. I pray for him to help you and he will . . . do, dear, wish to live for *all* our sakes. What should we *all* do without you here? Jim and Lizzie and I all need you. I always feel as though you were a mother to me. I wish I could do something for you. I can pray and I do and will . . . do not touch the nasty stuff . . . I should like to shield you from harm as I know you would me, dear dear Hannah. I cannot bear to think of your letters so I won't . . . Please! write again.[77]

Some of Hannah's remarks seem cold: she sounded as if she welcomed the chance that she could take care of Arthur:

> My darling Massa
>   I *am* sorry to know you've to go under such an operation with your one eye. Oh, I do trust it will be for *good* and nor for you to go blind – how should I feel if you couldn't see *me*? But if 'twas God's will and you *was* blind I should have to be your only servant then and do all for thee and that thou knowest I would do as long as I lived and had strength enough.[78]

Even though she knew the operation had been a success she reminded him about the role she expected to play, if he lost his sight: 'above all I like reading out to thee and if ever thou *was* blind, which God forbid, I'd tend thee as I always wished to do and for no other to do my work'.[79]

Hannah and Arthur's unusual sexuality continued into their old age. Her enjoyment of the role of slave to Massa meant that their marriage remained fetishized. More than once Hannah told him that even if she had not seen Kean's dazzling production of Byron's play she would have insisted on being his slave: '"I should ha' bin the same with you, Massa, even if I hadna sin that Myrrha in *Sardanapalus*. I couldna think myself no use to you else!"'[80] When they first met, fifty years before, he realized that she was the woman he had dreamed of and been looking for:

A robust hardworking peasant lass, with the marks of labour and servitude upon her everywhere: yet endowed with a grace and beauty, and obvious intelligence that would have become a lady of the highest. Such a combination I had dreamt of and sought for; but I have never seen it save in her. And from that day to this, my love for her and hers for me, has been in each of us a passion and a power that has stimulated and ennobled life, even through the very contrast of our lives.[81]

Written in Shropshire dialect, Arthur's poem 'The Shoeblack' describes Hannah's love of boot-cleaning. He struggled to stop her licking his boots, but never succeeded. Arthur felt that it was, in the end, wrong. Despite his protests, Hannah's stubborn desires had to be fulfilled when the mood took her: '"Eh Massa ... it's high time as I licked 'em" ... and straight away she threw herself on the floor at his feet. He took her by the shoulders, raised her, and clasped her and kissed her black lips, in a sort of shuddering rapture of humility and thankfulness':

So I brushes 'em and blacks 'em, aye an' kisses 'em
    an' all,
An' I sets 'em down to look at, they're that dainty an'
    that small:
If I puts my boots again' 'em, oh my patience don't I feel
What a clumsy foot my own is, aye an' bigger by a deal!
. . .
Eh, if I could be as near him as them boots is every day,
Why I'd stick to him like they do, I would never go
    away;
An' I'd carry him like they do, through the gutters in
    the street,
If I'd leave to do like they do, clip him always round
    his feet.
. . .
Still, I'd clean 'em like a good un, aye I would though,
    never fear!
An' I'd kiss 'em and I'd lick 'em, same as if I wasna
    theer;
Yes, I'd do it right afore him, till he couldna help but see
As I'd took it for a honour, such a job to come to me.[82]

Spitting on Arthur's boots was not enough to polish them brightly by her exacting standards. As she knelt before him she would lick the boots before pulling them off: 'I can always tell wheer you've bin by the taste o' your boots.'[83] Arthur felt this was 'offensive' but was thankful that the practice 'has not affected the sweetness of her lips – her country lips which have the velvet touch'.[84]

The last picture of Hannah was taken by Mr D. Fraser in Wolverhampton, while she was at her niece's house. (Plate 18) Arthur (Plate 17) was pleased with the photograph, comparing it with the one Dante Gabriel Rossetti had admired forty years earlier. Hannah, as a young woman, was a picture of 'grace and sweetness and purity': the older woman also had the 'face of a heroine ... though no one knows it save her husband'. He believed that the photograph did justice to her 'high noble character ... strong and resolute finely tempered nature' and her 'mature and inexhaustible love'. Arthur had it framed and hung in a secret place at Pyrford. It was 'curtained ... [so] that strangers may not intermeddle with its joy'. It was hidden behind black velvet and when he went away it was kept under lock and key.[85]

In 1903 Hannah left Hadley, driven out of the town by her spiteful and feckless neighbour Mrs Morris, and rented one of her brother Jim's cottages in Shifnal. Mrs Morris's theft of the ornaments Hannah put out for Arthur's visit was the last straw. Before this final chapter in Hadley, Arthur had asked the Reverend Borland and Vernon Lushington if he should move Hannah into his house at Pyrford: they said no. The Munbys' future was a source of concern when Hannah's equilibrium was shattered again, in June. In a letter of 9 June to Bill, a cousin, she spoke from experience of the pain and opprobrium of having a drink problem:

Drink is the curse of thousands in England and to those with a *heart* to feel and suffer over taking too much – it's a *tremendous* grief and overwhelming sorrow. You know *that* as well as *I* do as you know as well as me that no fellow creature in common has the least pity for them as torture themselves with drink and the only comfort is to know that God knows our hearts and the circumstances of *everybody*.[86]

A fortnight later, the theft of the ornaments upset Hannah enough to cause her to have a drink to calm her nerves.[87] Luckily this 'turn' did not last long and Arthur, Jim and Lizzie rallied round and were able to put her back together. Preparations were made for one of Jim's cottages to be redecorated quickly, and in the meanwhile, once her things were packed,

she would stay at Wombridge and with the Gibbses in
Wolverhampton, until she could move in September.

Hannah wrote her first letter to Arthur from her new home
in Wyke Place on 11 September: a harvest waggon and a farm
cart had been needed to transport her possessions. Looking
out of the back door, she could see her family home from
which Mrs Stubbs had recently moved. Hannah looked forward to being 'snug and quiet', off the main thoroughfare at
1 Bradford Street, but close enough to it for her daily errands.
Hannah was nostalgic about her childhood when she heard
the bells of St Andrew's church. She had come home: her new
neighbours were friendly, but after her experience with Mrs
Morris she was determined to keep them at arm's length.[88]
Hannah and Arthur spent Christmas together that year: his
description of the cottage in Shifnal creates an impression of
love and devotion being showered on the place. She made a
parlour for him in part of the kitchen: their books were
arranged there; pictures and photographs hung on the wall;
she bought an oil lamp for his reading; there was a vase of
flowers and 'a few other dainties'. In the same room there was
a range for cooking: on one side of the fireplace were
cupboards for crockery and food, on the other side were his
writing table and desk. They sat in armchairs on either side
of the fire; one was a 'handsome seventeenth-century chair of
carved oak' which faced her grandfather clock and 'ancient
brass warming pan'. The scullery was where she prepared the
food and washed herself. There was one bedroom upstairs,
'furnished as daintily as the kitchen' for his benefit. When he
was not there she rolled up the carpet and put it away, and
did not use the looking-glass and wash-stand and toilet-table.
Bare wooden boards were good enough for her, she insisted.
There was a privy in the yard and a pump for water.[89]

Hannah's time at Shifnal would have been idyllic but for
the cruel snobbery of a woman she met at a vicarage fête who

introduced her to Mrs McLean, the new resident of Aston Hall, whose flower borders Hannah had weeded as a charity girl sixty years before. Both women interrogated Hannah when she told them that her husband was a gentleman. The scene turned ugly when Mrs McLean gave Hannah a withering look and said, ' "You may be sure he has another wife in London." ' Poor Hannah felt obliged to go on: ' "I'm the on'y wife as he's ever had, and I know he loves me, same as I love him." ' Arthur was incensed, but Hannah begged him to let the issue drop.[90] She sometimes feared the return of her depression but rejoiced in her new feelings of contentment: 'I feel quite well and am happy thank God and I hope to be always so – it's nice to be alone and it's nicer to have thee to do for so it's good both ways.'[91] On his seventy-sixth birthday, she told him that she felt confident that her troubles were over and looked forward to their twilight years with optimism:

> Well, my own loving Massa, I wish thee *all* good and no more sorrow while thee livest and may God spare thee for me to do and work for as I have done these fifty years and more and I feel well nigh *sure* as I shall not suffer again as I have done something as you know from my own folly for I feel happier the older I get and that's a good sign and as long as I can find jobs to do I never feel mopey and that is when one is apt to fall.[92]

Hannah's physical well-being worried Arthur. In the winters of 1905 and 1906, a chest infection developed into bronchitis and he worried lest she caught pneumonia. Hannah begged Arthur not to fuss and 'wherrit'. But he did, taking out a subscription to Shifnal Cottage Hospital in case she needed a greater level of care. But his own health was also in decline: his sight was worse and the sciatica too. He worried about her health; about being able to post his letters to her; when he did not hear from her; about what would happen if they died without being able to reach each other. By this Arthur meant him not being able to reach her in time: it was inconceivable that she would be able to visit him before he died. Arthur could not ask her to come quickly unless he told his household of his secret wife and this he decided not to do. He needed spectacles and a large magnifying glass to read her letters and he dreaded the time when he could no longer read them and would be unable to ask anyone to read them aloud. Only two of the three close friends who knew about his marriage to Hannah were still alive, and they lived miles away. So he had to sit it out: in 1905 he had hurried to see her but she was too unwell to receive him and after a few nights at The Jerningham Arms, and some talk with Dr Gourlay, he returned to Pyrford to wait for better news. He was so fearful of the future, and guilty about all the times they had been apart, that he also spent Christmas 1905 with her at Shifnal.

Arthur's poem, 'In Eternum Domine', published in the *Spectator*, celebrated their love:

> This woman's soul and mine are one:
> One spirit, one career;
> Not only till the days are done
> Is our communion here.
> But after, though we singly brave
> The passage perilous,
> That small seclusion of the grave
> Has room for both of us.
> Both? we are as a single life, –
> And death itself shall spare
> The dust of husband and of wife
> That slowly mingles there.
> One may go first, and one remain
> To hail a second call;
> But nothing now can make us twain,
> Whatever may befall:

> For we have long since passed the bounds
> Of Self, of Time, of Space
> And felt the freedom that surrounds
> Love's final dwelling place.[93]

The last letter from Hannah to Arthur was written on 16 December 1907: she planned to spend Christmas with Jim and Lizzie and their grandchildren and looked forward to his visit in January. It was a warm and loving letter: after so many turbulent times, she sounded at peace with herself and 'darling Massa':

> I don't mind telling you now we are so old as I love thee more nor ever and I thank God with all my heart for giving me such as thou art and I shall always be for ever thy own loving servant wife.[94]

Arthur's near-blindness made writing very difficult for him, his description of a visit in the autumn of 1907 are his last words about their time together. He was hurt at the rudeness of the vicar of St Andrew's, the Reverend Malaher, whose disapproval of the marriage was blatant. Arthur made it his business to speak to the clergyman and explain their situation, telling him: '"I am the husband of that poor woman and my love for her and hers for me, has always been pure and that she lives here as a cottager simply because she prefers her own position to mine."' His notebook of this visit closed with the memories of 'colloquy' ending 'in the usual way, with kisses'.[95]

The following year Arthur returned for what would be his last visit to Shifnal, writing to Austin Dobson from the cottage on 17 September 1908. This was the last time they were together before Hannah died of 'failure of heart action and senile decay' on 9 July 1909. She was seventy-six years old. She was buried on 12 July. Another woman had been buried that day by the haughty Reverend Malaher: fifty-one-year-old

Love & Dirt

Mary Hayward, an inmate of Shifnal Workhouse. Hannah's years of hard work and her marriage had spared her the indignity of a pauper's funeral. Unable to attend, Arthur mourned on his own at Pyrford. He had dreaded not being able to see her before she died, the consequence of the years of secrecy they had endured. Eventually a stone was placed on the grave with the words: 'She was for fifty-six years the pure and unbroken wife of Arthur J. Munby of Clifton Holme . . .'

Arthur's final collection of poems, *Relicta*, was published in October 1909 and dedicated to 'the gracious and beloved memory of HER whose hand copied out and whose lifelong affection suggested all that is best in this book'. The title was carefully chosen – 'things which are left, or remain' – and shows that Arthur was willing to reveal some of the truth of his secret life. Her death, and his guilt, had emboldened him to start talking.

Arthur would have wondered what his family thought of the dedication, and asked his clergyman brother George to visit him at Pyrford in November. George was shocked to be told the context of his elder brother's most recent book:

> he told me that he wished me to know that, for years, he had been *married*, and that he never loved any one but her who had thus been his wife: and then he told me all the story. Not only his last book, but almost *all* his books . . . harping on the same string – which is the love of an *educated man for a peasant woman*.[96]

Arthur died of pneumonia on 29 January 1910, in his eighty-first year. At his deathbed were his servants and his landlord, John Cole. The Munbys knew the contents of his will, which was handled by the family firm, led by his brother Fred, and waited, dreading the moment when probate would be granted and the details of Arthur's life laid bare. They hoped that no one would take any interest, but Austin Dobson's obituary for

The Times, and other tributes to Munby, guaranteed interest in the will of a minor poet and man of letters known for his interest in social reform and the cause of working women. Hannah had also known what the will contained: Arthur had expected to die first and wanted to clarify the circumstances of their unusual union. On Monday, 4 July, the newspapers splashed: 'Romance of a Barrister's Marriage'; 'Servant Wife of a Barrister'; '45-Year-Old Secret'; 'A Wife's Noble Resolve'; 'Wife Who Would Be a Servant'; 'Strange Marriage Revealed'; 'Wife Prefers Obscurity', and 'Romance of a Helpmeet'. The Cullwicks had always known, but the Munbys must have felt as if they had been hit by lightning. They may have felt betrayed by Arthur.

His will, dated 1900, quickly came to the point: once the executors were named, he told the story of their lives:

> ... And whereas Hannah Cullwick servant born at Shiff-nall [sic] in the county of Salop and bred at the Charity School at Aston Brook by Shiffnall has for forty-five years and upwards been beloved by me with a pure and honourable love and not otherwise and she the said Hannah has during all that time been as faithful and loving and devoted to me as ever woman was to man And whereas after vainly trying to explain this state of things to my father I married the said Hannah (she being then in my service) publicly in the presence of all her kindred who could be got together at the parish church of Clerk-enwell in the county of Middlesex on the fourteenth day of January 1873 And whereas there has been no issue of the said marriage And whereas notwithstanding her said marriage the said Hannah has always refused and still refuses to have the position which as my wife she might and could have had and always insisted and still insists on being my servant as well as my wife her one grievance being that she cannot be my only servant And whereas

owing chiefly to this noble and unselfish resolve of hers I have never been able to make known my said marriage to my family or to the world at large and the same has been known and is known only to her kin and friends and to three of my most intimate college friends of whom the said Robert Spencer Borland is the only one who knows the circumstances of the case and who knows the said Hannah personally And whereas the said Hannah is now and for some years has been living among her own people at my expense and under my name and as my acknowl-edged wife in a dwelling chosen by herself and provided by me at the village of Hadley in the said county of Salop in which dwelling I am in the habit of spending as much of every year as is possible along with her . . .[97]

The *Daily Mirror* sent a reporter from Wellington, Shrop-shire, to interview Hannah's brother Jim. His alleged remarks about his sister and brother-in-law are the only words we have from him:

'they married for love, and they were lovers all their lives . . . She was very fond of cooking, and he used to like her cakes above everything, and sometimes he would read to her. They used to walk in the fields together, and he would talk to her about the trees and the birds and the flowers.'[98]

Arthur's estate was worth £26,000, the equivalent of £1,250,000 today. Eventually, Hannah's furniture, pictures, the samplers she and her mother had worked, the books Arthur had sent her, and the jewellery he had bought her were probably shared among her relatives: her niece, Emily Gibbs, received the annuity of £70 a year until she died in 1920.

The British Museum, to whom he had bequeathed his books and the two deed-boxes filled with Hannah's letters to him, her diaries, his notebooks and hundreds of photographs of working women, including Hannah, were unable to accept the legacy. In case of this eventuality, he willed the boxes to his old college, Trinity, who became the custodians. He added the proviso that 'I request that the said two deed-boxes may not be examined nor opened until the first day of January 1950 aforesaid.'

The Munbys must have been thankful that the contents of the boxes remained secret for forty years. They made no attempt to get to know their new relatives in Shropshire. As for Jim and Lizzie, they mourned Hannah, bemused at being in the spotlight for a brief moment. Lizzie died, aged eighty-six, on 12 December 1911. Her husband Jim died in 1915 near Shifnal, aged eighty-five; it is thought that Ellen died in 1919, in Plaistow, and Polly died aged seventy-nine on 6 January 1924. The Cullwicks' links with Trinity College in 1950 were maintained by Hannah's great-niece, Ada Perks, Emily's daughter, who had spent much of her childhood with her aunt. Ada, who was now seventy years old, awaited the opening of the boxes with interest. The date, 14 January, was Arthur and Hannah's wedding anniversary. She wrote to the Master and Fellows of Trinity asking if she could attend but they refused, telling her it was 'a private' occasion. Dr A. N. L. Munby, Arthur's great-nephew and librarian of King's College, was there to represent the family. The Master of the College, the social historian Dr G. M. Trevelyan, opened the boxes and left. The witnesses may have puzzled over the significance of those pictures of working women – dust girls, scantily clad, leggy gymnasts, hundreds of pit-brow lasses and the strange guises of Mrs Munby – and left the room to return to their studies. The College issued the following statement to the press about the Munby boxes:

The three boxes of A. J. Munby (ob.1910) were opened today (January 14th) by the college authorities, in the presence of a representative of the Munby family. They contain diaries and poems by Mr Munby, and letters to him by his wife. Also photographs and studies of working women of the late nineteenth century, in whose conditions of life Mr Munby took a sociological interest.

Notes

Sources

The Munby Papers at Trinity College, Cambridge, are the main source for this book. It is a rich archive which includes: Arthur Munby's diaries; a dozen notebooks on working women; almost thirty books titled *Visits to Hannah*; twelve notebooks and a two-volume study of Hannah; manuscript poetry; photographs of Hannah and hundreds of working women. Hannah Cullwick's memoirs and diaries referred to in the notes which follow are variously titled: *Hannah's Diary, Christmas 1854*; *1855–56 Kitchenmaid at Henham*; *1855 Westbourne Park and Kilburn*; *1857 Kilburn*; *1858 Kilburn*; *1860, A Few Fragments*; *1863*; *Hannah's Diary 1864*; *1864 A Maid of All Works Diary*; *1864 Margate*; *1865 St Leonard's*; *1866–1872 A Servant's Life*; *1870 Gloucester Crescent*; *1871*; *1872 Gloucester Crescent, Eaton Terrace and the Temple*; *Hannah's Places* and *Life of a Servant in the Temple*. Also at Trinity there are 850 of Hannah's letters to Arthur.

Preamble

1. Diary of Hannah Cullwick, 16 October 1863.

One - Arthur Munby

1. *York Courant*, 27 February 1827, p. 1.
2. *Directory of York*, 1843, p. 117.

3. A. J. Munby's Diary, 2 July 1879.

4. Wedding register of St Helen's Church, 1827, p. 29, and letter from Jane Munby to Joseph Munby, March 1827.

5. Baptism records of St Olave's Church and *Leeds Directory* for 1830, p. 434.

6. A. J. Munby's ms *Faithful Servants*, Hannah Carter's memorial copied in 1889.

7. Derek Hudson, *Munby, Man of Two Worlds: The Life and Diaries of Arthur J. Munby 1828–1910*, 1972, p. 7.

8. 1881 Census Surname data.

9. 1841 Census for York.

10. *Directory for Kingston-upon-Hull*, 1840, p. 563.

11. Hudson, op. cit., pp. 8–9.

12. Ibid., p. 398.

13. A. J. Munby, *Memorial of Joseph Munby*, 1875, pp. 1–2.

14. Hudson, op. cit., p. 10.

15. *Trinity College*, a guide book, no author or date given.

16. Nicholas Pevsner and David Hare, *The Buildings of York and the East Riding*, 1975 and 1995, p. 244.

17. Hudson, op. cit., pp. 10–11.

Two - Hannah Cullwick

1. Baptism records of St Andrew's Church, p. 187.

2. A. J. Munby, *Visits to Hannah*, June 1893.

3. Burgesses' Records for 1647.

4. *Salopian Journal*, 14 November 1804, p. 3.

5. Charles Dickens, *The Old Curiosity Shop*, 1841, pp. 346–400.

6. *Pigot's Directory*, 1828, p. 688.

7. *Salopian Journal*, 3 September 1800, p. 3.

8. *Hannah's Places*, 1872, pp. 34–5.

9. *Visits to Hannah*, 1903, p. 140.

10. *The Reports of the Charity Commissioners to Enquire Concern-*

ing Charities in England and Wales Relating to the County of Shropshire, 1819–37, 1839, pp. 258–9.

11. John Cannon, ed., *The Oxford Companion to British History*, 1997, p. 190.

12. *Hannah's Places*, p. 35.

13. *Visits to Hannah*, 1896, p. 306.

14. Ibid., January 1892, p. 101.

15. Munby's Diary, August 1874, p. 200.

16. *Visits to Hannah*, June 1899, p. 127.

17. Ibid., May 1897, p. 83.

18. Ibid., April 1885, p. 81.

19. Ibid., September 1893, p. 277.

20. Ibid., Christmas 1888, p. 19.

21. Munby's Diary, 13 March 1874, p. 88.

22. Census Return for Shifnal, 1841.

23. Baptism and burial records of St Andrew's Church, 1843, pp. 4–5.

24. Sylvia Watts, *Some Shifnal Buildings and People*, 2000, p. 26.

25. Letter from Hannah, 10 April 1891.

26. Letters from Hannah, 16 November 1886.

27. *Visits to Hannah*, March 1902, pp. 114–15.

28. Ibid., August 1892, p. 324 and *Pigot's Directory*, 1836, p. 371.

29. Ibid., May 1892, pp. 184–5.

30. *Slater's Directory*, 1850, p. 38.

31. *Hannah's Places*, pp. 1–2.

32. *Visits to Hannah*, October 1886, p. 150.

33. *Hannah's Places*, pp. 2–3.

34. *Visits to Hannah*, November 1899, pp. 166–8.

35. Ibid., 1 September 1891, p. 177.

36. Ibid., 1898, pp. 22–3.

37. *Hannah's Places*, p. 4.

38. Letter from Hannah, October 1903.

39. *Hannah's Places*, pp. 4–5.

40. Burial records, St Andrew's Chuch, 1847, pp. 51 and 52 and death certificates.

41. *Visits to Hannah*, September 1898, p. 117.

42. *Hannah's Places*, p. 6.

43. *Visits to Hannah*, June 1892, p. 253.

44. Hannah's Places, p. 7.

45. Letter from Hannah, 27 November 1907.

46. Munby, *Hannah*, vol. 1, 1875, p. 69 and *Visits to Hannah*, 1903, p. 114.

47. *White's Directory*, 1851, pp. 457–8.

48. Isabella Beeton, *Book of Household Management*, 1861, p. 988.

49. *Census Return for Aqualate Hall*, 1851.

50. *Visits to Hannah*, 1899, pp. 48–9.

51. *Hannah*, vol. 1, 1875/6, pp. 132–3.

52. *Casey's Directory*, 1874, p. 402.

53. Census Return for Woodcote Hall, 1851.

54. Mrs Beeton, op. cit., p. 43.

Three - 26 May 1854: A Defining Moment

1. *Men at the Bar*, 1885, entry for A. J. Munby; Derek Hudson, *Munby, Man of Two Worlds: The Life and Diaries of Arthur J. Munby, 1828–1910*, 1972, p. 12.

2. *The Concise Dictionary of National Biography*, vol. 1, 1992, p. 436.

3. *Kelly's Directory for London*, 1851, p. 284.

4. *Hannah's Places*, pp. 9–11.

5. Munby's Diary, 2 September 1874, p. 220.

6. Ibid., 8 July 1860, p. 199.

7. *Visits to Hannah*, Easter 1899, pp. 39–40.

8. Ibid., May 1899, pp. 90–2.

9. *Hannah's Places*, p. 11.

10. Ibid., p. 12.

11. Ibid., p. 14.
12. *Bagshaw's Directory*, 1851, p. 513.
13. *Visits to Hannah*, Christmas 1888, pp. 23–4.
14. Lord Byron, *Sardanapalus*, 1821, pp. 8–10.
15. Ibid., p. 30.
16. Ibid., p. 33.
17. Ibid., p. 41.
18. Ibid., p. 31.
19. *The Era*, 19 June 1853, p. 10.
20. Ibid., p. 12.
21. *Visits to Hannah*, Christmas 1888, pp. 24–5.
22. Ibid., March 1893, pp. 148–9.
23. *Hannah's Places*, p. 15.
24. *Visits to Hannah*, 1885, p. 83.
25. Ibid., May 1891, p. 18 and June 1904, p. 274.
26. Ibid., June 1893, p. 33.
27. Ibid., November 1892, p. 86. Conversations with Dr T. G. Hill, historian of Shifnal and Shropshire, 2001 and 2002.
28. Hudson, op. cit., p. 12.
29. *Munby's Diary*, 27 September 1860, p. 100.
30. *Hannah's Diary*, Christmas 1854, pp. 1–4.
31. Clare Market was demolished at the turn of the century to make way for the Kingsway and Aldwych improvement schemes.
32. *Visits to Hannah*, October 1899, p. 150.
33. *Hannah's Places*, p. 15.
34. Ibid., pp. 16–17.
35. *History, Gazetteer and Directory of Suffolk*, 1855, p. 339, and 1858, p. 619.
36. Census Return for Henham Hall, Suffolk, 1851.
37. *Hannah's Places*, pp. 17–18.
38. Ibid., pp. 18–19.
39. *Kelly's Directories*, 1855 and 1856.
40. *Munby's Diary*, 8 February 1862, pp. 94–5.

41. *Hannah's Places*, p. 19.

42. Ibid., pp. 19–20.

43. Hannah's Diary for 1855, pp. 7–8.

44. *Men at the Bar*, 1885.

45. Munby's Diary, 31 July 1863, p. 125.

46. *Hannah's Places*, p. 21.

47. Hannah's Diary, 1856, pp. 17–22.

48. Ibid., p. 24.

49. *Hannah's Places*, p. 21.

50. Hannah's Diary, 1856, p. 1.

51. Ibid., pp. 1–9.

52. Ibid., pp. 11 and 17.

53. Munby's Diary, 22 November 1873, p. 180.

54. *Hannah's Places*, p. 22.

55. Isabella Beeton, *Book of Household Management*, p. 1001.

56. Hannah's Diary, 1857, p. 5.

57. All images from Trinity College, Cambridge.

58. Hannah's Diary, 14 February 1857, p. 23.

59. Ibid., 7 September 1857, p. 57.

60. Ibid., 18 February 1857, p. 25.

61. Ibid., 11 June 1857, p. 46.

62. Ibid., 10 September 1857, p. 59.

63. Ibid., 19 September 1857, p. 64.

64. Ibid., 30 September 1857, p. 71.

65. Ibid., 3 October 1857, p. 73.

66. Hudson, op. cit., pp. 12–13.

67. *Kelly's Directory*, 1858.

68. Hannah's Diary, 18 November 1857, p. 87.

69. Ibid., 22 November 1857, pp. 90–1.

70. Hannah's Diary, 27 January 1858, p. 7.

71. Ibid., 4 March 1858, p. 18.

72. Ibid., 29th March 1858, p. 26.

73. Hudson, op. cit., p. 13.

74. Ibid., 30 June 1858, p. 56.

75. Ibid., 1 July 1858, p. 57.
76. Ibid., 4 July 1858, p. 60.
77. Ibid., 12 July 1858, pp. 65–6.
78. Ibid., 14 July 1858, p. 67.
79. Ibid., 12 December 1858, p. 88.
80. Munby's Diary, January–March 1860, p. 1.
81. Ibid., 29 January 1859, p. 10.
82. Ibid., 1 January–30 June 1859, passim.
83. Ibid., 1 February 1859, pp. 14–19.
84. Ibid., 30 July 1859, pp. 82–6.
85. Ibid., 18 August 1858, p. 24.
86. Hudson, op. cit., p. 43.

Four – 'I am a dreamer and observer'

1. Munby's Diary, 3 February 1862.
2. Hannah's Diary, 5 February 1872, p. 20.
3. Munby's Diary, 22 June 1862.
4. Munby's photographs at Trinity College, Cambridge.
5. Munby's Diary, 1 January 1860, p. 1.
6. Munby's Diary, 6 February 1860, pp. 85–6.
7. Ibid., 3 January 1860, pp. 102–7.
8. Andrew Saunders, Introduction to Charles Dickens, *Our Mutual Friend*, 1994, pp. xvi–xvii.
9. Dickens, *Our Mutual Friend*, 1907 edition, pp. 486–9.
10. Munby's Diary, 6 January 1860, pp. 12–16.
11. Ibid., 11 January 1890, pp. 117–22.
12. Ibid., 15 January 1860, pp. 30–4.
13. Ibid., 29 February 1860, p. 129.
14. Ibid., 12 March 1860, pp. 157–9.
15. Ibid., 22 March 1860, pp. 220–7.
16. Ibid., 5 April 1860, pp. 29–30.
17. Ibid., 23 April 1860, pp. 52–3.

18. Ibid., 12 June 1860, p. 135. During the 1860s Arthur's brothers Fred and John qualified as solicitors and practised in the family firm; George and Joe became clergymen; Edward went to agricultural college and Caroline, a spinster, lived at home.

19. Census Returns for Clifton Holme, York, 1861 and 1871.

20. Angela V. John, *By the Sweat of Their Brow: Women Workers at Victorian Coal Mines*, 1984, pp. 23–37.

21. Michael Hiley, *Victorian Working Women: Portraits from Life*, 1979, pp. 48–60.

22. Munby's Diary, 19 August 1859, pp. 23–7.

23. Ibid., p. 30.

24. Ibid., 27 August 1860, pp. 189–203.

25. Ibid., 1 September 1860, p. 61.

26. Ibid., 28 August 1860, pp. 58–9.

27. *Visits to Hannah*, November 1898, p. 164.

28. Ibid., August 1899, pp. 42–3.

29. Ibid., 2 September 1860, pp. 63–5.

30. Ibid., 14 December 1860, pp. 140–1.

31. Ibid., 9 January 1861, pp. 188–9.

32. *Hannah's Places*, p. 22.

33. Munby's Diary, 13 February 1861.

34. Ibid., 24 February 1861.

35. Ibid., 1 July 1860, p. 189.

36. Ibid., 21 March 1861.

37. Ibid., 12 March 1860. Michael Grant and John Hazel, *Who's Who in Classical Literature*, 1993, p. 195.

38. *Kelly's Directory for Brighton*, 1862, p. 1647.

39. Munby's Diary, 26 May 1861, pp. 172–3.

40. Ibid., 5 July 1861, p. 15.

41. Ibid., 20 July 1861, p. 51.

42. Ibid., 27 July 1861, p. 68.

43. Ibid., 22 August 1861, pp. 178–80.

44. Munby's Diary, 24 August 1861, pp. 209–12.

45. Ibid., 15 December 1861, pp. 232–3.

46. Ibid., 20 December 1861, p. 237.
47. Ibid., 19 January 1862, pp. 39–40.
48. Ibid., 7 January 1862, pp. 10–14.
49. Ibid., 14 January 1862, pp. 28–9.
50. Ibid., 26 January 1862, p. 52.
51. Ibid., 16 February 1862, pp. 125–8.
52. Ibid., 22 February 1862, pp. 145–7.
53. Ibid., 20 April 1862, pp. 47–55.
54. Ibid., 30 April 1862, pp. 77–82.
55. Ibid., 31 May 1862, p. 193.
56. Ibid., 22 June 1862, pp. 2–25.
57. Ibid., 23 June 1862, p. 27 and pp. 169–70.
58. Ibid., 25 June 1862, pp. 33–5.
59. Derek Hudson, *Munby: Man of Two Worlds: The Life and Diaries of Arthur J. Munby, 1928–1910*, p. 220.
60. Ibid., p. 67.
61. Ian Gibson, *The Erotomaniac: The Secret Life of Henry Spencer Ashbee*, 2001, pp. xii and xiii.
62. Munby's Diary, 7 July 1862, p. 71.
63. Ibid., 29 July 1862, pp. 139–41.
64. *Kelly's Directory*, 1862.
65. Munby's Diary, 16 August 1862, p. 192.
66. Ibid., 17 August 1862, p. 107.
67. Ibid., 20 August 1862, p. 115.
68. Ibid., 9 September 1862, pp. 171–80.
69. *Visits to Hannah*, June 1891, and January 1892, p. 91.
70. Munby's Diary, 24 September 1862, pp. 50–4.
71. Ibid., 14 October 1862, pp. 173–5.
72. Ibid., 24 October 1862, pp. 200–2.
73. Ibid., 16 November 1862, pp. 50–4.
74. Ibid., 26 December 1862, pp. 54–8.
75. Ibid., 10 January 1863, pp. 87–8.
76. Ibid., 11 January 1863, pp. 91–5.
77. Ibid., 18 January 1863, pp. 108–11.

78. Hannah's Diary, 1863, 17 January, pp. 16–17.
79. Ibid., 8 January 1863, p. 10.
80. Ibid., 1 February 1863, pp. 32–3.
81. Ibid., 28 February 1863, pp. 57–8.
82. Ibid., 7 March 1863, pp. 64–5.
83. Ibid., 15 March 1863, pp. 72–3.
84. Munby's Diary, 21 March 1863, pp. 74–8.
85. Hannah's Diary, 30 April 1863, p. 100.
86. Munby's Diary, journeys and excursions in 1863.
87. Ibid., 4 May 1863, p. 36.
88. Ibid., 10 May 1863, pp. 58–65.
89. Hannah's Diary, 26 May 1863, pp. 117–19.
90. Ibid., 31 May 1863, p. 122.
91. Ibid., 18 July 1863, p. 163.
92. Munby's Diary, 26 July 1863, p. 61.
93. Hannah's Diary, 31 July 1863, pp. 177–8.
94. Ibid., 3 August 1863, pp. 182–3.
95. Ibid., 7 August 1863, p. 191.
96. Hudson, op. cit., pp. 67 and 220.
97. Hannah's Diary, 9 August 1863, p. 193.
98. Munby's Diary, 9 August 1863, pp. 115–20.
99. Ibid., 15 August 1863, pp. 183–93.
100. Hannah's Diary, 10 September 1863, pp. 216–17.
101. Ibid., 14 October 1863, pp. 239–40.
102. Ibid., 16 October 1863, pp. 241–2.
103. Ibid., 31 December 1863, pp. 309–10.
104. Munby's Diary, 12 January 1864, pp. 43–6.
105. Ibid., 22 February 1864, pp. 180–9.
106. Ibid., 6 March 1864, pp. 231–6.
107. *A Maid Of All Work's Diary*, 1864, pp. 2–3 and 45–6.
108. Hannah's Diary, 9 March 1864, p. 50.
109. Ibid., 11 March 1864, p. 52.
110. Ibid., 12 March 1864, p. 53.
111. Ibid., 20 March 1864, p. 57.

112. *A Maid of All Work's Diary*, 1864, p. 3.

113. *Hannah's Places*, p. 25.

114. Hannah's Diary, 9 April 1864, pp. 78–80.

115. *Hannah's Places*, pp. 26–7.

116. *A Maid of All Work's Diary*, 1864, p. 11.

117. *Kent Directory*, 1862, pp. 29 and 930–1.

118. Munby's Diary, 14 May 1864, pp. 6–11.

119. Hannah's Diary, 26 May 1864, p. 144.

120. *Kelly's Directory*, 1864.

121. Munby's Diary, 27 May 1864, pp. 105–11.

122. Ibid., 4 June 1864, pp. 163–8.

123. Ibid., 5 June 1864, pp. 157–8.

124. Munby's Diary, 5 June 1864, pp. 169–71.

125. Ibid., 24 June 1864.

126. Ibid., 7 September 1864, no page citations.

127. Hannah's Diary, 23 September 1864, p. 242.

128. *Slater's General Directory for Yorkshire*, 1864, p. 64.

129. Munby's Diary, 27 October 1864.

130. Hannah's Diary, 2 November 1864, pp. 262–3.

131. Ibid., 4 November 1864, p. 264.

132. Ibid., 26 November 1864, pp. 268–9.

133. Ibid., 28 November 1864, pp. 269–70.

134. Ibid., 4 December 1864, pp. 274–5.

135. Ibid., 7 December 1864, pp. 276–7.

136. Ibid., 17 December 1864, pp. 285–7.

137. Ibid., 20 December 1864, pp. 289–90.

138. Ibid., 25 December 1864, pp. 291–2.

139. Ibid., 27 December 1864, pp. 293–4.

140. Ibid., 28 Decemer 1864, p. 296.

141. Ibid., 31 December 1864, p. 300.

142. Ibid., 3 January 1865, p. 6.

143. Ibid., 15 January 1865, p. 14.

144. Ibid., 23 January 1865, p. 19.

145. Ibid., 13 February 1865, p. 32.

146. Ibid., 15 April 1865, p. 62.

147. Ibid., 26 April 1865, p. 67.

148. Ibid., 13 May 1865, pp. 75–7.

149. Ibid., 13 May 1865, p. 80.

150. Ibid., 17 May 1865, pp. 86–7.

151. Munby's Diary, 23 May 1865.

152. Hannah's Diary, 13 June 1865, p. 103.

153. Ibid., 28 August 1865, p. 121.

154. Hudson, op. cit., pp. 124–5.

155. Munby's Diary, 1 May 1864, p. 215.

156. Ibid., May 1863.

157. Ibid., 11 September 1865.

Five - 'Out of Place'

1. A. J. Munby, *Verses Old and New*, 1865, pp. 157–8.

2. Hannah's Diary, 5 October 1865, pp. 140–1.

3. Derek Hudson, *Munby, Man of Two Worlds: The Life and Diaries of Arthur J. Munby, 1828–1910*, 1972, p. 225.

4. Ibid., p. 282.

5. Ibid., p. 220.

6. Munby's Diary, 27 May 1866, p. 45.

7. J. G. Harrod and Co's *Directory of Sussex*, 1867.

8. Munby's Diary, 25 August 1866.

9. *Visits to Hannah*, December 1893, p. 158.

10. Munby's Diary, 8 December 1866.

11. *A Servant's Life, 1866–1872*, p. 2.

12. Ibid., p. 3.

13. The Bazaar dated from 1816 and was founded by John Trotter who made a fortune in the Napoleonic Wars. He hired out stalls to the widows and daughters of army officers, who sold needlework, millinery, lace, gloves and potted plants. By Hannah's day there was a registry where servants paid a fee

to wait for an employer to inspect them and perhaps engage them.

14. *A Servant's Life*, pp. 3–4.
15. Ibid., p. 5.
16. Ibid., p. 7.
17. Munby's Diary, 5 February 1867.
18. *Hannah's Places*, p. 30 and *Visits to Hannah*, May 1899, pp. 89–90.
19. *A Servant's Life*, pp. 10–11.
20. Ibid., pp. 17–18.
21. Ibid., p. 27.
22. Ibid., pp. 30–1.
23. Ibid., p. 33.
24. Munby's Diary, 9 May 1866, p. 37.
25. Ibid., 13 November 1866.
26. Ibid., 6 June 1867.
27. *A Servant's Life*, pp. 35–7.
28. Munby's Diary, 4 August 1867.
29. Ibid., 5 August 1867.
30. *A Servant's Life*, pp. 42–5.
31. Munby's Diary, 14 September 1867, p. 89.
32. Ibid., 17 September 1867.
33. Ibid., 28 March 1868.
34. *A Servant's Life*, pp. 37–8.
35. Ibid., pp. 39–40.
36. Audrey Linkman, *The Victorians: Photographic Portraits*, 1993, pp. 38 and 48.
37. Michael Hiley, *Victorian Working Women: Portraits from Life*, 1979, pp. 68–70.
38. Munby's Diary, 7 March 1868, p. 22.
39. *A Servant's Life*, p. 41.
40. Ibid., pp. 51–3.
41. Ibid., pp. 58–60.
42. Ibid., pp. 60–1.

43. Ibid., pp. 64–5.
44. Munby's Diary, 15 October 1868, pp. 188–9.
45. *A Servant's Life*, pp. 67–9.
46. Hannah's Diary, 1870, pp. 2–3.
47. Ibid., 5 January 1870, p. 9.
48. Ibid., 5 March 1870, p. 6.
49. Ibid., 7 March 1870, p. 18.
50. Ibid., 11 March 1870, p. 20.
51. Ibid., 14 March 1870, p. 25.
52. Ibid., 21 April 1870, p. 53.
53. Ibid., 8 May 1870, p. 66.
54. Letter from Hannah, 9 May 1870.
55. Hannah's Diary, 12 June 1870, pp. 88–9.
56. Letter from Hannah, 16 June 1870.
57. Ibid., 16 June 1870.
58. Hannah's Diary, 19 June 1870, p. 99.
59. Letter from Hannah, 21 June 1870.
60. Hannah's Diary, 15 July 1870, p. 112.
61. Ibid., 4 November 1870, pp. 140–1.
62. Ibid., 16 December 1870, p. 154.
63. Hannah's Diary, 23 February 1871, p. 46.
64. Ibid., 9 March 1871, p. 57.
65. *General Servant*, 4 May 1871, pp. 98–9.
66. Munby's Diary, 4 May 1871.
67. *General Servant*, 10 May 1872, pp. 109–11.
68. Ibid., 11 May 1871, p. 112.
69. Ibid., 14 May 1871, pp. 116–17.
70. Ibid., 28 June 1871, pp. 148–50.
71. Ibid., 25 July 1871, pp. 168–9.
72. Ibid., 18 October 1871, p. 212.
73. Ibid., 1 November 1871, p. 222.
74. Ibid., 25 November 1871, p. 232.
75. Ibid., 5 December 1871, p. 237.
76. Ibid., 25 December 1871, pp. 250–1.

77. Ibid., 26 December 1871, pp. 241–52.

78. *Gloucester Crescent, Eaton Terrace and the Temple*, 1 January 1872, pp. 1–2.

79. Ibid., 6 January 1872, pp. 6–7.

80. Ibid., 8 January 1872, p. 8.

81. Munby's Diary, 24 January 1872.

82. *Gloucester Crescent*, 24 January 1872, pp. 18–19.

83. Munby's Diary, 28 January 1872.

84. *Gloucester Crescent*, 6 February 1872, pp. 26–7.

85. Ibid., 9 February 1872, pp. 27–9.

86. Ibid., 13 February 1872, p. 35.

87. Ibid., 18 February 1872, p. 39.

88. Ibid., 20 February 1872, p. 41.

89. Ibid., 21 February 1872, p. 42.

90. Ibid., 3 March 1872, p. 48.

91. Ibid., 5 March 1872, p. 49.

92. Ibid., 11 March 1872, p. 51.

93. *Gloucester Crescent*, 9 April 1872, p. 65.

94. Ibid., 10 April 1872, pp. 66–7.

95. Ibid., 15 April 1872, pp. 77–82.

96. Ibid., 21 April 1872, p. 85.

97. Ibid., 24 April 1872, pp. 88–9.

98. Ibid., 2 May 1872, p. 103.

99. Ibid., 3 May 1872, pp. 103–4.

100. Ibid., 16 May 1872, p. 107.

101. Ibid., 23 May 1872, p. 113.

102. Ibid., 26 May 1872, pp. 116–17.

103. Hudson, op. cit., p. 308.

104. *Gloucester Crescent*, 11 June, p. 125.

105. Ibid., 27 June 1872, pp. 141–2.

106. Ibid., 28 June 1872, p. 144.

107. Ibid., 31 July 1872, p. 167.

108. Ibid., 8 August 1872, pp. 172–3.

109. Ibid., 14 August 1872, p. 178.

110. Ibid., 17 August 1872, p. 179.

111. Hudson, op. cit., pp. 308–9.

112. *Gloucester Crescent*, 10 September 1872, p. 204.

113. Ibid., 13 September 1872, pp. 207–8.

114. *Kelly's Directory*, 1872.

115. Hudson, op. cit., p. 312.

116. *Gloucester Crescent*, op. cit., 14 November 1872, pp. 239–40.

117. Ibid., 23 November 1872, p. 245.

118. Ibid., 26 November 1872, pp. 247–9.

119. Ibid., 27 November 1872, p. 250.

120. Ibid., 28 November 1872, p. 251.

121. Ibid., 30 November 1872, pp. 252–3.

122. Ibid., 3 December 1872, p. 256.

123. Ibid., 7 December 1872, p. 265.

124. Ibid., 13 December 1872, p. 268.

125. Ibid., 21 December 1872, p. 275.

126. *Gloucester Crescent*, 31 December 1872, p. 281.

127. Munby's Diary, 1 January 1873.

128. Ibid., 6 January 1873.

Six - A Wedding in Clerkenwell

1. Munby's Diary, 14 January 1873.

2. *Visits to Hannah*, January 1892, p. 105.

3. Ibid., November 1893, p. 88.

4. Marriage certificate of Hannah Cullwick and Arthur Joseph Munby.

5. *Visits to Hannah*, January 1892, p. 105.

6. Letters from Hannah, 17 April 1896.

7. Derek Hudson, *Munby, Man of Two Worlds: The Life and Diaries of Arthur J. Munby*, 1928–1910, 1972, p. 319.

8. *Hannah*, vol. 1, 1875, p. 146.

9. Charles Dickens, *Pickwick Papers*, 1837, 1907 edition, pp. 418–19.

10. *Gloucester Crescent, Eaton Terrace and the Temple*, 7 December 1872, pp. 264–5.
11. Munby's Diary, 18 January 1873.
12. Ibid., 19 January 1873.
13. Ibid., 26 January 1873.
14. Ibid., 8 February 1873.
15. Ibid., 17 February 1873.
16. Ibid., 17 February 1873.
17. Ibid., 22 February 1873.
18. Ibid., 28 March 1873.
19. Ibid., 10 April 1873.
20. Ibid., 23 April 1873.
21. Ibid., 7 May 1873.
22. Ibid., 9 May 1873.
23. Ibid., 11 May 1873.
24. Ibid., 24 May 1873.
25. Ibid., 26 May 1873.
26. Munby's Diary, 29 May 1873.
27. Ibid., 30 May 1873.
28. Ibid., 21 July 1873.
29. *Visits to Hannah*, January 1892, pp. 123–5.
30. Munby's Diary, 5 August 1873.
31. Ibid., 16 August 1873.
32. Ibid., 17 August 1873.
33. Ibid., 20 August 1873.
34. Ibid., 21 August 1873.
35. Notebook for 1873, 24 August.
36. *Life as a Servant in the Temple*, 30 August 1873, pp. 1–2.
37. Munby's Diary, 30 August 1873.
38. *Life as a Servant*, 3 September 1873, p. 8.
39. Munby's Diary, 11 September 1873.
40. *Life as a Servant*, 11 September 1873, p. 16.
41. Ibid., 12 September 1873, pp. 18–19.
42. Munby's Diary, 12 September 1873.

43. Ibid., 13 September 1873.
44. *Life as a Servant*, 13 September 1873, pp. 19–20.
45. Ibid., 14 September 1873, pp. 22–3.
46. Ibid., 15 September 1873, p. 24.
47. Ibid., 20 September 1873, p. 31.
48. *Life as a Servant*, 22 September 1873, p. 35.
49. Ibid., 27 September 1873, p. 42.
50. Munby's Diary, 12 October 1873.
51. *Life as a Servant*, 30 September, p. 48.
52. Ibid., 30 September 1873, p. 46.
53. Ibid., 22 November 1873.
54. Ibid., 24 November 1873.
55. Ibid., 2 December 1873.
56. Ibid., 4 December 1873.
57. Ibid., 24 December 1873.
58. *Life as a Servant*, Christmas 1873, p. 60.
59. Ibid., 31 December 1873.
60. Munby's Diary, 3 January 1874.
61. Ibid., 26 January 1874.
62. Ibid., 10 February 1874.
63. Ibid., 28 February 1874.
64. Ibid., 7 April 1874.
65. Ibid., 20 April 1874.
66. Munby's Diary, 2 May 1874.
67. Ibid., 19 May 1874.
68. Ibid., 29 May 1874.
69. Ibid., 2 June 1874.
70. Ibid., 11 June 1874.
71. Ibid., 27 June 1874.
72. Ibid., 29 June 1784.
73. Ibid., 20 July 1874.
74. Ibid., 3 August 1874.
75. Ibid., 5 August 1874.
76. Ibid., 11 September 1874.

77. Ibid., 8 November 1874.
78. Ibid., 23 December 1874.
79. Ibid., 30 December 1874.
80. *Hannah*, vol. 1, 1 January 1875, pp. 9–10.
81. Ibid., 14 January 1875, p. 21.
82. Ibid., 10 March 1875, p. 40.
83. Ibid., 27 March 1875, p. 59.
84. Ibid., 3 April 1875, p. 70.
85. Ibid., 13 January 1875, p. 20.
86. Ibid., 10 April 1875, p. 73.
87. *Hannah*, 20 May, p. 83.
88. Ibid., 2 June 1875, pp. 91–3.
89. Munby's Diary, 3 August 1875, p. 32.
90. Ibid., 19 August–21 Sepember 1875, pp. 34–9.
91. Ibid., 2–4 December 1875, pp. 49–50.
92. Ibid., 6–8 December 1875, p. 50.
93. Ibid., 31 December 1875, p. 53.
94. Memorial of Joseph Munby, 1876.
95. Munby's Diary, 1 January 1876, p. 1.
96. Ibid., 14 January, p. 2.
97. Ibid., 20 May, p. 10.
98. *Hannah*, 21 June 1876, pp. 111–12.
99. Munby's Diary, 3–6 July 1876, p. 17.
100. *Hannah*, 6 July 1876, p. 147.
101. Ibid., 7 July 1876, p. 152.
102. Ibid., 12 July 1876, pp. 154–5.
103. Munby's Diary, 2 August 1876, p. 20.
104. *Hannah*, 11 August 1876, pp. 170–1.
105. Munby's Diary, 18 August 1876, p. 34.
106. Ibid., 19 August 1876, p. 34.
107. Ibid., 20 August–2 September 1876, p. 36.
108. Ibid., 5 October 1876, p. 41.
109. Ibid., 17 October 1876, p. 43.
110. Ibid., 26 October 1876, p. 44.

111. Ibid., 18 November 1876, p. 47.
112. Ibid., 4 December 1876, p. 50.
113. Ibid., 23 December 1876, p. 52.
114. Ibid., 31 December 1876, p. 54.
115. *Hannah*, vol. 2, 15 January 1877, p. 22.
116. Munby's Diary, 15 January 1877, p. 4.
117. *Hannah*, vol. 2, 15 January 1877, pp. 8–12.
118. Ibid., 23 January 1877, pp. 42–9.
119. Ibid., 31 January 1877, pp. 85–8.
120. Ibid., 2 February 1877, pp. 105–6.
121. Ibid., 13 February 1877, p. 120.
122. Ibid., 25 March 1877, p. 149.
123. Ibid., 3 April 1877, p. 164.
124. Ibid., 4 April 1877, pp. 166–8.
125. Munby's Diary, 23 April 1877, p. 18.
126. Ibid., 27 June 1877, p. 27.
127. Ibid., 5 October 1877, p. 41.
128. Ibid., 6 October 1877, p. 41.
129. Ibid., 16 October 1877, p. 43.
130. Ibid., 25 October 1877, p. 44.
131. Ibid., 27 October 1877, p. 44.
132. Ibid., 22 November 1877, p. 48.
133. Ibid., 24 November 1877, p. 48.

Seven - Hannah's Story 1877–1909

1. Unpublished poem, 27 December 1878.
2. Letter from Hannah, 2 August 1880, pp. 1–8.
3. Ibid., 23 September 1881.
4. Ibid., 1 June 1882.
5. *Kelly's Directory for Bearley*, 1880, 1884.
6. Letter from Hannah, 9 June 1882.
7. Ibid., 23 June 1882.

8. Ibid., 28 July 1882.
9. Ibid., 2 August 1882.
10. Ibid., 1 September 1882.
11. Ibid., 6 April 1883.
12. Ibid., 31 July 1883.
13. Ibid., 28 September 1883.
14. Ibid., 6 October 1883.
15. Ibid., 14 November 1883.
16. Ibid., 28 December 1883.
17. Ibid., 16 January 1884.
18. Ibid., 9 February 1884.
19. Ibid., 7 March 1884.
20. Ibid., 24 March 1884.
21. Ibid., 18 April 1884.
22. Ibid., 2 May 1884.
23. Ibid., 27 August 1884.
24. *Kelly's Directory for Stratford-upon-Avon*, 1884.
25. Letter from Hannah, 29 October 1884.
26. Ibid., 5 November 1884.
27. Ibid., 15 May 1885.
28. Ibid., 12 March 1885.
29. Ibid., 1 May 1885.
30. Ibid., 11 December 1885.
31. Ibid., 25 January 1886.
32. Ibid., 5 February 1886.
33. Ibid., 10 February 1886.
34. *Visits to Hannah*, 28 April 1886.
35. Ibid., 1 May 1886.
36. Letter from Hannah, 20 July 1886.
37. Ibid., 13 August 1886.
38. Ibid., 18 August 1886.
39. *Visits to Hannah*, June 1899, p. 112.
40. Ibid., 6 October 1886.
41. Letter from Hannah, 23 December 1886.

42. Ibid., 11 February 1887.
43. Letter from Richard Cullwick, 19 April 1887.
44. Ibid., 1 May 1887.
45. Letter from Hannah, 24 May 1887.
46. Ibid., 18 September 1887.
47. *Visits to Hannah*, September 1887.
48. Ibid., 3 April 1888.
49. Letter from Hannah, 9 May 1888.
50. *Visits to Hannah*, 3 April 1888.
51. Letter from Hannah, 31 August 1888.
52. Ibid., 11 September 1888.
53. Ibid., 18 October 1888.
54. *Visits to Hannah*, 23 December 1888.
55. Ibid., 1 April 1890.
56. Letter from Hannah, 25 January 1890.
57. Ibid., 10 April 1891.
58. *Visits to Hannah*, 8 June 1891.
59. Letter from Hannah, 7 July 1891.
60. *Visits to Hannah*, 27 August 1891.
61. Ibid., 7 September 1893, pp. 235–6.
62. Letter from Hannah, 19 December 1892.
63. Ibid., 13 January 1893.
64. Ibid., 8 July 1893.
65. *Visits to Hannah*, 3 June 1893, p. 34.
66. Ibid., 28 June 1895, pp. 277 and 289.
67. Letter from Hannah, 22 January 1895.
68. Ibid., 25 January 1895.
69. Ibid., 2 February 1895.
70. Ibid., 8 February 1895.
71. Ibid., 19 February 1895.
72. Ibid., 29 February 1895.
73. Ibid., 11 April 1895.
74. Munby's record of days spent with Hannah, 1892–1902.
75. Letter from Hannah, 7 April 1897.

76. Munby's Diary, 20 June 1897, p. 81.
77. Letter from Mary Ann Cullwick, 2 September 1897.
78. Letter from Hannah, 11 June 1897.
79. Ibid., 13 July 1897.
80. Munby's Diary, 11 September, p. 255.
81. *Visits to Hannah*, 8 June 1904, p. 274.
82. 'The Shoeblack', 26 April 1898.
83. *Visits to Hannah*, June 1901, p. 149.
84. Ibid., September 1898, p. 56.
85. Ibid., September 1902, p. 25.
86. Letter to Bill Cullwick, 9 June 1903.
87. Letter from Hannah, 23 June 1903.
88. Ibid., 11 September 1903.
89. *Visits to Hannah*, 7 October 1903.
90. Ibid., August 1904, pp. 5–12.
91. Letter from Hannah, 18 July, 1904.
92. Ibid., 18 August 1904.
93. 'In Eternum Domine', *Spectator*, 18 February 1905.
94. Letter from Hannah, 16 December 1907.
95. *Visits to Hannah*, October and November 1907, p. 74.
96. Derek Hudson, *Munby, Man of Two Worlds: The Life and Diaries of Arthur J. Munby, 1828–1910*, 1972, p. 435.
97. Last Will and Testament of A. J. Munby, 1900, pp. 1–2.
98. *Daily Mirror*, 4 July 1910, p. 3.

Index

OTHER PAN BOOKS

AVAILABLE FROM PAN MACMILLAN

SUSAN GRIFFIN
THE BOOK OF THE COURTESANS   0 330 48807 4   £7.99

ALEX KERSHAW
BLOOD AND CHAMPAGNE   0 330 49250 0   £8.99

ANDREW BARROW
QUENTIN AND PHILIP   0 330 39185 2   £8.99

MIRANDA CARTER
ANTHONY BLUNT   0 330 36766 8   £8.99

All Pan Macmillan titles can be ordered from our website,
www.panmacmillan.com, or from your local bookshop
and are also available by post from:

Bookpost, PO Box 29, Douglas, Isle of Man IM99 1BQ
Credit cards accepted. For details:
Telephone: 01624 677237
Fax: 01624 670923
E-mail: bookshop@enterprise.net
www.bookpost.co.uk

Free postage and packing in the United Kingdom

Prices shown above were correct at the time of going to press.
Pan Macmillan reserve the right to show new retail prices on covers
which may differ from those previously advertised in the text
or elsewhere.